MEXICAN LOBBY

MEXICAN LOBBY

Matías Romero in Washington, 1861-1867

Edited and translated with an introduction by

THOMAS D. SCHOONOVER

Assisted by Ebba Wesener Schoonover

THE UNIVERSITY PRESS OF KENTUCKY

Library of Congress Cataloging-in Publication Data

Romero, Matías, 1837-1898.
  Mexican lobby.

  Translation of: Correspondencia de la legación
mexicana durante la intervención extranjera, 1860-1868.
  Bibliography: p.
  Includes index.
  1. Romero, Matías, 1837-1898—Correspondence.
2. Diplomats—Mexico—Correspondence.   3. Diplomats—
United States—Correspondence.   4. Mexico—Foreign
relations—1861-1867.   5. Mexico—Foreign relations—
United States.   6. United States—Foreign relations—
Mexico.   I. Schoonover, Thomas David, 1936-
II. Title.
F1233.R75A4   1986   972'.07'0924   86-5530

ISBN 978-0-8131-5423-7

Contents

Acknowledgments

Many people and institutions have helped me in the preparation of this book. I wish to thank particularly the library of the Secretaría de Hacienda (Mexico City), the Indiana University and University of Southwestern Louisiana libraries, and the Archivo Histórico de Matías Romero (Banco de México). I wish to thank my colleagues Robert Butler for helping me translate the difficult passages; Stanley Ross, Bill Evans, Robert Kirkpatrick, and Judy Gentry for reading the translated texts for style and readability; and my wife, Ebba, for helping throughout the entire process of translating, typing, editing, and proofreading the manuscript, and compiling the index. I wish to thank Kinley Brauer for his advice and intellectual stimulation.

I also wish to thank the National Endowment for the Humanities for its support of my research in Central America and Mexico in 1972–73. I first discovered Romero's ten-volume *Correspondencia de la legación mexicana en Washington* while working on my doctoral dissertation with the generous support of the Chicago Civil War Roundtable Fellowship.

The Universität Bielefeld, Germany, where I spent 1981–82 as a Fulbright senior lecturer, provided me with spiritual and material support during the final revision of this manuscript. Although I was a transient instructor, not officially attached to the Universität Bielefeld, its faculty and staff willingly and eagerly aided my work in any way they could. Their interest in scholars and scholarship enlightened me regarding what a university could and should be.

Introduction

Historian Eric Foner has pointed out that the reports of foreign diplomats, who, like Georges Clémenceau, were "fascinated contemporary observers," are a long neglected source of information about American Reconstruction history.[1] This book attempts partially to fill that gap by offering the insightful comments of Mexican chargé and minister Matías Romero, who resided in the United States during the secession crisis, the Civil War, and Reconstruction. During that residence, Romero composed some seventy-five memorandums to his superiors in Mexico summarizing private conversations with key American political, military, and business figures (as distinguished from official meetings with the president or State Department officers). These memorandums, written soon after the conversations they record, are translated here from the published correspondence edited by Romero himself.[2]

Vital, dramatic events—the Mexican *reforma*, Civil War and Reconstruction in the United States, and French intervention in Mexico—demanded Matías Romero's attention during the years 1860 to 1867. Romero recorded his impressions of meetings with such important figures in both Mexico and the United States as Abraham Lincoln, William H. Seward, Ulysses S. Grant, Jefferson Davis, Benito Pablo Juárez, Porfirio Díaz, Maximilian, Napoleon III, and many others. Mexico experienced a civil war, the *reforma*, from 1857 until 1860, followed by the allied intervention of late 1861. The latter quickly became a unilateral French action to sustain a client regime under Archduke Maximilian, with the collaboration of the defeated Mexican conservative elements from the *reforma*. The United States assumed that the French under Napoleon III were seeking to take advantage of the American Civil War to undermine U.S. influence in the Caribbean and to lay the groundwork for a revived French presence. Still, the United States assigned priority to its Civil War and later to Reconstruction, thereby rejecting any aggressive policy regarding Mexico. The United States formally protested French intervention in internal Mexican politics, but not until mid-1865 did attention from the press (occasionally subsidized by Juárez's faction), military leaders including Grant, and economic and political factions interested in loans, arms sales, public statements, and in-

---

1. Eric Foner, ed., "Andrew Johnson and Reconstruction: A British View," *Journal of Southern History,* 41 (August 1975):381.
2. Matías Romero, ed., *Correspondencia de la legación mexicana durante la intervención extranjera, 1860-1868,* 10 vols. (México: Imprenta del Gobierno, 1870-92) 2:294.

formation dissemination create noticeable opposition to French activities. In response to this pressure, Secretary of State Seward issued veiled, moderate formal warnings to the French. Thus, the U.S. role in inducing Napoleon III to abandon his dreams of empire in the New World and withdraw from Mexico was modest and indirect. The primary reasons for French withdrawal seem to have been financial costs, deepening European crises, and Mexican resistance. Naturally, given the comparative power relationships of the United States (even during the Civil War era), Mexico, and France in the early 1860s, Juárez's Mexico wished for material as well as moral support from the Lincoln government. It would not have sought aid from the Confederacy because Mexico recognized that the Confederacy was nearing collapse; moreover, Mexican liberals believed the Confederate leadership to be responsible for the annexations and expansion in the prewar decades and assumed that, if victorious, the South would favor expansion of slavery.

The translated correspondence sent by the Mexican chargé and minister to the United States, Matías Romero, to his government should be of interest primarily to historians of the Civil War and Reconstruction era, but this book was not prepared with only these readers in mind. Some diplomatic historians sense that there is a close interrelationship between domestic and foreign politics and that a society's foreign policy goals are normally extensions of the domestic goals and aspirations of the governing elite. Other diplomatic and many political historians, however, seem to focus so sharply on domestic politics that they largely ignore foreign policy. Historians of the Civil War and Reconstruction have not avoided this pitfall. These documents will offer the opportunity, both for those seeking personal informal learning as well as those in formal learning situations, to consider the relationship they reveal between internal and external affairs.

Matías Romero was an active and competent representative of his government. His voluminous correspondence with his superiors in Mexico amounted to five to seven hundred dispatches averaging more than a million words annually. The memorandums included here, although a small part of the total, reveal important aspects of Romero's and Mexico's relationship to domestic United States politics; they frequently show Romero himself as a lobbyist, manipulator, and behind-the-scenes political fixer.

Romero held important posts in the Mexican government for thirty-seven of the forty-two years of his life between 1857, when he joined the Relaciones Exteriores (Foreign Relations) ministry, and his death in 1898. His service included two years in Relaciones Exteriores (1857-59); three periods, for a total of twenty-six years, as secretary of the legation, chargé, or minister to the United States (1859-68, 1882-92, and 1893-98); three periods, a total of about seven years, as secretary of the treasury (1868-72,

1877-79, and 1892-93); and two years in the Mexican Senate (1875-77). As his voluminous private correspondence in the Banco de México and official correspondence in the Relaciones Exteriores archives testify, he played a key role in inducing North American capital to enter Mexico and in furthering closer Mexican–United States relations.

Romero was born in 1837 in Oaxaca, in southwestern Mexico, the birthplace of fellow Mexican Liberal leaders Benito Pablo Juárez, Porfirio Díaz, and Ignacio Mariscal. He was educated as a lawyer, but immediately upon finishing his studies he joined the Liberal government under President Benito Juárez during the War of the Reforma (1857-61). As a protégé of Juárez, Romero served for a time as an unpaid employee in Relaciones Exteriores before being given a salaried post. Thus although he was young when he entered diplomatic service in the Mexican legation in the United States early in 1859, he was not totally inexperienced. When the outbreak of the American Civil War thrust considerable responsibility upon him, the twenty-four-year-old Romero already had spent four years in the Mexican foreign service, including two years in the United States as secretary of the legation and chargé d'affaires. Romero served as chargé until mid-1863, when he resigned because he lacked sufficient funds to conduct a proper lobbying campaign to persuade the United States to act against the French in Mexico. He returned to Mexico hoping to serve in the army against the French. Juárez and Minister of Foreign Relations Sebastián Lerdo de Tejada, however, persuaded him to return to the United States by promising prompt payment of his salary, adequate funds to maintain an active legation, and the rank of minister. By October 1863, Romero was back in Washington, where he remained until late 1867. The need to resolve outstanding American claims so as to preserve Mexico's credit rating with potential investors brought him back to the United States in mid-1868. After negotiating the United States–Mexican claims agreement of 1868, which arranged for the adjudication of all outstanding claims, Romero again returned to Mexico. At the age of thirty-one, he became Juárez's secretary of the treasury.

Displeased by Juárez's decision to seek reelection in 1872, Romero resigned to pursue an activity he had long advocated—coffee culture in southern Mexico. This phase of his life lasted only three years, in part because of the hostility of Guatemalan President Justo Rufino Barrios, who feared that Romero's presence near Guatemala's frontier portended future Mexican expansion into his country, and in part because in 1875 Romero was elected to the Mexican Senate. Two years later, Porfirio Díaz named Romero secretary of the treasury. Romero's health declined in 1879, compelling him to resign. Battling recurring stomach problems that had plagued him since his youth, Romero traveled to the United States to consult medical specialists. In 1880 and 1881, while recuperating, he was involved in several railroad schemes with former United States President Ulysses Grant, Albert K. Owen, Hiram Barney, and others. From 1882 until his death, Romero served as Mexican minister to the United States, except for a short period from mid-1892 until early 1893, when he returned to Mexico for his third period as secretary of the treasury. Porfirio Díaz's second marriage to Romero's daughter no doubt secured and stabilized Romero's role in Mexican politics and increased his influence within the Díaz administration. Romero died in Washington on December 30, 1898, after an attack of appendicitis.

Throughout his service in the 1860s in the United States, and especially after his return in 1863, Romero viewed it as his chief responsibility to lobby for moral and material support against the French. His memorandums are valuable in revealing the specific actions and policies he planned or adopted to achieve his purposes. Romero believed that he could shape Union political and public opinion by distributing information, by coordinating his work with people who seemed to share Mexico's objectives, by traditional lobbying devices such as subsidies to create a favorable press, by the use of congressional resolutions to bring key ideas and documents to the public attention, and by wining and dining the political elite. Shaping opinion, he hoped, would result in public attitudes and political actions advantageous to Mexico in its struggle against foreign intervention. His plan required inching toward his goals rather than advancing by dramatic giant steps. He hoped to change opinion and policy over the long run by constant, slow pressure.

Support from key public figures would enable Romero to enlighten Northern politicians and the public about the plight of the Republic of Mexico, convince them that Mexico and the United States shared a liberal ideology, and persuade them that the disruption of the Union was tied to the French invasion of Mexico. He sought to convince the Northern public that French troops had come to Mexico because of the disruption of the Union and encouragement from the Confederates, who shared their conservative outlook. Hence Romero used his influence in Congress to draw attention to such matters as Maximilian's resurrection of slavery in Mexico, William Gwin's scheme to colonize Confederates in northern Mexico under land grants from the French and Maximilian, and the friendly relationship between Confederates and imperial military leaders along their common frontier. Romero was successful in persuading many Union military leaders that the Civil War would not end until Confederate support in Mexico—support from Maximilian and the French—was ended. The evidence suggests that Romero's lobbying campaign was more successful with the military leaders than with the business community, the congressional leadership, or key administration figures. Romero's friendly relationship with Grant opened doors to the military elite of the country, who, as the memorandums reveal, were at times willing to act on their own initiative, particularly when it seemed that the executive authority would act very slowly or not at all.

Romero's correspondence discloses his involvement in a variety of issues, some of which concerned United States–Mexican relations, others internal United States matters. Those apparent intrusions into domestic American life were for the purpose of ultimately influencing Mexican–United States relations. Among the chief topics of Romero's correspondence were trade ties, communication links both by sea and by rail, and United States military intervention in Mexico. Romero also persisted in meddling in domestic politics. He supported various efforts to oust Secretary of State William H. Seward, who, Romero was convinced, successfully opposed taking aggressive steps to compel the French to withdraw from Mexico. Romero generally cooperated with the Radical efforts to defeat Lincoln in the election of 1864 and to carry the elections of 1866; he welcomed the early efforts to impeach President Andrew Johnson in 1866-67; and he sought to influence appointments to the foreign relations committees in Congress in 1866.

Another interesting element in this story is Romero's interaction with such Radical leaders as Benjamin Wade, Henry Winter Davis, and Zachariah Chandler. Romero supplied these House and Senate opponents of Seward, Lincoln, and Johnson with resolutions and information for their speeches and debates with the intent of embarrassing the administration or its officials. Romero worked with the Radical leaders in part because he hoped to use their access to the public press or the Government Printing Office to distribute information about the struggle in Mexico and to awaken American public opinion against the French intervention.

On occasion Romero supplied evidence of a more grandiose plan to obtain Union sympathy or support for Mexico. A clear move to obtain influence among powerful people occurred in mid-1862, when Romero explained his conduct toward Montgomery Blair and others to his government:

Attempting to take advantage of Blair's position and of the friendly consideration which he shows me, I have managed to cultivate his friendship and have attempted to influence the president through him. Unfortunately, Blair is not in harmony with Seward and in matters of foreign relations it seems that the president gives more weight to the latter than the former. Therefore I have not been able to obtain all the benefits I have hoped for through the good offices of Blair.

I have attempted to cultivate in other influential people the same [friendly] spirit [toward Mexico] which Blair has exhibited, but either because the internal affairs of the country dominate their attention, without permitting them to dedicate it to other affairs, or because they do not have Blair's natural good disposition, my labors in this direction have also not been as fruitful as I expected. This, nevertheless, will not prompt me to reduce my labors.[3]

This letter did not signal the failure of Romero's methods. It merely indicated his inability to obtain the fast start and quick success he desired. His resignation in 1863 and subsequent return to the United States were closely tied to his insistence upon being given adequate funds to win the personal goodwill and assistance of Union politicians, businessmen, and military leaders so he could generate the political influence and public sympathy necessary to maneuver United States legislation and policy favorably for Juárez's Mexico. Thus when Romero returned to Washington in late 1863, he launched a concerted lobbying effort toward the sources of power and influence in the capital. He attempted to make personal contacts at dinners, private meetings, and public festive and ceremonial events. He summarized his activities: "I have given about twenty dinners to almost all the senators, members of the cabinet, some judges of the Supreme Court and the Court of Claims, some members of the House, some members of the diplomatic corps and other distinguished persons. I have had about two hundred guests to dine, and through that means have made slow but sure progress. When I return from New York [where he would attend a public banquet in honor of the Mexican Republic, which he had helped arrange through friendly business and political leaders], I will have still some more [dinners]."[4]

Several brief items of official correspondence for late 1862 are included in the documents printed here because they reveal that several sources within the State Department were leaking information to Romero. Circumstantial evidence suggests that these sources were Robert Chew, Henry Roy de la Reintrie, and Edward Lee Plumb, all State Department employees.

Romero initiated the project to publish all his official correspondence from the era of the French intervention to aid the claims commission investigations required by the 1868 Mexican–United States Claims Treaty. Before 1868 the United States had published much more documentation on Mexican–U.S. relations than Mexico had, often in response to the demands of Romero's congressional allies while he was serving as minister to the United States. But in 1868 Romero had decided that Mexicans should learn about the intervention from their own documents and in their own language.

---

3. Romero, *Correspondencia* 2:294.
4. Romero to Plumb, Washington, March 15, 1864, Edward Lee Plumb Collection, Stanford University.

Moreover, he believed that the Mexican government should be as interested in the story as was the United States government. Yet the publication of the ten-volume *Correspondencia* caused him some embarrassment. In the introduction Romero published a disclaimer, denying that the occasional expressions of ill-feelings toward the United States found in the published official Mexican documents expressed his true sentiments. Rather, he explained, these words reflected his feelings of tension and the importance of the conditions that threatened Mexico. In other words, they were the product of his patriotism and frustration.

The historical significance and rareness of the original Spanish-language edition of Romero's official correspondence (only about six copies in the United States and very difficult to find in Mexico) and the significance of these selected documents for U.S. domestic history makes their translation desirable. I have selected about sixty thousand words from Romero's dispatches—less than 1 percent of the total—for translation and inclusion in this volume. The full edition contains about seven million words in ten large volumes averaging more than one thousand pages with about seven hundred words per page. The original edition is, of course, still valuable not only for United States–Mexican relations but also for insights into United States domestic history. Many specialists in United States history, however, cannot read Spanish well enough to examine such a large collection with ease. Moreover, very few bibliographies even suggest that Romero's published correspondence might be of value to historians specializing in internal United States history.

To test the accuracy and reliability of Romero's published correspondence, several hundred dispatches from the published edition were checked against the originals in the Archivo Histórico de la Secretaría de Relaciones Exteriores in Mexico City. This comparison disclosed a degree of accuracy and reliability that made it unnecessary to check every dispatch. Generally, when Romero found it desirable to depart from the manuscript text, he inserted a series of dots in the printed document roughly equivalent to the length of the passage omitted. Rarely did he alter a document, and then normally because of an orthographic or other minor error in the original. Only once did I discover a significant change in the wording of a document. In this case, where the original document read, "we [Mexicans] desire to have some of the most distinguished soldiers from the United States [go to Mexico] as much so that they would serve as a species of nucleus for our army as for making more useful the sympathies of that people for our cause," became in print "it would not be disagreeable to us to have some of the most distinguished soldiers." The meaning was altered to suggest that the initiative in proposing that American soldiers go to Mexico came from the United States and not from the Juárez government. This is an important point if one recalls the remnants of bitter feelings toward the United States in Mexico and the Mexican fear of further loss of national territory to the "Colossus of the North."[5]

The accuracy and reliability of much of Romero's alleged and reported activity can also be checked in other sources. For example, his claims that Union congressmen had promised to introduce calls for correspondence, legislation, or resolutions can be verified in the *Congressional Globe* or the papers of the congressmen. Other information can be found in the correspondence of North American politicians, businessmen, and soldiers and Mexican officials and friends of Romero. My efforts to verify Romero's assertions have convinced me that he was an honest reporter and that he possessed a good ability to evaluate the rumors and allegations that often found their way to him. He did not merely accept those stories or rumors that were favorable to Mexico and discount those that were unfavorable. He evaluated, investigated when possible, and exercised a reasonable amount of cynical, critical pessimism even toward stories he wanted to believe. Although he was honest and critical, at times he misunderstood, miscalculated, misinterpreted, or was misled. Occasionally he passed along unfounded rumors and baseless stories. Still, his acceptance of bad information did not occur frequently. An intelligent, talented, serious, and prudent person, apparently both from training and inclination, Romero was, in short, a trustworthy agent for his government and a reliable, accurate source for historians.

Quantitative information taken from Secretary of State Seward's papers and from *El Siglo Diez y Nueve,* the official Mexican government newspaper, reveals Romero as a persistent and accomplished lobbyist and a prodigious worker. According to Seward's statistics, from 1861 to 1865 he addressed 49 notes per year to the Mexican legation in Washington; it was the fifth most active correspondence he maintained with a foreign representative. Romero, however, calculated that from 1861 to 1866, counting annexed documents, the Mexican legation received 80 items per year from the secretary of state. Romero's data reveal that he had submitted almost 300 items per year, totaling 500 pages, to Seward's consideration. Romero's statistics also show that he submitted about 600 items per year, totaling 4,000 pages, to his own government. Perhaps the average yearly incoming and outgoing correspondence statistics for Romero while serving in the United States best indicate his vigor and activity. For the years from 1861 through 1866, Romero wrote, on the average, 2,850 items containing 8,230 manuscript

---

5. These two items are in Romero, *Correspondencia* 5:297, and the Archivo Histórico de la Secretaría de Relaciones, H/110 (73-0)"865"/1.19-C-R-1, pp. 724-27.

pages, and received 1,860 items containing 4,030 manuscript pages. One can truly say that Romero labored for his government.[6]

In translating the documents contained in this volume, I have followed certain guidelines. For clarity, I have occasionally substituted more customary, familiar names for the names used by Romero. For example, Romero referred to "the committee to consider the facts relative to the conduct of the war" for "the Committee on the Conduct of the War." Sometimes Romero used names or labels that would not be clear in English. For convenience I have retained several of these to avoid repeating longer descriptions or terms. For example, I allow Romero's "gobierno supremo," literally, supreme government, to mean the Mexican government of Juárez. Likewise, Romero's "this ministry" appears as he used it, as an abbreviated form for the Mexican Ministería de Relaciones Exteriores (Ministry of Foreign Relations). Romero referred to Grant as "the general" and Mexico as "the Republic"; both terms are preserved when their meaning is clear to avoid the repetitive use of "Grant" and "Mexico." Romero inconsistently used words and figures for numbers; I have followed his usage even when it appeared inconsistent. Romero always used a title of address before proper names. I have dropped these when the title was honorific or formal. As examples, Romero used "Mr." very often; I have dropped it in almost every case. I have changed or dropped Romero's formal "excellency," or "your excellency"; he used "His Excellency the Minister, etc.," which I have shortened to "minister." I have excluded the formal ending of Romero's dispatches.

Romero's writing is so stiff, formal, and awkward that it posed translating difficulties; I have taken the liberty of rendering it somewhat loosely, while maintaining as much of his style as possible. For example, many of his sentences run on for several hundred words. I have often broken up the longest ones. His use of pronouns would be impossible in English because of the lack of precision. I have substituted nouns for pronouns when necessary for clarity. Explanatory material has been included in the text in brackets to eliminate the need for footnotes. Material in parentheses is from Romero's original text. Except for excluding some extraneous material and the formal endings, the translated documents are published essentially in full.

Despite his awkward style, at times Romero's observations have a succinct, biting quality. Commenting on the U.S. attitude toward slavery in late 1862, Romero observed that it was "very far from arriving at the point de-

---

6. *El Siglo Diez y Nueve*, July 18, 1867, p. 4, and July 19, 1867, p. 2; and "Comparative Statement of the number of communications made by the Secretary of State, in each year, to twelve of the principal Foreign legations, from March 4, 1860, to March 4, 1866," Miscellaneous, Public Papers, 1861-69, box 62, folder 13, William Henry Seward Papers, University of Rochester Library.

manded by civilization and humanity." This remark is intriguing in light of
repeated U.S. intervention in Mexico and Latin America during the next
120 years in the interest of "civilization and humanity."

For those wishing a deeper understanding of Matías Romero and his
role in Mexican–United States relations, I have included an essay on
sources relative to his life and career and a bibliography of the works he
edited or wrote. The reader who wishes to pursue external sources to verify
Romero's reliability can best begin by checking the sources cited in the footnotes and bibliography of my articles and book mentioned in the last two
paragraphs of this work's essay on sources. I must warn, however, that although my article on the "swing-around-the-circle" will guide a reader to
Gideon Welles's *Diary* or contemporary newspapers that verify the public
manifestations described by Romero, only rarely will the primary sources
reveal in detail the private exchanges Romero committed to the memorandums. Therein lies their special value.

MEXICAN LOBBY

1861

Mexico experienced a long, bitter struggle, the *reforma*, between conservative and liberal factions in the 1850s, terminating in the victory of the Liberal party under the leadership of Benito Juárez in 1859. Although victorious within Mexico, the Liberals faced continuing Conservative maneuvers in Europe to persuade Spain or France to intervene, depose the *reforma* Liberals, and return the Conservatives to power. The American secession crisis occurred simultaneously with the sharpening of Mexico's problems. The Mexican chargé to the United States, twenty-four-year-old Matías Romero, rejoiced at the victory of Abraham Lincoln and the Republican party because he interpreted the party's platform to signal a liberal transformation of the United States. Immediately after the U.S. Congress certified Lincoln's election, Romero traveled to Springfield, Illinois, to congratulate him and to seek cooperation and aid from the new administration. Romero particularly hoped to find a sympathetic ear for his request for support in blocking any use of European funds or forces to return the conservatives to power in Mexico. Romero was pleased when Lincoln's administration appointed a ranking and esteemed Republican "dignitary," Thomas Corwin, former secretary of the treasury, as minister to Mexico.

Romero immediately began groping for ways to induce the North American political system to take the steps he and his government judged necessary to preserve Mexican autonomy. The method he developed was lobbying: use of the press, public speeches, dinners, contacts with politicians, and socializing with the wealthy and powerful to gain support for his cause. Romero believed that, with proper cultivation, individuals with broad followings such as Postmaster General Montgomery Blair and Massachusetts Senator and Chairman of the Senate Foreign Relations Committee Charles Sumner could be won over to the Liberal Mexican position. Such political gains would help solidify the ideological bonds that he believed already existed between the two nations. A practical goal was a U.S. loan to pay the interest due on loans that had been made by European powers to Mexico when the conservatives had been in power. As an inducement to U.S. interests, Mexico agreed to negotiate treaties on extradition, postal matters, and commerce to facilitate commercial exchange, investment, and other economic links between the two liberal regimes and stimulate market expansion, growth, and development. A loan treaty was negotiated and presented to the U.S. Congress. Congress, however, refused to provide a loan unless the European powers guaranteed that they would not intervene in Mexico. When such a guarantee was not forthcoming, Congress was unwilling to risk millions needed for the domestic war in an uncertain situation. Nevertheless, this first formal effort of a U.S. administration to make a government loan to another government merits attention. It certainly indicated that both the U.S. Republican and Mexican liberal governments seriously desired a rapprochement. Apparently, the United States did not again consider a loan to another nation until World War I.

In December 1861, Spain, France, and Great Britain initiated a tripartite intervention in Mexico. Several months later, the Spanish and British withdrew, but the French—alone at first, then with Austrian Archduke Maximilian as stalking horse—remained for six years.

JANUARY 23 Complying with the president's orders . . . I left Washington on January 7th and arrived in Springfield, Illinois, the residence of Abraham Lincoln, president-elect of the United States, on the 18th.

The following day I went to his residence, disclosed to him the object of my visit, read your . . . note, and, at his request, left him a copy in English which I had prepared for that eventuality. Entering into the subject of Mexican affairs, the machinations of the clergy and the army were, I explained to him, entirely responsible for the constant revolutions that had devastated Mexico since its independence. To conserve their privileges and impose their rule on the nation, they had overthrown every constitution and maintained the country in constant turmoil. According to official reports received that very day, however, both these groups had now been completely conquered, therefore remaining unable to raise the standard of rebellion again. Now Mexico's hopes to enjoy peace and prosperity are not only solidly based but assured. I told President Lincoln that the constitutional government desires to maintain the most intimate and friendly relations with the United States, to whose citizens it proposes to dispense complete protection and to concede every form of facilities toward developing the commercial and other interests of both republics. Mexico wants to adopt the same principles of liberty and progress which are followed here, traveling the same path to arrive at the grandeur and unequaled prosperity currently enjoyed in the United States. I told him also that the constitutional government had viewed the recent triumph of Republican ideas in this country with satisfaction. Such ideas are very much in harmony with the principles rooted very deeply in the hearts of Mexicans. Therefore, the policy of the Republican administration with regard to Mexico is expected to be truly fraternal and not guided by the egotistic and antihumanitarian principles which the Democratic administrations had pursued in respect to Mexico, principles that resulted in pillaging the Mexican Republic of its territory in order to extend slavery.

Lincoln appeared to listen to all that I said with pleasure. When I had concluded, he explicitly, almost vehemently, insisted that he was very interested in the peace and prosperity of Mexico. During his government, Lincoln claimed, far from placing any obstacles to the attainment of those ends, he will do what he can to assist their realization. While he is in power, he added, Mexico should be assured he will do her entire justice on all questions that are pending or that will subsequently occur between the two republics. In all matters, Lincoln concluded, he will treat Mexico with sentiments of the highest consideration and of true sympathy. During the conversation and in conclusion he expressed his belief that no question would arise that would suffice to dampen his determination in this particular.

He immediately made clear to me that he intended to meditate on Mex-

ican affairs and, as soon as time would permit, he would write me regarding
the sentiments he had just expressed and on any considerations that might
later occur to him in view of what I told him and of the various pamphlets
I left with him concerning the situation in Mexico. . . .

Among the various questions he asked about Mexico was one inquiring
into the condition of the peons in the Republic because there exist exaggerated ideas here of the situation among the Indians working in the hacienda
system. They are allegedly in a more abominable servitude than the Negroes
on Southern plantations. Furthermore, it is believed that the abuses which,
unfortunately, are committed in some areas of Mexico are general throughout the Republic and are authorized by law. I explained in detail how such
abuses were committed. He professed great pleasure in learning that such
practices were contrary to the laws of the Republic and that, when Mexico
has a solidly established government, it will attempt to correct these abuses.

On January 21st I visited Lincoln again to take leave of him. . . .

My trip to Springfield was, I believe, very opportune, and I expect it
was very profitable for Mexican interests. Lincoln was evidently not very
well informed on Mexican affairs. Furthermore, considering that the foundation of his policy toward Mexico will rest upon the manner in which he
views our situation, my first concern was to inform him of the causes of our
past turmoil, which had already become proverbial here and were considered by many to be without remedy. I informed him that now the causes of
past turmoil had been radically removed. In addition, the fact that Mexico
is presently the only nation that has congratulated Lincoln upon his eleva-
tion to power ought to convince him of the positive sentiments of that Republic with respect to his principles and his country. Our exchange will
influence his mind in a manner clearly favorable to Mexico. Quite certainly
during his term of office he will be guided by the good sentiments he expressed to me because he is a simple, honorable man, and his words carried
the stamp of sincerity and not of pompous phrases, empty of meaning,
which, when used by the people educated in the school of false policy, cus-
tomarily offer much and fulfill nothing.

During my days in Springfield, the capital of Illinois, I was presented to
the governor and other state authorities. By chance the legislature was in
session and all the principal state functionaries were present. In my informal conversations with state functionaries, I expressed to them frankly the
sympathies of Mexico and of me personally for republican principles and
my wish that we might succeed in our present experiment with these principles. The question presently being painfully aired in this country, I reminded them, is the consequence of United States acquisition of Mexican
territory. They were so pleased that they published an article in the official
newspaper of the state greatly honoring me. . . . I mention this incident

only because I suspect that it might have a significant effect upon the mind of Lincoln because all the persons referred to in the article are his close friends. His acquaintances since infancy, they have followed the same ideas, and everything that one might achieve with them is achieved in the mind of Lincoln.   [Matías Romero, ed., *Correspondencia de la legación mexicana*
en Washington durante la intervención extranjera 1:686-87.
References hereafter are to volume and page only.]

JUNE 1   Edward E. Dunbar has proposed to establish a mail steamship line between Veracruz and New York, either direct or with a stop at Havana. Believing that such a line will favor the interests of the Republic, I have encouraged him in his undertaking. The supreme government, I suggested, will probably concede him a moderate subvention, insofar as its current financial difficulty permits. Together we visited the postmaster general [Montgomery Blair] and the secretary of the navy [Gideon Welles] to explain to them the desirability of establishing the steamship line and to learn if one could count on a subvention from the United States government. Both cabinet members recognized the advantages of the project. Since no postal treaty existed between Mexico and the United States, Blair pointed out, he was not obligated to take any step to establish communications. He asked me if I was not currently negotiating some arrangement of this nature. I informed him that [José María] Mata had presented a draft postal treaty to the State Department. This proposal was passed on to the postmaster general as a matter properly within his prerogative. Until now, however, no response in this matter had been communicated to the Mexican legation. Referring to that project, Blair then suggested that it would be good to write to the secretary of state proposing the desirability of establishing postal communications. Such a course would bring the matter to the consideration of the cabinet, which would do everything possible.

Finding that suggestion very reasonable, today I directed a note to Seward. . . .

The most which his department could do, Secretary of the Navy Welles told us, would be to allot a warship to the postal service. Under the current circumstances, however, such a step was entirely impossible because the ships of the United States Navy were not equal to the most pressing military demands, and his department's business did not require regular communications with Mexico.   [1:404-5]

JUNE 6   If this Civil War is prolonged, I believe it will be converted into a servile war, and a large number, if not all, of the Negroes in the South will obtain their freedom. The people directing the present administration are abolitionists at heart, and soon their ideas will predominate in the Northern states.

One recent incident supplies clear evidence of what can be expected. Several Virginia slaves residing near Federal-occupied Fortress Monroe escaped from their owners and presented themselves to General [Benjamin] Butler, commander of the United States forces in eastern Virginia. The interested parties claimed the return of their slaves under the Fugitive Slave Law. Not wanting to return them, General Butler arbitrarily declared them contraband of war because the rebels were using slaves to construct fortifications, transport war equipment, and so forth. Using this line of reasoning, General Butler stated he would return runaway slaves only in cases where the owners swore an oath of loyalty to the United States government. Naturally, General Butler's proceedings have received the fullest approval of this government.

Under such a system, as they advance into the South, the Federal forces will soon have more slaves than they can physically take care of. The press has been discussing what to do with them. . . .

Last night in a conversation with Postmaster General Blair, one of the most influential men in the cabinet and considered a Radical Republican, while attempting at the same time to learn my opinion, he ventured the thought that it would be good if the slaves in the United States would immigrate to Mexico. "Mexico has much land," he told me, "called *tierra caliente* (tropical), where one could greatly enrich oneself cultivating cotton, sugar, and other fruits if there were sufficient labor and, above all, people who could survive in this unhealthy climate. Our Negroes are precisely such a people. It is a law of nature," he added, "that Negroes live in hot climates. Mexico has these hot climates. It would be as advantageous for the Mexicans as for the Negroes that the latter should be established on those lands since they are not able to remain here except with great violence."

We do not need the labor of the Negroes in our hot climates, I explained, adding that the whites and our Indians cultivate cotton and sugar in small quantities because of our small population and the difficulty of exporting those products, not because we need the labor of the Negroes. "On the other hand," I told him, "we have no prejudice against colored people; we believe all human beings are endowed with the same rights without distinctions about their place of birth or the color which nature painted their faces with. We desire immigration, and I do not believe it would be difficult to admit into Mexico as immigrants those who appeal to our hospitality, particularly if they come cast out and persecuted from a country that considers them as an inferior race, whose social perfection consists in being reduced to slavery."

These observations, perhaps, will not be applicable or they might need modification in case the movement of four million slaves from the South to Mexico should be attempted. This possibility will probably never material-ize because, if the South should succeed in conserving its independence in the present struggle, the Negroes of those areas not occupied by Federal forces will remain in slavery, and, if the South is subjugated, the majority of Negroes will continue living in the same states, either as slaves or freedmen.

In my judgment, Blair's project has been proposed before the cabinet by himself or by someone else, hence it appears necessary to inform you of what has occurred, so that the supreme government knows what plans are held here, and, therefore, it might give me instructions that would permit me to express my government's opinion if another occasion offers itself. . . .

I have had the satisfaction of finding Blair very well instructed about Mexican affairs, about the cause of our constant revolutions, and entirely in favor of a popular, liberal government. His influence in the cabinet could be very useful to us, if one knows how to exploit it. I propose therefore to cultivate an acquaintanceship with him.   [1:411-13]

JUNE 28   During this week I have had two conferences with Charles Sum-ner, senator from Massachusetts and chairman of the Senate Foreign Rela-tions Committee. The principal theme of our conversation has been the manner in which it would be desirable for the president to discuss Mexico in his opening address to the special session of Congress on the 4th of next month. As chairman of the Foreign Relations Committee, Sumner has great influence on the foreign relations of the country and the right to advise the president on what he ought to say regarding them.

In the first meeting, Sumner told me that, because the approaching session of Congress was extraordinary, the president was considering dedi-cating the main part of his message to the internal questions of the country and speaking very summarily of foreign relations—only one paragraph stat-ing merely that everything continues on a good footing and that the govern-ment is at peace with the whole world. If I wanted the president to say something special in regard to Mexico, he graciously added, he would gladly indicate such to the president. But because the president had com-plete liberty to say whatever appeared suitable to him, he could not assure me that it would be accepted.

If each nation would not be spoken of individually, as is the custom in the annual message at the beginning of each regular session of Congress, I suggested it would be better not to single out Mexico now. Moreover, under the present circumstances, I judged that whatever might be said would not lead to any important results.

Sumner is one of the most prominent men of the Radical faction of the Republican party. He holds abolitionist ideas in regard to slavery. During the war of 1846-1847 he sustained the Mexican position as arduously as a Mexican might have done. I have read his letters and speeches on this matter and believe it would be desirable to translate and publish them in the Republic.

Today, in my second conference with Sumner, we spoke of the Santo Domingo question. He asked me if Mexico had recognized the independence of Haiti. His government still had not recognized Haiti, he informed me, because, being a Negro republic, its recognition would refute the policy the United States has followed since its establishment, based upon the supposed principle of the impossibility of the Negro race governing itself. Sumner fears that France, following the example of Spain, might annex the Republic of Haiti.

Sumner's influence in the Senate will be very important if some treaty between Mexico and the United States should be submitted to the approval of that body.   [1:446-47]

AUGUST 31   Yesterday I met with the president of the United States. . . .

I desired to give him some information and explanations, I told him, which I considered important, concerning Mexico's situation and the difficulties arising with the French and English ministers accredited to the Republic, before his government might make any decisions regarding the matter. I began by explaining that in Mexico there are two parties. One party is the Liberal, formed from the mass of the Mexican people, whose ideas and tendencies are the same as those of the people of the United States. The Liberals propose to imitate the United States in order to arrive by the same path at the important goal of fabulous prosperity and wealth which this country has already achieved. The other party is the reactionary, composed of the clergy, the demoralized part of the old army, some moneychangers, and a few other illusionaries and fanatics who collectively are in an evident minority. Their tendencies are to establish an aristocratic and monarchical form of government, for which purpose they have solicited and ardently desire the aid and intervention of the European powers. Out of sympathy, identity of ideas, or convenience, I observed, European powers have always aided the second party. This fact was most obvious in the last Mexican civil war, when European diplomacy supported the reactionaries in opposition to the United States, which supported the liberals. Now that the Liberal party has been victorious in the battlefield and in the election urns, establishing a popular constitutional government, European diplomacy does not hide its disgust for this government and its sympathy for the principal leaders of the reaction (some of whom the French minister has in his house, favoring them with the flag of his country). The European governments have sought by every means at their disposal to place obstacles in the way of the Liberal government with the intention of toppling it and establishing the reactionary party in power. The Europeans have such influence over this faction that, once it is in command, the Europeans could consider themselves arbitrators of the Republic's destiny. This goal was, I told him, the key to the conduct the English and French ministers had followed in Mexico. The decree of July 17 [suspending Mexico's payment on its foreign debt], I added, was only a pretext which they conveniently seized upon to further their ulterior designs. I explained at once the urgent necessities that had determined the Mexican government to adopt this extreme measure [debt payment suspension], the manner with which the European diplomatic agents had protested against it, and all the other details relative to this affair in the terms of your July 29 instructions to Juan Antonio de la Fuente [Mexican agent in Europe].

In the present case, I continued, the interests of the United States could be considered identical with those of Mexico. If, as I fear, the French and English governments approve the conduct of their respective agents and blockade our ports, then the United States would not be able to move its troops from California across Mexican territory via Guaymas to Arizona although the necessary permission had just been granted them. To make this mutual interest even more palatable I used another example which I was certain would produce a stronger effect. If England took Matamoros, I observed, she could extract all the Southern cotton through that port.

The president listened with marked attention and without interrupting during the preceding report. He stated that [United States minister to Mexico Thomas] Corwin had informed this government of all these developments and that his report differed in no way from what I had just told him. To make clear that he had penetrated to the heart of the problem, he summarized his understanding of it in a manner which I found highly satisfactory. He and his cabinet were, Lincoln added, deeply aware of the importance and significance of the matter. Since receiving Corwin's concerned dispatches, they had dedicated their fullest attention to this matter, occupying themselves with it in preference to all other important problems. Their purpose, Lincoln continued, was to try to prevent the armed intervention of France and England in Mexico, or, failing in that, to defer it as long as possible. As soon as [Secretary of State] William H. Seward returns from the North, he stated, they would send the corresponding orders and instructions, which he expected would be satisfactory to Mexico. Lincoln did not indicate, nevertheless, anything about the means this government had considered undertaking to obtain that goal, nor did it appear suitable to question him in this regard because, if upon Seward's return, he should also judge it desirable to maintain reserve, I have a sure route to learn government policy. The president, however, appeared to lack confidence in the success of his efforts because of the present situation in the United States. . . .

Finally, expressing my recognition of the favorable disposition he had demonstrated toward Mexico, I took leave of him. [1:729-30]

SEPTEMBER 9 On Saturday, for the purpose of learning the tenor of the reserved instructions sent to Corwin last week . . . I met with the postmaster general. Favoring me with his friendship, he is more communicative than Seward, thus offering me the opportunity to learn what otherwise would escape me. Blair asked my opinion in respect to the action [Corwin's offer of a United States loan to Mexico spread over six years to satisfy her European creditors] taken by the United States in the present difficulties of Mexico. The course adopted, I frankly told him, did not appear the most desirable to the interests of Mexico, since upon expiration of the six years during which the United States would undertake to assume payment of the interest on our debt, we would be in worse condition than we are now. "Or, if not," he responded, "within six years the Mexican crisis will have terminated in one form or other, since it is not possible for the Republic to remain that much longer in its current state." With this phrasing he wanted to make clear that, if we have not succeeded in achieving peace and establishing order within six years, either the United States or Europe would intervene.

Then Blair told me: "Be assured that in our present circumstances it is the most that we could have done. We know the importance and significance of the affair, but presently we are only trying to obtain its postponement until we have exited from our difficulties."

Then I asked Blair if he believed that Great Britain and France would accept the expedient proposed by the United States. He replied: "Evidently not. For a long time European nations have been deliberating upon plans to establish their influence on this continent. They have matured them already and now with Mexico's conduct and the United States' difficulties, they have a unique opportunity. They will certainly take advantage of it. In turn we also are arranging to defend the traditional policy of this government, which does not permit the establishment of European influence on this continent. What Europe considers our embarrassment is nothing but a proof of our strength. When we have snuffed out the Southern rebellion, which would require no more than six months, we will find ourselves with a magnificent and numerous army, well organized and amply provided for, which we could use against those who are now trying to profit from our misfortune."

All Federal cabinet members express very great and blind confidence in their army's speedy reduction of the dissident states. The partisan spirit blinds them, in my judgment, suggesting an easy result, which, if obtainable, will be achieved only after years of fighting.

We turned to discuss the postal treaty. I told Blair that Corwin had proposed a similar treaty to the supreme government and that negotiations were sufficiently advanced. "Could you assure your government," he said, "that the United States will definitely prefer the one which we conclude, as much because it already has Senate approval as because it was negotiated with use of Postal Department data? Besides," he added, "I am almost positive that the provision [in Corwin's treaty] for conceding the privilege to a specific person would not be acceptable to the Senate. Our policy in this as in other business has been to leave an open field for competition because experience has shown us that this is the best and cheapest way to do anything. I believe that if the Mexican government ratifies our treaty, a direct line from New York to Veracruz can be established with little expense."

[1:732-33]

DECEMBER 4   Since Montgomery Blair is . . . one of the most influential members of the cabinet, it seemed desirable to see him to express my ideas about the advantage occurring to the United States if it would take part in the European [French-British-Spanish] expedition against Mexico. He would, I hoped, support this position in the councils of the president if he found the idea reasonable.

Today then, I had an interview with Blair during which I expounded my views on this matter in detail and was pleased to find my ideas completely in agreement with his views and with the policy he believed the United States should follow in the present emergency. He had meditated thoroughly on this matter, he claimed, and had informed Seward of the results of his investigations. His views were entirely consistent with what I had proposed to him, namely, that the United States would participate in the expedition solely to introduce discord and to hasten disagreement among the European powers, thereby impeding the realization of their plans. Blair's opinion so pleased Seward that he requested its submission to him in writing, thus making it more useful and leaving a record in the archives of the State Department. I asked Blair for a copy of that document, but he told me that he had not retained one. He did not believe it convenient, he added, to ask Seward for a copy now because he did not want it to appear that he gave great importance to, or that he was making an ostentatious display of, his opinion. Certainly Seward referred to this report when informing me at our last meeting on November 30th that he had consulted with another cabinet member on this matter.

In the course of our conversation Blair told me with characteristic frankness: "In the form the expedition against Mexico has taken and because of the motives the European powers allege in carrying it through, we can oppose them in conformity with international law." I consider this the real opinion of the administration. The outcome of the [French-English-Spanish] expedition [to Mexico], Blair maintained, will depend on the course events take here. If the Civil War ends rapidly and the Federal government recovers its authority over the states in rebellion, the European powers will not attempt to consummate their plans. In the contrary case, however, the consummation of the European schemes can be prevented only with intrigues and cunning. This is why, Blair claimed, the Federal government has sent one of the most apt men [Thomas Corwin] to Mexico as United States minister. He will be capable of counterchecking the influence of the European diplomats. Corwin is an able man, Blair said, but lacking in the experience and tact necessary in the present situation. He had favored sending another person, Blair added, a man of the category of Reverdy Johnson, a distinguished Maryland lawyer. This leads me to believe that Corwin will not represent the United States in the conferences with the intervening powers.

Blair is fully informed of the real intentions of the European powers and of all the dangers contained in the present situation. We share the most perfect uniformity of views and ideas on this matter as well as on the best manner to counter the European maneuvers under the present circumstances. . . .

I have also spoken with Senator [James F.] Simmons of Rhode Island, and I had the satisfaction of seeing that he approved my plan, considering it the best way to exit successfully from the present difficulties. [1:620-21]

DECEMBER 22 Senator Sumner told me . . . today that the Senate Foreign Relations Committee had met yesterday to consider the special message of the president relative to Mexican affairs. Although no action had been agreed upon, the opinion prevailed among the members that it was not desirable to approve the loan Corwin proposed for the Mexican government because they believed that the loan would not effectively prevent the European expedition being organized against the Republic and because the loan could alienate the goodwill of France and Spain from the United States. The United States is now cultivating this friendship more than before because of the menacing aspect developing in relations between this country and England. Speaking for the Senate committee, Sumner informed me: "We do not see that any advantage will occur to our country in making the loan to Mexico."

Although I am already accustomed to observing that even the statesmen of this country ignore the state of Mexican affairs, Sumner's words surprised me. It was necessary, I knew, to begin by informing him of negotiations between France, Britain, Spain, and Mexico. I also explained to him in detail the present condition of Mexico, the desires and actions of the Conservative party in favor of establishing a monarchy with a European prince at the head of it, the arrangement between that party and the cabinet in Madrid, the true plans and designs of the French and Spanish governments, and everything else I considered necessary. The contest would be not only between Mexico and Spain, I observed, but between republican institutions and monarchy, between America and Europe, because undoubtedly the large naval force, which the allied powers have already placed or are going to place in the Gulf, indicated very clearly that they intend something more than to attack Mexico and seize its ports.

All this took Sumner by surprise, apparently, because he raised various questions to which I attempted to respond in the best possible manner. He noted the sum total of our exterior debt, with specification of its diverse classifications. If the United States is persuaded of the delicacy and significance of the case, I said, it could aid us in no better manner than by facilitating the financial resources we need to resist our invaders effectively.

I asked Sumner when the Senate considered adjourning its session. He responded that it would adjourn on Wednesday, the 25th of this month. Did he believe, I inquired, this matter would be settled before that date? He assured me it would not, because it is not considered very urgent. Then leave it until after the New Year, I suggested, because meanwhile news could come from Mexico that could change the opinion of the Foreign Relations Committee members. This idea appealed to him. . . .

I invited Sumner to dine with me tomorrow, when I will take the opportunity to speak of this affair again.   [1:659-60]

1862

Matías Romero insisted that the purpose of the tripartite intervention was not primarily to achieve the repayment of European loans or even the return of the Mexican conservatives to power, but rather conquest and empire. He sought throughout early 1862 to persuade the Lincoln administration and the U.S. Congress that the loan would effectively counter the French, Spanish, and British violation of the Monroe Doctrine, as well as encourage Mexican liberal resistance to the European powers. Romero continued his lobbying, concentrating on Senator Charles Sumner out of recognition of the senator's powerful position, Postmaster General Montgomery Blair, and Representative Jacob Cox of Ohio.

Negotiations on extradition and postal treaties moved toward completion because these two treaties involved low-cost matters of obvious, mutually shared liberal interest. The commerce treaty between Mexico and the United States bogged down because, although both sides saw advantages in the pact, the Mexicans judged it to be of such major importance to the United States that they could use it as leverage to extract a loan or, at the very least, outspoken U.S. opposition to the intervention. In the midst of a Civil War of uncertain duration and intensity, the Lincoln administration and U.S. Congress were not prepared to pay such a price. Despite his expressions of deep sympathy for the Mexican Liberals and condemnation of European intervention, Montgomery Blair finally decided that steps should be taken to enable Juárez to continue to resist until the U.S. Civil War was terminated and the United States could intervene in Mexico with force.

As the prospect of a major Mexican diplomatic victory in the form of a U.S. loan or some equivalent activity on the part of the Lincoln administration faded, Romero sought to locate alternative avenues of influence and support. He established confidential access to State Department materials, most likely through Edward Plumb, Robert Chew, and Henry Roy de la Reintrie, all of whom served in permanent or temporary positions with the department during much of the 1860s. In mid-1862, when the tripartite intervention disintegrated (Spain and England withdrew) and it became evident that France expected more than mere repayment of the loans and its citizens' investments, the Lincoln administration used the occasion to try to resolve a domestic military problem and to alleviate the foreign policy crisis in Mexico with one dramatic act. General Winfield Scott was considered a hindrance to the proper military conduct of the war because of his age and infirmity, yet he retained a reputation as a great soldier. The Lincoln administration sought to shuffle Scott off to Mexico as a special minister to complement Corwin's political role by lending military weight to the U.S. mission. His appointment would underscore to the French the U.S. commitment, while simultaneously removing the aged general from Washington and permitting the promotion of men such as General George B. McClellan. Ultimately, Scott was unwilling, unable, and unsuited for the Mexican mission.

Another Union scheme occupied Romero during 1862. Many in the North wished to remove the blacks—both slave and free—from the United States. The matter became urgent as the war lengthened into mid-1862 because such men did not want it to be interpreted as a war to free the blacks. Nor did they want the blacks free to live in the North. Various schemes surfaced to colonize the blacks back to

Africa (some had already returned to Liberia), to the Caribbean islands (Haiti or elsewhere), to Central America, Brazil, Ecuador, or Mexico. Those who promoted colonizing blacks in Mexico, Central America, and the Caribbean islands usually pointed out that their removal from the United States could be converted into an act of great material and strategic benefit for the Union. Assuming a wise selection of locations for colonies, the blacks sent into these regions would settle along the main transit lines linking the Atlantic and Pacific oceans. Thus they would represent a permanent U.S. influence in areas of vital importance to the United States; they would serve as economic, political, and cultural entering wedges into these vital areas. Montgomery Blair, claiming to speak for the Lincoln administration, discussed with Romero the prospects of obtaining colonial sites under U.S. control in Mexico. Like the Central American diplomats, Romero proved skeptical. Ultimately, he made it clear to Blair that the blacks could enter Mexico only if they surrendered their U.S. citizenship and became Mexicans. Whenever U.S. domination of the black colonists was rejected, however, the forces in the United States urging the colonization projects lost interest in the schemes.

JANUARY 5   On the second of January the disagreeable news that Veracruz had been occupied by the Spanish was received here. . . .

The preceding news, which I had anticipated, furnished me good arguments to defend Corwin's projected [loan] treaty before the Senate Foreign Relations Committee. Taking advantage of the opportunity then, I conferred with Sumner, chairman of that committee. . . .

The occupation of Veracruz without a previous declaration of war and without motives that justified hostilities, I informed him, was additional proof of Spain's intentions to reconquer Mexico. "My government," I added, "considers itself sufficiently strong to wage a war with Spain successfully because the Mexican people are as much as anyone else jealous of their independence, which our old rulers wish to snatch from us again. However, we can hardly fight against the combined power of Spain, France, and England. Our policy should be, then, to isolate Spain from the other two powers by conceding to them whatever is within the limits of our capabilities. Since the interests of both in Mexico, and especially England, are primarily pecuniary, it is natural to believe that if we could offer them the [financial] guarantee of the United States, we should move close to the conclusion of an honorable and suitable agreement. But if the United States refuses us her aid, we will find ourselves with all ports sealed and in imminent danger of succumbing."

Sumner asked me if I believed that once Corwin's treaty is approved it would produce the effect of disarming France and England against Mexico. I immediately replied in the negative, but added that it very probably would produce this result as soon as those nations realized the resistance the intervention would encounter from the Mexican people. I knew from a trustworthy source, I related, that both powers had agreed to the intervention with the understanding that they would receive the assistance of a large majority in my country without resistance from a hostile party. When they are disabused of this idea, however, they will most certainly desist from an undertaking that would cost them a great deal if carried to a conclusion, but from which they can extract little profit. "Quite likely," I continued, "they will then attempt to negotiate an advantageous peace, which could be more easily concluded if we can count on the guarantee of the United States to satisfy the pecuniary interests of those powers."

My ideas seemed very reasonable, Sumner observed, and since our first conference, his attention had been drawn to the moderation of my wishes. "We have the greatest sympathy for Mexico," he added, "and we sincerely desire to help her, but you know our difficult, critical position. We have too many foreign complications to look for new ones. If we can remove France and England from Mexico by pacific means and without offending either of those two powers, we will do so with great pleasure."

This, I noted, is precisely what we desired. Then he asked me what I wanted done with the treaty now in the Senate. I wanted it approved if this were possible, I replied, and, in case that were not possible, it should not be taken under consideration until present circumstances change. He appeared to decide for the latter course.

In conclusion, at the coming Foreign Relations Committee meeting on Tuesday, he told me, he will inform it of what I had just communicated to him. At that time, he added, he would see what could be done in the matter. . . . From what Sumner told me the first time I saw him and from what he indicated today, I believe that, if the treaty were submitted now for Senate approval, it would be rejected. Considering the harm this would cause us, I propose to maneuver so that, if it is not possible to approve the treaty, it remains pending in the committee for the present.   [2:2-4]

JANUARY 7 Today I visited the Senate with the intention of learning what the Senate Foreign Relations Committee had decided in regard to Corwin's draft treaty at its morning meeting. Sumner informed me that he had expressed the ideas I had explained to him at the meeting on the 5th in detail to his colleagues. . . . Finding my observations well founded, Sumner reported, the committee had decided to table all action on the matter for now to permit future developments to change the appearance of the question. At that time there might be greater probability that the negotiation would be successful. Amicably, Sumner offered that no action would be taken in regard to this matter without advising me previously. He also requested me to communicate to him any news that I might receive.   [2:6]

JANUARY 28   Last night I had another conversation with [Sumner]. . . . I informed him of the most recent news from the Republic and of the desirability that, after the Senate approves the Corwin draft treaty with some modifications, this government should offer to mediate the present difficulties between the European powers and Mexico in conformity with what Seward told me. . . .

I told Sumner everything that seemed necessary to persuade him that the present is a good time to work in that direction because, according to all reports, the allies have begun to be discouraged upon seeing the opposition they faced. They might accept an honorable way to exit from the difficulty. In reply he voiced his judgment that it was not the time to make any decision. Mexico and the United States, Sumner pointed out, would gain as much with the passage of time as the allies would lose. His cardinal idea is, as he made clear, that while this government has no important advantage over the rebels, it ought not to make proposals of any kind. He has told the members of the Foreign Relations Committee, he informed me, that all the energy and all the resources of the government ought to be destined to suffocating the rebellion, and that proposals made, while this goal remains unobtained, ought to be rejected, or, at least postponed, if they would contribute toward weakening the resources of the government, or toward distracting it from that goal. Nevertheless, if the president sends another message urging Senate action, he claimed the committee would take account of that and its report would be submitted for the Senate's consideration.

I offered to submit some written considerations if he would do me the favor of communicating them to the committee when it might occupy itself with this affair.

A majority of the committee is favorably disposed, I believe, and would decide for immediate action. I am going to assure myself of that, and if it appears so and there is the probability of success, I will continue to work for a prompt consideration of the matter. I have also visited some other senators, discovering their attitudes to be satisfactory. In the process of speaking with the senators and informing them of our affairs, I have been aided by [Edward Lee] Plumb, secretary of the United States legation in Mexico City.   [2:26-27]

FEBRUARY 1   Today I met with Montgomery Blair. . . . He related to me that [New York businessman Edward] Dunbar and [Cuban general and filibuster Domingo de] Goicuria had visited him to propose the sale of the island of Cozumel to the United States government. This project pleased him because he believed Cozumel to be a very apt place to send the Southern Negroes. He inquired if Goicuria had authorization from the supreme government to negotiate an arrangement of this kind with the United States. According to my understanding, I replied, he did not, since his current commission was solely for the purpose of obtaining money in New York. Moreover, I did not believe it would be possible to celebrate a convention in that form, I told Blair, because the government and the people of Mexico were firmly decided against alienating another inch of national territory. "If the United States government," I said, "wishes to transport to that island some or all of the Southern Negroes, it can conclude an arrangement with Mexico. I do not doubt that my government will be favorably disposed toward such an arrangement. Consequently, the colonization will be done in the form the United States desires, provided, however, Mexico does not lose sovereignty over the island." "This would not be possible," replied Blair, "because the Negroes do not wish to go anywhere, except under the protection of the United States flag."

"This difficulty," I answered, "can easily be surmounted, because, conserving their character as United States citizens, the Negroes will be under the protection of that government." "Certainly," said Blair, "but then they would not be able to acquire real estate." Our laws now permit foreigners to acquire real property, I informed him, and therefore this difficulty does not exist either. Blair appeared persuaded by my reasons, and he began to mention the motives that had led him to believe that the project was acceptable for both governments. "Cozumel," he told me, "is a deserted island which in no way serves the Mexicans, and the white race could not possibly acclimatize itself on Cozumel or in Yucatan, which is inhabited by Indians. These regions are destined to be populated by Negroes. We need to rid ourselves of them, and we could not encounter another place more appropriate to send them to than that island." Together with the antecedents, which I will mention below, this was adequate to illuminate immediately Blair's real project. In the best way I could, I told him that if the United States desired to gain the goodwill of Mexicans, it must begin by persuading us that the ancient policy of constant aggressions against our territory has been abandoned absolutely and permanently. The government and the people of Mexico, I added, expected the present administration to pursue a more elevated policy than that followed up to the present of acquiring our territory, even by the most reproachable means, with the sole object of introducing slavery into it, or Mexico would not have entertained such a project for a moment. The United States, I continued, would receive more benefit from Mexico as an independent nation with its actual boundaries than if it were inside the Union, forming an integral part of its territory, because then the lack of homogeneity of population, which has been the cause of the present Civil War, would be greater and therefore would present more difficulties in conserving the Union. I illustrated this concept with the example of the

United States itself, which has produced a hundred times more for England since its independence than it produced for her when it was her subject. "We can celebrate," I added, "commercial arrangements, by virtue of which the manufacturing states of the North acquire in Mexico the market they have lost in the South, but from which they have been prohibited until now by the jealousy and distrust with which Mexico naturally saw this country. Because our political tendencies and interests are identical, we can make other equally satisfactory arrangements, permitting the United States to obtain from Mexico all of the advantages that would have come from annexing it to the American Union without having to suffer any of the inconveniences born from such a step."

Blair manifested his complete agreement with me. He gave me additional reasons for making the annexation of Mexico to this country less desirable. The principal one was that in all the territories that would be annexed the South would tend to preponderance, which is contrary to the policy of the present administration. He attempted to quiet my fears entirely in respect to the projects of this government, telling me that it had considered purchasing Cozumel, not precisely to acquire territory, but because it seemed easier to accomplish the colonization in this way. Naturally, I appeared to be entirely satisfied. Unfortunately, I am not. What the president said in his annual message in regard to the purchase of territory for the colonization of Negroes; the questions Seward asked me about Yucatan; Blair's previous conversations concerning the same matter; a bill proposed by [Francis P. Blair, Jr.] the brother of Montgomery Blair, a Missouri congressman, authorizing the president to purchase territory he should judge proper for the colonization; and my recent conversation regarding the island of Cozumel with Senator [James] Doolittle of Wisconsin, chairman of the Senate Foreign Relations Committee, indicating that he approved the schemes, are more than sufficient grounds to indicate that this government has been meditating the acquisition of Cozumel and even the Yucatan Peninsula for some time. For more than one reason it would be very advantageous for this country and an irreparable loss for us.

The United States has a large part of its coasts on the Gulf of Mexico and controls one of the outlets of this sea, the one formed by Cape Cayo Hueso on the Florida peninsula and the northeast corner of Cuba. If it should obtain Yucatan, then it will be owner of both entrances into the Gulf, and this sea, on which half of our coasts and our major ports are located, will be converted into a North American lake, without any hope of our reconquering control in the future. The least astute policy cannot hide that Yucatan is the most important possession remaining to us in the Gulf of Mexico.

For the same reason, I was very surprised that Domingo de Goicuria, who showed me an official note expressly warning him not to compromise the sovereignty of Mexican territory under any circumstances, should have commenced by making promises and offering hope to this government which it should never have been allowed to entertain. This surprise diminished markedly after considering that Goicuria is not Mexican, nor interested in the fate of Mexico, except insofar as he can use us to obtain his personal ends. On occasion he has frankly told me as much.

I have been tempted to use the press to clarify the nature of the powers under which Goicuria acts in order to prevent the occurrence of similar cases. Only because he is an agent of the supreme government have I abstained from doing so. We would not present a very instructive example if we initiated a polemic contest over the extent of the powers with which this ministry had invested him.

At the conclusion of this matter I spoke to Blair about the attitude of this government with respect to European intervention. He told me that Seward had charged him with approaching the Senators who were his friends to prepare them favorably. Blair said he had already seen several. The United States, Blair believed, would send an agent to Veracruz to confer with the allied diplomatic agents. The mission's success, he thinks, will depend entirely upon the person chosen to undertake it. He has spoken in this sense with the president and Seward, both of whom received the observation well. The person whom he considered most appropriate for this mission, Blair intimated, was Edward Everett of Boston. He asked my opinion concerning Everett's appointment. Since Everett is one of the prominent people of this country, with a very well-established European reputation, I told him that I believed it would be difficult to make a more suitable selection. Everett's long experience in diplomatic service and the respectability of his personal character would make him very appropriate for assuring the complete success of the mission.   [2:32-34]

FEBRUARY 9   I met with Sumner to ask if the draft resolution on Mexican affairs which will be presented to the Senate had been written. It still was not, he replied. Although in the abstract he was already persuaded of the desirability of working quickly and had already coordinated his ideas, he still had not overcome various difficulties which arose upon expressing them in practical terms. From his remarks, I infer that the resolution will contain the following points: (1) an offer of mediation; (2) payment by the United States of the *immediate* claims of the allies against Mexico, which also will be done immediately; (3) payment for five years of the interest on Mexico's foreign debt; (4) payment of the foreign conventions, consolidating them into a fund that will be paid off within a period of five or ten years;

(5) no arrangement except in concert with and to the satisfaction of the allies [Britain, France, and Spain].

He was thinking, Sumner said, of reducing the period during which the United States would assume payment of the interest on the Mexican debt to three years. In that case, I responded, the allies might not accept the arrangement.

He asked what guarantees the Mexican government would like to give for the repayment of the money advanced by the United States. The same ones, I replied, stipulated in the Corwin draft treaty. To this he responded that he did not like the establishment of a mixed commission to supervise the sale of Mexican federal lands in case of default because it would permit favoritism and fraud; he preferred the guarantees requested by Seward . . . which consisted of a lien on unclaimed land in the frontier states. I did not believe, I explained, that the Mexican government would agree to giving such guarantees or that the allies would ever accept such a stipulation. If the United States insists upon inserting this idea as a necessary condition, I added, the result will be lost time, and, if the United States sincerely desires to carry the negotiations to a satisfactory conclusion, it ought to start by placing a clause in the treaty expressly pledging itself not to acquire Mexican territory as a result of this transaction.

If he writes the resolution before Tuesday the 11th, the meeting day for the Foreign Relations Committee, Sumner told me, he will present it then. If it should receive the approval of his colleagues, he continued, he would report it to the Senate the same day. It is uncertain whether approval of a resolution of this nature requires a simple majority or a two-thirds vote of those senators present. Even in the latter case, it probably would pass the Senate. If it does pass, the negotiations will probably be conducted at Veracruz or at the point where the allied plenipotentiaries reside. . . .

Sumner told me that Seward visited him yesterday, expressing great concern because the Senate was occupying itself with this matter.

Sumner also informed me of the present Senate disposition of the extradition treaty and of the postal convention, both signed this past December 11. Regarding the second, he encountered no objection. Concerning the first, he is undecided whether he will or will not request the deletion of the clause authorizing the extradition of criminals charged with theft of private property.   [2:44-45]

FEBRUARY 16 Recently the rumor arrived here that Emperor Napoleon's speech at the installation of the French Corps Législatif would propose an armed intervention in United States affairs. Since this rumor had some credibility, Sumner was moved to suspend all proceedings in our affairs until he received the text of the imperial address. The text arrived shortly thereafter and was entirely satisfactory to this country. While the United States respected the rights of neutrals, the emperor merely noted, France ought to limit itself to wishing for a prompt termination of the difficulties that divided this country. After this, Sumner decided to await the arrival of the Mexican mail for January so he could gauge the most recent appearance of things. The mail arrived on the 14th, and this other difficulty was surpassed.

This morning I saw Sumner to inform him of the news I had received recently from Mexico and Paris and to learn whether he had drafted the resolution on Mexican affairs. He intended to do so this evening, he told me, and to present the resolution to his colleagues at the next meeting of the committee on Tuesday the 18th. That this will be done soon does not encourage me much because Seward is going to send instructions to Corwin without waiting for the Senate resolution.

Sumner continued to contemplate the guarantees that need to be requested from Mexico in return for the money advanced by the United States. Edward Lee Plumb has suggested that the United States demand the transit right over Tehuantepec and over the northern frontier, with the privilege of sending troops to protect the transit in the terms stipulated in the McLane-Ocampo treaty. I immediately considered such pretensions inadmissible, as much for Mexico as for the allies. Such a transit privilege could not be considered a guarantee but rather a concession, I informed Sumner, something not currently under consideration and something France and Spain certainly would not approve. I informed Sumner . . . that the previous report of permission conceded by the Mexican government for United States troops to pass over its territory had been a major factor contributing to Emperor Napoleon's decision to intervene in Mexico to overthrow a government that acted so favorably toward the United States. In my judgment, I concluded, the nature of the guarantees ought to be left to Corwin's discretion because none could possibly be adopted without the agreement of the Mexican government and the allies.

Sumner told me that he had spoken with Seward yesterday, expressing in detail his views on Mexican affairs and the form in which he intended to draft the resolution. Seward asked him if he thought the Senate would possibly approve the resolution by the 19th, in which case it could leave here with this mail. Sumner told Seward he did not think that would be easy to do. If Seward sends Corwin the general authorization which he mentioned to me yesterday, there is a danger that Corwin might undertake some arrangements in Mexico that are not in conformity with the Senate resolution, thereby complicating the matter very much. [2:52-53]

FEBRUARY 19 Yesterday the Senate Foreign Relations Committee discussed the resolution Sumner presented on Mexican affairs. At midday I went to the Capitol to learn the result. Sumner was occupied in a Senate debate, so I could not talk to him. Another senator, a member of the committee, informed me nevertheless that Sumner's resolution had been adopted with modification.

In the evening I had the opportunity to speak at length with Sumner at a dinner to which the secretary of the treasury had invited us. He did not consider himself at liberty, he told me, to show me the resolution as approved by the committee because Senate rules strictly prohibited that. He found no obstacle, however, in telling me the essence of it. With minor differences, his words were: "Our minister in Mexico is authorized to demand sufficient guarantees, excluding the acquisition of territory, since the United States declared that it does not propose to acquire any territorial advantage by means of this transaction, nor to prejudice or diminish the sovereign rights of Mexico. He can negotiate the necessary arrangements with the government of that Republic, the allies consenting, so that the United States would assume for a fixed period of time the payment of the interest on Mexico's foreign debt and of those claims against her whose immediate satisfaction is demanded. It is understood that upon such agreement the allies would retire their forces from Mexican territory."

Sumner has been charged with drafting the report that ought to precede that resolution. When I saw him yesterday evening he informed me that he had already written it. . . . As soon as it is printed he will present it to the Senate. . . . Seward, I have also learned, has already written his instructions to Corwin, which will go out on the same steamer as this note. The Senate, Seward states in these instructions, is occupied with the matter, and it almost unanimously thought that only the interest on the Mexican debt and the reclamations and convention [debts] should be paid, with the understanding that this action would result in the allied troops withdrawing from Mexico.   [2:55-56]

FEBRUARY 24   Yesterday, reliable people assured me that this government was determined to send General [Winfield] Scott on an extraordinary mission to Mexico and that he would depart immediately in a warship of the United States. Appearing almost unbelievable in view of Seward's conduct of a few days ago in sending Corwin general instructions to make suitable arrangements to place Mexico in a position to fulfill its financial commitments to the allies, this news drew my attention. Desirous of ascertaining its truth, I went to see Blair in the evening (even though it was Sunday and people here are not accustomed to making calls on holidays). At the cabinet meeting this past Friday the 21st, Blair told me, Seward had proposed sending General Scott to Mexico. The other cabinet officers had concurred in this measure, thus leaving the matter definitely settled. Before sending the nomination to the Senate for confirmation, Seward had personally communicated the cabinet decision to the members of the Senate Foreign Relations Committee and asked for their opinion. As I am told, all professed themselves in favor of the nomination.

Blair told me that he considered the selection of General Scott very imprudent. General Scott is very advanced in age, suffers greatly from the failings and pains of his age, and, moreover, because of military habits and the custom of command, is inappropriate for the delicate mission entrusted to him. The diplomatic agents of the allies, Blair added, could confound Scott easily. It would not be difficult for Scott, Blair feared, to place United States interests in Mexico in a worse condition because, if the allies take him unawares and he expresses himself favorably toward them in his dispatches, later the allies will oppose us in the same terms communicated by our envoy. What we need in Mexico now is a good lawyer who knows how to gather unimpeachable evidence of the allied projects. Although already well aware and morally certain of allied projects, we lack the tangible proofs that could serve as the basis for our future action on this matter.

Blair also told me that one of the most influential senators had informed him that he [the senator] and some of his colleagues were opposed to the resolutions presented by the Senate Foreign Relations Committee and to General Scott's trip to Mexico. If Scott's terms were not accepted by the allies, they believed, the United States ought to intervene immediately in Mexican affairs with force because the refusal to accept the terms would be the best proof of the allies' designs. Since the United States still is not in a position to intervene, this senator added, it would be more convenient to delay the proposed measures a while longer until the Civil War was terminated. This opinion appeared very reasonable to Blair. . . .

I have spoken with various other people regarding General Scott's nomination. All disapproved of it, unanimously expressing the opinion that he is not suited to discharge that delicate task. The only good aspect they saw in the nomination was that the allies would know through his appointment that the United States appreciates the magnitude of events now taking place in the Mexican Republic because it will have selected one of its most prominent men, highly considered and respected in Europe, to go there.

If General Scott finally does go, he will most likely carry in his retinue some able person as his adviser, who, having the confidence of this government, will really discharge the work of the mission. I know of some men who are already working to receive this nomination. . . .

Some people believe that General Scott will not accept the mission because he recognizes he is physically unable to discharge the duty. . . .

This nomination will probably produce Corwin's recall.   [2:63-65]

MAY 9 On May 5 . . . Blair mentioned the attitude the United States will take in the Mexican complications. His opinion merits attention, not only as that of a statesman, knowledgeable about his country, who could more easily than others judge what it might do in the future in light of such complications, but also as a member of the present cabinet and an adviser to the president.

As soon as the Southern insurrection is defeated, Blair believes, the United States will send an army to Mexico to throw the French out. This is an indispensable necessity for the United States, he claims, and, although a wise counsel might not advise it, the people of the United States would demand it. If the president or some cabinet officer refused to do so, he judged, the reluctant secretary would fall and the president would be over-ruled by Congress, representing the most immediately popular spirit. "Even the difficulties of organizing an army and providing it with armaments and munitions of war, which in another situation would have sufficed to make the government and the nation hesitate before undertaking a foreign war, are already removed," Blair told me, "because now we have the armies prepared for combat, the martial spirit developed in our people, and our own strength concretely demonstrated. If you can sustain yourselves a little longer," he added, "do so, confident that shortly we will come to your aid."

I have heard similar ideas with notable uniformity from all classes of society, from a senator to a day laborer, with whom I have discussed our matters. This nation knows that Europe is taking advantage of its weakness to dispose of Mexico's destiny and that only the favorable course of events here has made England and Spain retire from the undertaking. Many be-lieve that the news of the recent and important advantages obtained by this government will make France change its policy.

The representative for Missouri, Frank P. Blair, Jr., brother of the post-master general, expressed these same ideas in a speech given on April 11 in the House of Representatives . . . although he mixed it with his pet idea of making Southern blacks migrate into the tropical or equatorial regions of this continent.

The New York newspaper editorials . . . uniformly express the same idea that France will be thrown from the continent when peace is reestab-lished here.   [2:170-71]

MAY 12   Desiring to learn . . . how the House Foreign Relations Commit-tee would present some resolutions on Mexican affairs in light of the cor-respondence the president has sent it, I have conversed twice with John J. Crittenden, representative from Kentucky and chairman of that commit-tee. . . .

I told him I had received reports that placed French intentions beyond doubt, informing him in detail of what these were. He asked me if the United States government had a report of these facts. Two days ago, I in-formed him, I had communicated them to the State Department and I also assumed Corwin had communicated them. If it appeared convenient to have these data in hand before discussing the matter, I observed, he could request them from the president. I did not believe, I added, there would be any difficulty in sending them to the House. He told me that he would do so.

In the course of our conversation, I explained to him how desirable it would be to have someone present resolutions, in suitable terms and in a suitable form, protesting, for example, against the allied armies forcibly reestablishing a monarchy in Mexico. Such action would make clear to Europe that the United States did not view intervention in Mexico with indifference and that the United States reserved the right to take the necessary steps when circumstances permitted. I indicated also the desirability of making a speech in the same vein, even if only to make noise.

Crittenden appeared persuaded of the suitability of taking these steps. When things were regulated here, he claimed, the United States Army would undertake to throw the European intruders out of Mexico. He entreated me to make a recommendation to the supreme government, which I will do when I receive the letter he offered to send on this matter.

[2:176-77]

MAY 16 Wishing to inform the president of the United States of the condition of our affairs, while at the same time learning his ideas and views for the future regarding French intervention on this continent, I have resolved to call upon him with the required frequency. Although my character near this government is not the most appropriate for possessing the right to be received by the president, I have determined to commit this small irregularity for my country's sake.

This morning I had the first interview with Lincoln. To see him I adopted the pretext of expressing my condolences at his loss of a son this past February. . . . Shortly before taking leave of him, I congratulated him on the success of his recent trip to Fortress Monroe, expressing my wish to see peace reestablished in the United States, because, in great part, the settlement of things in Mexico depends on that. I expounded a little on the themes that the European expedition was undertaken in the belief that the United States was permanently divided, that the French policy in Mexico was hostile to this nation, and that an identity of interests exists between our two countries. He had always believed, he replied, that the settlement of Mexico's present difficulties depended upon the course events would take here.

Since Mexican affairs were a matter of such importance to the United States, I told him, I would take the liberty of coming occasionally in an unofficial capacity to speak with him on these matters.   [2:184]

JULY 3 Today the Senate Foreign Relations Committee had its weekly meeting. Before the meeting I went to see Sumner to inquire whether he had considered continuing the discussion of the Corwin treaty and to repeat my request that, in case there would be no chance of a favorable vote, as there is not, he would leave the matter pending for the next session of Congress.

In the afternoon I went to the Capitol to learn what had been the outcome of the committee's deliberations. After carefully considering the matter, Sumner told me, the committee had decided that the treaty was not acceptable because France would consider it as a hostile measure and it could produce complications which are necessary to avoid. Out of consideration for Mexico, however, for which the committee has the greatest sympathy in its present condition, and out of consideration for Corwin, the treaty was not rejected. It was left pending, without approval or disapproval.

In consequence of this, the committee charged Sumner with writing a report that proposes to table the treaty. This is a special procedure permitted by the rules of debate in the United States Congress, and it is the equivalent of leaving a matter without resolution. Later, a majority vote of the Senate could bring the matter under consideration.

Tomorrow or the day after, Sumner will probably present the committee report to the Senate, which will approve it without discussion, and thus this affair will be settled.

I regret this result very much. It destroys the supreme government's plans to obtain [financial] resources. I did what I could to avoid it. The current circumstances, however, have made it almost impossible to obtain approval of the treaty now.   [2:286-87]

SEPTEMBER 13 I have had an opportunity to see the August 28 dispatches which Corwin sent his government by this month's English steamer. . . . [This and the next two items are examples of Romero's access to confidential U.S. government documents.]   [2:383-84]

OCTOBER 10 I have had the opportunity to see this government's dispatch instructing Corwin that, if some government should establish itself in Mexico City, he should not recognize it but should refer the matter to the president's decision.   [2:537]

NOVEMBER 12 Accompanying the coming president's annual message to Congress, I have learned, the Department of State will send several of Corwin's notes on Mexican affairs, omitting, nevertheless, everything related to the April 6, 1862, [Corwin-Doblado] treaty.   [2:581]

DECEMBER 22   Animated by the uniformity with which the press of all political colorations has censured Corwin's conduct for intervening in favor of [the Swiss banker Jean-Baptiste] Jecker [Jecker had lent money to the conservative government in Mexico in the 1850s, the repayment of which became one basis for the French intervention in Mexico] because of Jecker's expulsion by the supreme government, I wanted the House of Representatives to take notice of this affair by requesting the relevant correspondence from the president. I spoke about this with Congressman [Jacob D.] Cox of Ohio, Corwin's home state. Whether because he was convinced of the impropriety of Corwin's conduct or out of a spirit of partisanship, because he and Corwin belong to different parties, Cox said he would present the resolution I suggested in the House and in the terms I would draft. Taking advantage of this offer, I drafted the resolution in such terms that, although merely requesting the correspondence, it encompassed a direct censure of Corwin's conduct. I gave it to Cox in the Capitol on the 15th. Since it was not presented this past week, I went to the House today to remind him of the resolution. While I was there he presented it without changing a single word. It was approved without discussion. . . .

the fact that Cox, a member of the Foreign Relations Committee, submitted the resolution, which was approved, should produce some effect on Corwin. He will be, perhaps, more cautious in the future.   [2:735]

1863

The year 1863 proved a turning point for both the American Civil War and Matías Romero's role in the United States. The persistent and increasingly effective blockade of the South, the major campaigns culminating in Union victories at Gettysburg and Vicksburg, and the restructuring of the Union military command are often viewed as the turning point in the Civil War. Romero resigned his post as chargé in early 1863. He expressed frustration because he was receiving neither his pay check nor adequate expense money to conduct a campaign to influence and shape U.S. policy with even a remote chance of success. After Romero had been in Mexico a short time, President Benito Juárez persuaded him to return to the United States with a promotion from chargé to minister and with assurances that funds would be available for his salary and for legitimate legation expenses to conduct a lobbying campaign to maximize Mexican effectiveness within the U.S. political system. During the brief period of Romero's resignation, the Mexican Liberals had correctly become convinced that French Emperor Napoleon III would send Archduke Maximilian to govern Mexico. Thus, upon Romero's return, he struggled more urgently to harness U.S. power and goodwill to the Mexican Liberal side. In the fall of 1863, Romero discovered that California Congressman James McDougall was a determined ally. McDougall labored long and hard against the French-Maximilian intervention in Mexico.

JANUARY 18 In this and the past sessions of Congress, Senator [James A.] McDougall of California has manifested the most interest in Mexican affairs. From the beginning he has believed that the emperor [Napoleon] proposes to acquire territory on the Pacific. . . . I have managed to keep him current with events [in Mexico], and I have supplied him, at his request, with copies of some of my notes to Seward. He offered the resolution mentioned in my note No. 17 of January 14 as proof of his favorable disposition toward us. . . . He told me that soon the Mexican question will be discussed in the Senate in public sessions. Naturally I supported him in that idea. I have arranged to give him whatever information is within my reach so that his speech will be favorable to us and solidly founded in fact.

Today McDougall asked me to come to see him. After I arrived at his house, he showed me some resolutions. . . . He asked me if I had any objection to them. After reading them carefully, I indicated some minor modifications, which he cheerfully accepted. Tomorrow, he told me, he would present them and he would request the Senate to set a day for discussing them, arranging for it to be next Thursday. Then he would make a well-prepared speech. He had indicated his intentions, McDougall informed me, to some senators, among them Sumner, chairman of the Senate Foreign Relations Committee, who had entreated him not to present anything or say anything that would be offensive to France, the only nation in Europe which is friendly to the United States. The public men of this nation are blind in this respect. The emperor [Napoleon] has deceived them like children. Through the medium of his dentist, an American citizen, Napoleon assures them that he is a friend of the Union and desires its reestablishment and indicates to them that they must fear England. Although he has failed to keep his word and even his sworn promises, they believe in his sincerity on this occasion. Even his decidedly partial conduct in favor of the South, acknowledged by President [Jefferson] Davis in his message of January 12 and by Secretary of State [Judah] Benjamin in correspondence recently intercepted by this government, is not sufficient to persuade them otherwise.

I do not have the remotest hope that McDougall's resolutions will be approved by the Senate, but the mere fact of their presentation and the subsequent discussion, I believe, will produce results favorable for us.

[3:123]

NOVEMBER 5 During my stay in New York I conversed with Robert McLane, former United States minister to Mexico, a very wise person, knowledgeable about the situation and about the tendencies of the European powers. During this conversation he communicated his opinion on Mexican affairs . . . which appeared in large degree judicious and well-founded. . . .

McLane has just returned from Paris, where his family presently resides. While there he had various conversations on the Mexican question with Duke Victor Fiolin de Persigny, who was then the French minister of government [roughly equivalent to secretary of the interior]. In these conversations, he sought to demonstrate to de Persigny, drawing upon his own experience, the impossibility of France establishing anything permanent in Mexico. Blindly confident that his government would succeed in tying one or more of the Liberal *caudillos* to the intervention, the French minister believed in the easy fulfillment of the French undertaking, provided that they had the perseverance to carry it to the end and were skillful in the mode of developing it.

The United States, McLane assumes, is in a situation where its influence in the Mexican question is entirely nonexistent. There is absolutely nothing, he believes, the United States can do in our favor. Even more, if it does succeed in doing something, he presumes it could not produce the French withdrawal from an enterprise to which France is already very committed. In his judgment it is more suitable for Mexico's interest that things remain in their present situation, because if by our action war breaks out between France and this government, France will immediately ally itself with the South and this alliance would produce two lamentable results for Mexico.

First, instead of having only one enemy as we now have, we would have two, France and the Confederate States. Second, the United States would be thoroughly defeated in a conflict undertaken against a combined France and Confederacy. The little influence the United States might have had otherwise would be entirely nullified. It must be remembered that McLane is and has been a partisan of the South. In his conversation with me, he has compared the strength of this government to subdue the rebel dissidents with that of France to impose a monarchy on us and of Russia to subdue Poland.

In McLane's opinion, the success or failure of the French forces in imposing monarchy on Mexico will depend exclusively on the means that are chosen to make it appear in Europe that the Mexican people really desire monarchy or would accept it with pleasure. If public opinion in Europe accepts such a view, England, Spain, and the other continental powers would recognize the monarchical government and the fate of Mexico would be sealed. If, on the contrary, the efforts in that direction were fruitless and in the eyes of Europe the Mexican people were evidently opposed to monarchy, neither England nor Spain would recognize it, and France would see the complete impossibility of carrying its enterprise to completion. This mode of viewing things appears quite valid because the French government persists in making it appear that the intervention is popular in Mexico, that the intervention is received everywhere with demonstrations of the greatest sympathy, and that everywhere the intervention is anxiously desired as the remedy for all the evils.   [3:489-90]

1864

Since 1862, some Republican politicians, called Radicals, had become increasingly irritated by their inability to align the Lincoln administration behind their program for freeing slaves and prosecuting the war more energetically and punitively. Radical Republican hostility toward President Lincoln and Secretary of State William H. Seward was not restricted to their differences on domestic policy and the conduct of the war. They differed markedly on the proper foreign policy for the United States to follow in face of the French threat in Mexico in the form of the puppet Maximilian empire. This dispute between Lincoln's administration and many Radicals came to a head when Maximilian formally accepted the Mexican throne under Napoleon's protection. Romero had labored hard, for example, not only with Representative Henry Winter Davis (Maryland) but also with Senator James McDougall (California) and Representative John Kasson (Iowa) to produce a resolution condemning French action in Mexico. The Davis resolution stated U.S. refusal to recognize any monarchy created in the New World under foreign influence and upon the ruins of an American republic. Although Romero preferred the Davis resolution, he realistically developed a strategy of keeping various resolutions alive by offering modest encouragement, while laboring diligently behind the scenes for the toughest resolution. If Romero's first choice failed, there were fall-back plans. Finally, the Henry Winter Davis resolution passed the House of Representatives on April 4, 1864, by a vote of 104-0. But Senator Charles Sumner prevented its passage in the Senate because he believed it unwise to challenge the French while in the midst of the Civil War.

By early 1864, Romero had become convinced that Lincoln and Secretary of State William Seward would provide no effective aid or assistance for Mexico. In response to the Lincoln administration's stance, Romero became interested in ousting Seward or unseating Lincoln. Toward this end an informal alliance of convenience bloomed between the Radicals (and other opponents of the administration) and Romero. For example, Romero supplied resolutions or calls for information which friendly Radicals introduced in Congress to embarrass the administration. Romero's sources kept him privy to the secret sessions of the Senate Foreign Relations Committee. He supplied information and documents and critiqued speeches for opponents of the administration during the summer and fall of 1864.

After interviewing the various Republican and Democratic candidates for the presidency in 1864, Romero lent his confidential support to the effort of Radical favorite General John C. Frémont to win the nomination from Lincoln. When Frémont's candidacy failed, Romero tried to encourage him to run independently. When this hope failed, Romero met with and aided Senators Benjamin Wade, James McDougall, and Zachariah Chandler and Congressman Schuyler Colfax through subtle means to defeat the Lincoln-Seward team.

A central goal of the Mexican minister was to end the U.S. Civil War so as to free the power of the Union to hang as a Democlean sword over the neck of Maximilian and Napoleon. In late 1864, Romero offered to undertake a trip to the Confederate capital in Richmond, alone or with the other Latin American diplomats in Washington, in search of a mediated end to the war. Seward expressed appreciation for the offer without requesting its implementation.

When Union military and political leaders could anticipate victory in the winter of 1864-65, Romero kept pointing to the unpleasant possibility that the French-Maximilian forces would offer refuge to the defeated, fleeing rebels, enabling them to recover from their wounds and renew the attack alone or aided with French-Mexican forces at some time in the future. Although many rejected such a scenario as unlikely, the possibility of guerrilla or raiding activity from rebel forces based in Mexico could never be dismissed. General Ulysses S. Grant repeatedly declared in 1865 that the Civil War would not be over until the French were expelled from Mexico.

JANUARY 19 Last night John Kasson, congressman from Iowa, visited me to inform me that he was considering presenting some resolutions on Mexican affairs in the House. Although lacking the character of hostility toward France which [James] McDougall's resolutions possess, these resolutions nevertheless would convey complete disapproval of the French invasion of Mexico and a manifestation of sympathy in our favor. Moreover, they would not commit the United States government to make war on France in the immediate future. Kasson claimed assurances that his resolutions would be unanimously approved in the House of Representatives. He intended to see the president and the secretary of state to obtain their opinions on the suitability of presenting his resolutions and on the terms in which they should be drafted, after which they would be presented without delay. He concluded by asking me various questions concerning the pretexts the French use for making war on Mexico and various other matters, which presented me with the opportunity to inform him of those things we desired him to know. I also offered him all the data and documents in my power relative to our war with France. Early in the coming week, I propose to invite Kasson, the Speaker of the House of Representatives, and various members of the House Foreign Relations Committee to dinner. At that time I shall attempt to make clear that they should expedite this important business in the best possible manner.

Since Congress will probably approve Kasson's resolutions, whereas McDougall's would not be approved, I judge it more important that the former are presented and passed. . . .

Today the Senate Foreign Relations Committee had its weekly session. Because McDougall, who is a member, did not attend, they did not consider his resolutions. That committee will not reconvene until Tuesday of next week. It seems unlikely it will do more then than it has until now. Therefore, I believe the Senate debate on this matter will still be delayed many days.   [4:9]

JANUARY 31 Henry Winter Davis, chairman of the House Foreign Affairs Committee, acting in advance of my own desires to see him, came to visit me today. We had an important conversation. Was he considering speaking in favor of Kasson's resolutions, I inquired? He still had not read them, he replied, but would study them this coming Tuesday. Moreover, he informed me, he had prepared other resolutions on the same matter. If Kasson's agreed substantially with his, he not only would approve them, but would be pleased that they had emanated from outside his committee.

He requested various information about different matters and about the intrigues of the French government. I noted his serious effort to concern himself with our affairs and to present them to the House's consideration in a prominent manner.

In the last few days, responding to the *London Daily News* story that the French commander in Mexico, General Eloy Forey, had obtained the assurances of the United States president that this government would not interfere with Archduke Maximilian in Mexico, the New York newspapers have published several articles in our favor. Fearing some foundation to that story, some dailies have suggested that Congress ought to investigate this delicate matter. Then I showed Davis the articles. . . . At the same time, I revealed to him a draft of a resolution [requesting an inquiry into the matter] written in what I considered were able terms. I inquired whether he considered it unsuitable to present the written resolution himself because he was invested with the position of chairman of the House Foreign Affairs Committee. In such a case, I informed him, I would ask another congressman, also a friend of mine, to present it. He would encounter no difficulty in presenting the resolution, he said, if the House and the whole country desired the information requested in it. Then he left with my draft resolution.   [4:21]

FEBRUARY 17   Last evening I had a conversation with Postmaster General Montgomery Blair. . . .

On the 9th of this month, the *Commercial Advertiser,* a New York evening newspaper, published an item translated from *El Continental* of January 12, referring to my remarks at a dinner for some of New York's leading men at Delmonico's restaurant on December 16, 1863. Blair had read this article and, at a reception he gave in his house on February 11, he told me it had struck him as very good. He has shown it to various of his friends, believing that it should be more widely circulated. On the night of the 16th at the house of John P. Usher, secretary of the interior, Blair told me that he had reread my speech (as he referred to it) and that he had read it to the president during a cabinet meeting. The president, Blair added, encountering many things in it which he had not been aware of, was pleased that it was read. Seward had requested Blair's copy. Returning again to the desirability of giving it wider circulation, Blair suggested that, since in general Congress was completely ignorant of the state of our affairs, it would be desirable at least for all the representatives and senators to read it. If Thomas Hart Benton were alive, Blair added, he would have taken care to inform Congress and the whole country of the actual situation in Mexico from his Senate seat, because he was a highly informed man concerning the policies and tendencies of foreign nations, who was always up to date on foreign events. Since Benton's death, no one had replaced him; and, therefore, the most complete ignorance of events outside the United States reigned in Congress. Blair concluded by suggesting that I should order the speech printed in pamphlet form, with large print to facilitate reading, and then distribute it to the members of Congress and to other persons who have a role in public affairs. I decided to follow these suggestions, which came from such a significant source as Blair, not only because of the high office he presently occupies, but also because of his wide experience in public affairs. . . .

In turn, I explained to Blair the objective I had in mind when I offered a banquet for some of the most prominent citizens of New York, speaking to them about the attitude of this government on Mexican affairs. As if wishing to defend Seward's policy, Blair mentioned that the United States government wanted to avoid involving the pride of the French nation in the Mexican conflict. Until now, he added, this war was unpopular in France. In addition, if the French government is left to fight internal discontent and the opposition of the Corps Législatif, this government believes, it will soon find itself compelled to withdraw the expedition. If the United States intervenes in the matter and requests the withdrawal of the expedition, however, French national pride will be offended, and under these circumstances the emperor would find sufficient grounds not only to prolong his Mexican intervention indefinitely, but even to make war on the United States. Moreover, a large part of the data that [Louis-Adolphe] Thiers used so effectively in his speech against the expedition, Blair informed me, came from this government. Combining this confidential information with impressions Seward conveyed on the day he lunched with me and regarding the intelligence links between this government and the opposition in the Corps Législatif . . . this government's policy in Mexican affairs appears more favorable under the new light.

Meanwhile, Seward continues in the same pattern of compliance with the French government that has distinguished his direction of United States foreign relations. As proof of his excess in this respect, I find it necessary to mention an incident that occurred a short while ago in the house of John L. V. Pruyn, congressman from New York. Pruyn had invited Seward, Salmon P. Chase, and various members of the diplomatic corps to dinner. At the dinner, Secretary of the Treasury Chase said in a jocular tone that he was going to open the port of Brownsville to Mexican commerce; Seward replied at once to Chase, remarking that "being neutrals, we ought to treat

both belligerents in an entirely equal manner, and if you contemplate opening a port for Mexico, it is necessary to open another for France."

The Sunday *New York Herald* published a telegram from Washington
which asserted that the United States government was about to lodge an
energetic protest against the French intervention in Mexico. Seward had
the press association correspondent in this city immediately deny this report. This government, Seward added, did not propose to follow any other
policy than that indicated in the recently published State Department correspondence. [4:52-53]

MARCH 2 A few days ago I asked [Henry Winter] Davis if the House
Foreign Relations Committee . . . had already taken up Kasson's resolutions
on Mexican affairs. He replied affirmatively, but added that it had resolved
not to take any steps in this matter until the French government's position
became clearer. He had received, Davis said, reports of an official character,
which assured him that the French government was disgusted with and
tired of the Mexican expedition, desiring to end it as fast as possible. In
addition, it had been suggested to him that if the United States should demand the retirement of the French forces in a more or less directly imper-
tinent way, the sensibility of the French people would be wounded. Such
an action would produce results entirely opposed to those desired. Finally,
if I had some indicator, Davis said, that the French government persisted in
its policy of intervention, such as, for example, that the Archduke Maximilian had accepted the crown and visited Paris as emperor, or, even better,
that he actually had embarked for Mexico, his committee would immediately approve the aforementioned resolutions. Then I mentioned to Davis
that the rumors of the alleged desire of the French to terminate their Mexican intervention had come to my knowledge and at first appeared reasonable. After reading Eugène Rouher's speech in the Corps Législatif this past
January 27 on the policy the imperial government intended to follow in
Mexico, however, I believed that far from having the slightest desire to
withdraw the expeditions, the emperor firmly intends to continue in Mexico until his plans are fulfilled. I offered Davis the issues of the Paris *Moniteur*, which published the entire debate on Mexico. A House declaration on
this matter, I surmised, is made much more urgent in the present circumstances because the French government is attempting to persuade Europe,
by means of its official press organs, that the United States government is
far from hostile to the projected intervention and establishment of monarchy in Mexico, looking upon it in fact with pleasure, and that a secret
agreement exists between the United States and the French, in which the
former has promised not to undertake any action that could frustrate the
success of the French plans. Up a certain point, I added, this had been con-

firmed by the Paris publication of Seward's dispatches on Mexican affairs, which were interpreted there as being very favorable to the intervention. Davis accepted my offer and, on February 17, I sent him the *Moniteur*. . . . Reading Rouher's speech apparently changed Davis's opinion.

This morning I went to the Capitol and conversed with Kasson in the House before the above-mentioned resolutions were discussed. I learned from him that the so-called authentic notices concerning the French government's desire to end the intervention emanated from Seward, who, pursuing his policy of condescension toward France, appears to have assumed the duty of preventing the approval of these resolutions.

I presented Kasson with the same information I had passed on to Davis and immediately sent him the *Moniteur*. If he encountered sufficient grounds for not lending credence to Seward's notices, Kasson claimed, he would have his resolutions immediately taken into consideration and approved.

Then I went to Davis. It would be desirable, I suggested, to inform the members of the committee of the conclusion he had arrived at regarding the intentions of the French government. If they agreed, there should be no more hesitation in this business.

For more than a month I have lobbied Congress to ask the president for the correspondence on Mexican affairs, without my yet having obtained even the presentation of the resolution. Today I again lobbied for this and fortunately obtained the presentation and approval of the resolution. . . . Having refused to present the resolution in the terms I had drafted because it contained implicit disapproval of French policy, Davis modified it to a request only for the above-mentioned correspondence and correspondence relative to Venezuelan affairs.   [4:76-77]

MARCH 16 A few days ago during a long conversation with Senator McDougall, I explained the necessity of discussing as soon as possible the resolutions on Mexican affairs presented in the Senate. Probably, I told him, Kasson's resolution would be discussed and approved soon, and, if that happened, his would not receive consideration. In the Senate Foreign Relations Committee session scheduled for yesterday, he suggested that he would try to obtain committee agreement on the report to be presented to the Senate. Then he would attempt to fix the nearest date possible for discussing the resolutions in the Senate. Today I saw him in the Capitol. In yesterday's session, he informed me, the committee had not wished to occupy itself with the cited resolutions, believing it inopportune to take this matter under consideration. He would not cease in his efforts, he added, to obtain an early Senate discussion of these resolutions.

I have also spoken to McDougall about the convenience of requesting the president for the correspondence concerning the intrigues France is nurturing to establish monarchies in South and Central America. I have learned from an unquestionable source that such correspondence exists in the State Department. Since McDougall agreed with me on that point, I left him a draft resolution which he presented yesterday in the Senate. It was approved.

A member of the House Foreign Relations Committee, who attended a dinner I gave at home last night, informed me that immediately after Kasson presented his resolutions, Seward made appointments with the committee members in the State Department. Seward imparted to them his hope that they would not take action on the resolutions for the reasons Kasson and Davis had previously mentioned. . . . Learning then the real difficulty that had arisen to prevent the approval of said resolutions, which I had only presumed before, I believed it necessary to work to neutralize Seward's efforts. This morning I had a long conference in the Capitol with Henry Winter Davis, chairman of that committee. Davis had told me that when I knew for certain that Archduke Maximilian had accepted the Mexican crown, these resolutions would be approved. That act would doubtless take place, I informed him. Considering the archduke's adventurous character, evidently he will not permit this opportunity to elevate his position to pass without taking advantage of it. If, after a year or two in Mexico under the protection of French bayonets, he learns, as he will have to learn, that he can sustain himself only with the support of [foreign] elements within a country that is essentially opposed to him, thereby obliging him to return to Europe, he will claim he left because he became convinced that the majority of the country were not in favor of the monarchy and he respected their right to choose. In Europe this would assure him the treatment and consideration of an emperor for the rest of his life. At the same time, it will preserve the respect, even the admiration, of those who believe he acted in good faith. Thus he would remain the most prominent candidate for the first monarchy that, as frequently occurs in Europe, might change its dynasty. In this manner he could also get out of his financial predicament, if, as the newspapers assert, this is another reason that has induced him to accept the crown. These considerations seemingly impressed Davis, who offered to bring them to the attention of the committee at the next session.

Moreover, if the House approved the resolutions, I told Davis, desirable consequences would follow: the expedition against Mexico would become unpopular in France, causing the French government to terminate it as soon as possible; the archduke would hesitate longer before going to Mexico; and the Mexican people, seeing the sympathy of a great nation officially expressed on their side, would redouble their effort to resist the intervention. Meanwhile, I continued, no inconvenience would result from the approval of these resolutions. Since they also needed Senate approval, and since Seward had more influence in the Senate than in the House, he would certainly succeed in having them swept under the carpet, which would satisfy the scruples of even the most timid.

The desire not to delude the supreme government concerning what the Congress of the United States will do compels me frankly to express my opinion that unless something extraordinary should occur, such as, for example, the complete defeat of the principal Southern armies and the capture of Richmond, there is no possibility that even Kasson's very inoffensively worded resolutions would obtain approval from both houses. Perhaps they could be approved after it is known that Maximilian has embarked for Mexico. Nevertheless, this conviction will not impede my continued, totally dedicated effort to obtain, through any means at my disposal, the approval of the aforementioned resolutions or other similar ones.   [4:100-102]

MARCH 23   On the 21st of this month I received a letter from President Juárez. . . . Since the news it contained, the only authentic material that has come to my knowledge, is favorable for our cause in comparison with those emanating from the French sources circulating here, I communicated it immediately to the newspaper. I also informed our friends in Congress of the letter's contents to encourage the passage of the resolutions on Mexican affairs now pending in both houses.

On the 21st, then, I went to the Capitol and communicated to several senators and congressmen not only these news reports but also those from the Austrian minister. . . . [Henry Winter] Davis . . . was not at the Capitol, so I sent a letter to his house . . . containing the substance of the information I had passed on to the other congressmen and senators.

With pleasure I inform you that my efforts have produced excellent results. . . . On Tuesday the 22nd the Senate Foreign Relations Committee met. McDougall proposed that it consider his resolutions. Sumner, chairman of the committee, whose fear of France makes him as condescending with that nation as Seward, attempted to prevent a decision on these resolutions. . . . The opinion of the majority of the committee did not appear to be so much against the resolutions as against the desirability of discussing them at that time. Of the seven members on that committee, only two, [Lafayette] Foster and [Thomas T.] Davis, appeared to agree with McDougall, who is resolved that the committee shall not indefinitely delay Senate debate on the resolutions. Last January, when he presented the resolutions, McDougall reminded his colleagues, he had requested that they be passed to the Foreign Relations Committee, not because he expected a favorable report, but because, being a member of that committee, he felt obligated to submit them first to that committee out of courtesy. Now he

merely asked the committee to return the resolutions to the Senate, requesting that it be excused from reporting, which would allow him the opportunity to speak on this matter. Because the committee does not intend to do
so, however, he cannot submit to the continued delay in this important
matter during the present session. He said that in yesterday's session he
would present different resolutions even more explicit and more hostile toward France. This time he would not request that they be sent to the committee, but rather that they lie on the table so that he could speak regarding
them when convenient. In fact, he wrote and presented the resolutions . . .
and obtained consent this past Friday to discuss them, but he will probably
need two or three weeks to prepare his speech.

Although Senate committee meetings are secret, I have learned these
details in a confidential manner from a member of the Senate Foreign Relations Committee who visited me this morning. . . .

Desiring to know what had occurred in the House Foreign Affairs Committee, I went to the Capitol at noon. The committee had decided at its last
session, Winter Davis informed me, to present its report on Kasson's resolutions, [which, however,] would be replaced by one he read to me. I re-
member it sounded approximately like the following:

> In order that the silence of the United States would not be interpreted as assent
> to the events that are currently taking place in Mexico, it is declared that the United
> States government will never consent to the erection of a monarchical government
> under European influence upon the ruins of an American republic.

He has had no opportunity, Davis added, to present his report to the
House, and probably he would not have a chance until next Monday. He
does not fear that the report will encounter opposition.   [4:112-13]

APRIL 9 I had a long conversation with General [John C.] Frémont, candidate of the abolitionist faction for president of the United States in the
coming election. Naturally, I spoke to him almost exclusively of Mexican
affairs, informing him in great detail of our situation and of what this government has done and could have done in regard to the intervention. I was
pleased to find him very favorably disposed toward our cause. Bitterly censuring the administration's policy in the Mexican question, he is disposed
to adopt a bold attitude if he should be elected. Speaking of his possibilities
in the next election, he knew with complete certainty and could emphatically assure me that Lincoln would not be reelected. All the probabilities of
the election favored him, he implied.

I tried to see General McClellan, another of the candidates, but did not
find him at his residence. Nevertheless, he also highly disapproves of the

administration's policy, I know, and favors the Monroe Doctrine, although apparently he will not go as far in this respect as Frémont.   [4:126]

APRIL 13 Today's *New York Times* published a telegram . . . asserting that, in conformity with the administration's wishes . . . the Senate Foreign Relations Committee decided not to occupy itself for the present with the April 4 House resolution on Mexican affairs. This is equivalent, the reporter claims, to a complete disapproval of that measure. . . . Today . . . I visited Sumner. . . . The committee, he informed me, had occupied itself yesterday with that matter, but without arriving at a definite decision. The resolution, he understood, had been approved against Seward's wishes and he needed to talk with Seward before resolving what he would do. Sumner strongly professed his sympathy for Mexico and his desire to aid us in every way possible. At the same time, however, he believed we ought not take any step that would compromise, or make more difficult, relations between the United States and France. These were clearly his general ideas; still, he had not begun to examine how they should be applied to the case of the previously mentioned resolution.

The resolution, I strove to explain to him, could not compromise the relations of this country with France in any way. In the form approved, the resolution was reduced to a simple question of recognition. Thus the fact of Senate disapproval, or simply nonapproval, would be equivalent to a declaration that the United States might recognize Maximilian's government, if it managed to establish itself in Mexico. This would, I observed, leave the question in a worse condition than it had been before the House approved the resolution. I also stated my belief that even Seward would rejoice that the resolution was approved so he could shield himself with it when France asked for recognition of Archduke Maximilian as emperor of Mexico. I made him weigh the consideration that public opinion had received this resolution with singular pleasure. It should be, I insisted, approved in legal form. . . .

Before adopting any resolution on this matter, Sumner expressed his wish to speak with Seward and Davis. . . . At the same time, he added, he would gladly receive any suggestions I had to offer on the matter. Without prejudicing the approval of the pending resolution, which seemed to me in any event indispensable, I expressed the belief that it would be desirable for Congress also to approve a resolution expressing, in a polite and conciliatory tone, the view that the United States could never look with indifference at European intervention in the affairs of the American republics. If the European powers insisted upon intervention, there would be danger of a deterioration in relations between the intervening powers and the United

States and even the possibility of major complications arising. The United States should desire to avoid this by means of a frank declaration.

Since Sumner had presented some similar resolutions regarding European intervention in United States affairs in the previous Congress, I did not imagine, I told him, anything better being done than to apply the previous resolutions generally to European intervention in the domestic affairs of American republics, of which the United States is the principal and most directly interested. Sumner received this idea with pleasure. He would write the resolution in the form that appeared most agreeable to me, he said, and he would take it under serious consideration, presenting it to the committee he chaired and doing all that he could in favor of the Mexican cause.

I always believed that any legislative disposition that would manifest, even indirectly, disapproval of French policy would encounter great opposition in the timid character of Sumner, whom I consider even more complacent toward the French than Seward himself. Nevertheless, in spite of that senator's scruples, I do not lose hope that the legislative body to which he belongs might sanction the cited resolution. For this goal I am going to do everything within my power. [4:127-28]

MAY 26 During this past week . . . I have visited various senators, friendly to Mexico, to obtain their cooperation concerning a suitable course regarding the resolutions about Mexico pending in that chamber. The most widely held opinion here is that it is best for Congress not to occupy itself with Mexican affairs until General [Ulysses S.] Grant's campaign results in the destruction of the Confederate army under General [Robert E.] Lee's command and the subsequent capture of Richmond. Then, the senators and other high functionaries unanimously agree, the Senate will not only immediately approve the aforementioned resolution, but the government will take more efficient steps against the French intervention in Mexico. Senator [Benjamin] Wade of Ohio, one of the most influential members of that body, who was almost elected president of the Senate in the last election, is also one of the most energetic critics of the administration's timid policy in Mexican affairs. Wade has demonstrated complete sympathy for our cause.

Some Democratic senators have told me that they favor immediate action, whether out of opposition to the government or out of conviction I don't know. In accord with them and with McDougall . . . we agreed that . . . McDougall would seek to discuss the resolution introduced on April 27. This resolution ordered the Foreign Relations Committee to present a report on the House resolution relative to Mexican affairs. Instead, it seemed more advisable and easier to petition the Senate to excuse the committee from presenting a report, thus permitting the House resolution to be discussed without waiting for the committee to present it for discussion. With this objective our resolution was presented. . . . Yesterday our resolution was supposed to be discussed and voted on, but the Senate was occupied with other affairs. . . .

On May 19, during a conversation about Mexican affairs requested by Senator Wade, I offered to send him a draft resolution requesting the president to submit the correspondence concerning the current situation in Mexico and concerning the intrigues of some European powers to subvert republican institutions on this continent, establishing monarchies with European principles in their place. Since the resolutions on the same subject which Davis offered this past February at my request were not sufficiently explicit, it seemed to me advisable for a distinguished senator energetically to present a resolution in the Senate.

Yesterday Wade presented such a resolution. To the draft resolution I gave him . . . he added another section relative to the correspondence concerning exportation of contraband of war from this country to Mexico. . . . The resolution was unanimously approved. Even if Seward should not send the requested correspondence, claiming that the national interest does not permit it, we still have obtained the advantage of calling the attention of the American people to our affairs through the repeated congressional resolutions.

On March [May] 18 . . . I saw Winter Davis in the House of Representatives. The tenor of [Seward's explanation to the French regarding the House's April 4 resolution rebuking French intervention in Mexico] was such, I observed, that this government's explanations became more than explanations: they were apologies. They must have been offered spontaneously, I added, because sufficient time had not passed to allow the French government to ask for them. If France had asked for explanations, it would have made the request in Paris and news of the request would have arrived here. At the same time, I suggested to Davis the desirability of requesting the correspondence on this matter from the president, at least to avoid the appearance that the House helplessly submits to the humiliation which the executive has obviously exposed it to. Davis adopted the idea immediately. On the 23rd he presented a resolution . . . which was approved unanimously. Yesterday the House received the president's reply accompanied by the requested correspondence. . . . From the correspondence it seems that the French chargé d'affaires here requested the explanations. The response Seward gave him, as well as those communicated to [William Lewis] Dayton, did not justify by any means the [demeaning] terms in which the *Moniteur Universel* has alleged the explanations were given. The explanations are, in my judgment, decorous and dignified. When they become known in Europe, they will furnish another incident exposing the low degree of veracity of the *Moniteur.*   [4:183-84]

JUNE 14 According to Sumner's formal promise to McDougall, today the Senate Foreign Relations Committee should have decided upon the report it will present to the Senate with the April 4 House resolution on Mexican affairs.

With the purpose of learning what the decision had been I . . . saw McDougall in the Senate. When the committee met, he informed me, Sumner commenced to speak in favor of the resolution, saying that it was necessary to approve it and that it must be done therefore, but that it still was not desirable to take this step, although the opportunity soon would arrive. He spoke the whole time the committee met. When the Senate session opened at noon, the committee meeting adjourned without having adopted any action. The matter remains pending for next week. Certainly then, what has occurred up to this point will repeat itself. If this government's circumstances do not notably improve, the cited resolution would most likely not be approved during the present session of Congress. . . .

The day before yesterday McDougall told me that he was considering presenting a resolution on Mexican affairs, using the same wording as the eleventh resolution from the platform of the Baltimore convention. . . . Since the administration [faction] wrote that resolution, the idea seemed very good to me. It would contain the principles on which the administration pretends to base its policies. Since the administration has a majority in the Senate, it would not be possible to conceive of anything that body ought to approve with fewer objections. The nature of the resolution would, nevertheless, change radically if the Senate approved it. Then it would have the official character which it now lacks and would obligate the government, which currently is not obligated in any manner. I supported, then, McDougall's idea. This morning he had already decided, he informed me, to present the resolution. Moreover, although he was unable to present it in the Senate today, he would present it tomorrow if possible. . . .

Today I also saw Winter Davis, who, being sick yesterday, could not present the report referred to in my note of June 8. He expects, however, to present it next week. In the present circumstances, I do not believe that this report will be approved. In a vote taken in the House of Representatives on June 6 upon Davis's request to suspend the order of business in order to present his report, the House denied his petition by 55 votes against 43.

[4:226-27]

JUNE 21 Today the Senate Foreign Relations Committee had another meeting in which nothing was said or agreed to concerning the resolution on Mexican affairs pending before that body. Sumner gave an account of the message the president sent at the end of last week to accompany the correspondence on Mexican affairs which the Senate had requested. By an error of the president of the Senate, the president's message was not sent to be printed but only passed on to the committee. Sumner was wary because the best part of the correspondence submitted has emanated from the Mexican legation. Nevertheless, Seward, who certainly would not have included anything whose publication was disagreeable to his view and to his policy, forwarded the correspondence. Sumner reacted to his swelling fear by stating that the correspondence would not be published, or that some might be published but only after a thorough examination. The committee discussed this until adjournment, when it agreed to hold an extraordinary meeting this Friday.

As soon as I learned what had happened in the secrecy of the committee, I informed Senator Wade. Wade had presented a resolution asking for the publication of the aforementioned correspondence . . . the normal procedure with messages received from the president. In addition, I saw other senators and I propose to see Sumner himself this evening or tomorrow. The desirability of publishing the correspondence seems so obvious to me that doubtless in the end it will be done. . . . The current session is near conclusion and there are many matters of private interest pending, which in such circumstances and in this epoch always obtain preference over the public interest. Moreover, because the military position of this government has not improved, nor is there hope it might improve, the Senate will certainly close its session shortly without approving the resolution on Mexico which the House passed unanimously this past April 4.

On June 14 McDougall presented a resolution on Mexican affairs. . . . This morning McDougall told me that he had purposely not sent his resolution to the Senate Foreign Relations Committee so as to be able to discuss it when the opportunity arises. . . . It still seems unlikely that McDougall will be able to make his prepared speech.

Last week, Winter Davis was ill at his house in Baltimore and thus could not present the Foreign Affairs Committee's report to the full House. . . . He left it in the care of two members of the committee, one of whom, [Samuel S.] Cox, I will see tomorrow. Cox expects to present this report before the House adjourns. He is preparing a speech which he proposes to make on that occasion, but it seems unlikely that he will be able to present it.   [4:234-35]

JUNE 23   Yesterday I had a long conference with Sumner . . . about the resolution on Mexican affairs now pending in his committee. A very few people, he told me, believed that a war with France suited the interests of the United States because it would arouse the public spirit, not only to fight that power, but also more easily to subjugate the South. However, only a very small number of people shared this opinion. There are others, Sumner said, who believe it advisable for the United States to assume a decisive, public position in opposition to the French intervention in Mexico, certain that this course will not lead to war and that the French will do what they want to do, whatever the conduct of this government might be in the meanwhile. Sumner told me that he shared this opinion to a certain point. Believing it proper to sin more on the side of excess precaution, however, he had joined with those who formed the majority. While the Civil War lasts, or at least during its current favorable period, he believed it undesirable to give the French the slightest pretext of an excuse to intervene in favor of the South or indirectly to aid the Confederates.

In turn I managed to explain to Sumner the danger, not to say the error, of his position, which will lead to great inconveniences. Although he was convinced of the justice of many of my observations, the road he has proposed to follow seemed safer to him. . . .

My conversation with Sumner has confirmed me in the view . . . that probably, indeed almost certainly, the Senate will not approve the aforementioned resolution during the present session.

Then I spoke with Sumner about the correspondence concerning Mexican affairs which the president recently sent to the Senate. If it were not possible to do anything else, at the very least, I entreated him, the Senate could offer the public authentic information about the events taking place in Mexico. Before deciding whether to publish the correspondence or not, Sumner told me, he was going to ask Seward if it were desirable to publish it. Other committee members have indicated to me that they favor publication, so the correspondence will probably be published.

Yesterday I also saw McDougall in the Capitol. He mentioned that he was just returning from presenting his new resolution about Mexico in the appropriate form. Although it elicited some opposition, it was finally admitted. He is prepared to discuss it when the opportunity presents itself. . . .

I went at once to the House of Representatives and entreated Speaker [Schuyler] Colfax to do all in his power so that Davis could present the report to the Foreign Affairs Committee. . . . Colfax, who is among our best friends, told me that Davis has had and would have opportunity to present the aforementioned report. In presenting it, however, Davis wanted to make a speech in regard to the report, which had not been and would not be possible. As soon as Davis returns, I shall endeavor to persuade him not to make a speech so that we do not forego both things. Meanwhile, I will state the same thing to Cox and [Godlove] Orth, who are charged with presenting the report during Davis's absence. [4:236-37]

JUNE 29 Today I must inform you that, although not by express agreement, the Senate Foreign Relations Committee tacitly agreed not to occupy itself with the April 4 resolution.

On the 27th, Davis managed to present the report . . . and he even requested a vote on its concluding resolution. He did not obtain the vote. The report was merely sent to be printed. On the same day I saw Davis, who expressed his hope that the resolution would be voted upon during the week, although he thought it would be done without discussion because the House now had very little time at its disposal.

Last Friday, the Senate Foreign Relations Committee did not occupy itself with the matter of printing the president's message accompanying the correspondence on Mexican affairs. Yesterday, upon reconvening, the Senate considered this matter. Wishing to put the correspondence aside without proposing frankly that it should not be printed, Sumner moved that the Senate consider matters that remain pending at the close of this session during its next session. McDougall opposed this maneuver, declaring that its intention was to avoid the printing of that correspondence. He moved to take it from the committee and print it.

McDougall's resolution was disapproved and Sumner's was approved. Nevertheless, the purpose of his resolution having been revealed, this morning Sumner proposed that the message should be passed on to the committee on printing. By that act seemingly he desired to pass the responsibility for printing the documents to others. I will continue to seek the printing of the correspondence. . . .

Following my suggestion of several days ago, Wade communicated to me that he has presented the resolution asking the president for copies of all orders sent by the War and Treasury departments in relation to the exportation of arms and contraband of war from the United States. He added that this resolution had been approved. . . .

I fear the president will not reply to the resolution, principally because so little time remains before Congress adjourns.   [4:241]

JULY 31   At the end of last week I saw McDougall in New York. . . . He had decided, he told me, not to return to San Francisco because he thought he could be more useful to the country by remaining here to work toward having the Chicago convention nominate a candidate whose excellent prospects for success would prevent Lincoln's reelection. Toward this goal and to accomplish what he would have done if he had gone to California, he was writing a letter to his constituents expounding the very powerful reasons, in his judgment, for not reelecting Lincoln. McDougall would consider Lincoln's reelection a public calamity; he believed it necessary to avoid this very deplorable prospect at any price.

Among the reasons counting against the reelection of Lincoln, McDougall maintained, a principal one was his very objectionable conduct of United States foreign affairs, most especially his policy in regard to Mexico. Not being well informed of the details of the Mexican question, although he knew the story in general, McDougall wished me to supply him the facts and necessary details to enable him vigorously to attack the government on this subject, but from an unassailable position. Then he read me what he had written on the subject. Although in general very good, there were various omissions and inexactitudes which I offered to correct by sending him a memorandum containing all the points it would be desirable to touch upon and all the facts necessary to speak with certainty. [A long passage is left out in the printed text.]

McDougall's letter will appear ably and judiciously written and will encompass all that could be said against this government's policy. He has extended to other public men with some special knowledge or interest the same invitation to review his ideas which he made to me. In this way he has obtained the advice and counsel of various eminent men, all of whom are enemies of the administration. McDougall and his friends are quite confident that they can prevent Lincoln's reelection. They are now directing all their efforts to this task. [4:282-83]

SEPTEMBER 10 Last night, while traveling by train from Washington to this city [New York], I encountered [Zachariah] Chandler from Michigan, an adherent of the Radical Republican faction and a member of the Joint Committee on the Conduct of the War.

He was very interested to learn what news I had from Mexico. Upon my reply that relatively speaking everything was going well, he asked me if I believed the supreme government could sustain itself for six months more. Most certainly, I responded, it could even sustain itself for six more years. Demonstrating great satisfaction at hearing this reply, on his behalf he requested me to tell President Juárez to make an effort to sustain himself for six more months, which period would not pass without [Mexico] receiving the effective aid of the United States.

You know, Chandler added, my position as a member of the Committee on the Conduct of the War makes me aware of current developments. In this sense, before next January 1, I can assure you, the organized armies of the South will be destroyed and only a guerrilla war will continue, which will soon be crushed.

After that, he continued, we will have a very considerable army, which it will be impossible to muster out and which will find no better occupation than to help you throw the French out of Mexico. This step will not only conform to United States interests but, in our situation, will also become such an imperative necessity that no government could oppose it.

Although Chandler's concern with General Grant's capability to destroy Lee's army was not unusual, accomplishing this task could easily still require a year or more. Regarding the rest, he merely expressed the senti-

ments and opinions of an American statesman. His ideas were in agreement
with others on this subject.   [4:343-44]

NOVEMBER 24   In my note of July 28, all we needed to make our affairs
take a more favorable turn, I explained to this ministry, was for the Civil
War in this country to end. If this occurred, I added, it alone could make
the French emperor withdraw his forces from Mexico. In the same note I
expressed my desire to do anything within my reach to obtain that result
which offered some probability of success.

Pending the presidential election, it was not possible to do anything in
that regard. Once the election was past, and in view of some indications
suggesting this government would not be ill-disposed toward a peace proposal and the Southern government even less ill-disposed, I decided the
time had arrived to mention to Seward my desires and dispositions with
respect to this matter. We desired, I told him, to see the Civil War that presently afflicts the United States terminated as soon as possible. When the
South recognized, I conjectured, that Lincoln's reelection firmly committed
the North to continuing the war until the reestablishment of the Union and
that at least another four years of unequal war awaited it, consuming its
resources and destroying its country and its inhabitants, it would be more
disposed to consider peace proposals and a negotiated termination of the
question. The South's disposition might change, particularly if it realized
that while the two sections of this country were destroying themselves in a
family quarrel, Europe was stirring up discord and rejoicing at seeing the
only republic that inspired respect on this continent divided and debilitated.
France is preparing soon to do to the United States what it has been doing
to Mexico and the other Hispanic American republics.

If he believed, I added, that a journey by me to Richmond would produce a good result, I would go, not as a commissioner of this government
but rather as a representative of a nation most directly interested in the Civil
War in the United States. If he desired, I observed, I would arrange for the
ministers of Venezuela, Colombia, and perhaps Chile to accompany me on
this mission. This would be a majority of the Hispanic American representatives resident in Washington.

I have had this desire for some time, I also explained, but I had not
communicated it because previously its realization seemed very unlikely to
succeed. With Lincoln reelected and things at their present state, however,
I thought something could be achieved by offering an amnesty to all who
have taken part in the insurrection. Furthermore, proposing to recognize a
part of the Southern debt would perhaps make some settlement easier to
arrive at.

Confidentially and with complete frankness, Seward replied, he would explain the government's policy on this point. "There is a question which is insoluble in the present circumstances," he said, "and it is the matter of slavery. No compromise was possible with regard to it. Slavery not being legally abolished, and there remaining a considerable faction in the North favorable toward it, if we concluded some arrangement with the South now, we would recognize slavery in some manner. We desire to remove the basis of the rebellion by making its prime cause, slavery, disappear. Any negotiations, then, that might be undertaken in the present circumstances would divide the Northern people on this key issue, with a great danger of leaving the cause of the conflict in existence. In the next Congress," he added, "the antislavery party will have a majority of more than two-thirds. This majority will be able legally to amend the articles of the Constitution that recognize slavery. To obtain this goal, it will be necessary to call Congress into special session next April or May. Once slavery is legally abolished, we could offer the South peace terms without dividing ourselves and with greater probability that the peace terms would be accepted. We shall offer them a reasonable compensation for the manumitted slaves, provided they submit. If the South continues in insurrection, however, it faces the prospect of losing its slaves and other things without any compensation."

In light of these explanations, and already having communicated my wishes in respect to this important matter, I wished only to state that, if at some time he believed my efforts and those of my colleagues could produce some good result toward putting an end to the Civil War, he had only to advise us when he thought the opportunity had arrived. I would do anything in my power on this matter, I affirmed.

Seward thanked me for my good wishes and good disposition to cooperate in reestablishing the United States.   [4:442-43]

1865

Although Romero's offer to travel to Richmond to initiate negotiations to terminate the war was not acted upon, Montgomery Blair obtained permission for his father, Francis P. Blair, Sr., kitchen cabinet member and editor during Andrew Jackson's administration, to visit his old friend Confederate President Jefferson Davis. The senior Blair hoped to persuade Davis to end the war so a joint military campaign could be undertaken to oust Maximilian and Napoleon from Mexico. This plan offered the Confederacy a face-saving way to terminate the war while upholding the Monroe Doctrine. Romero was privy to the early discussions of the project and authorized the senior Blair to offer Jefferson Davis command of one of two corps that would enter Mexico under General Ulysses S. Grant's overall command. One corps would consist of former Confederate troops, the other of former Union soldiers.

A few days after Lincoln's assassination, Romero met with President Andrew Johnson, believed to be a staunch advocate of applying the Monroe Doctrine to the French intervention in Mexico. Johnson wanted arms made available to the Mexican Liberals and directed General Grant to act on his own authority to aid them. The president welcomed the creation of a private military force made up of former U.S. troops and approved the appointment of General John Schofield to command the volunteer force. Seward continued to obstruct effective U.S. action, however, and Johnson revealed no desire to circumvent him.

The Radicals also distrusted Seward's power and intent, and they altered the diplomatic appropriations bill to prevent the recognition of Maximilian's regime by permitting funds only for a minister to the Republic of Mexico. Romero continued his lobbying and political contacts with a wide variety of opponents of a soft policy toward the empire in Mexico. Congressmen John Conness (California), Thaddeus Stevens (Pennsylvania), Elihu Washburne (Illinois), Samuel S. Cox (Ohio), Godlove Orth (Indiana), Jacob Howard (Michigan), Robert C. Schenck (Ohio), Nathaniel Banks (Massachusetts), Speaker Schuyler Colfax (Indiana), Senators Zachariah Chandler (Michigan), Benjamin Wade (Ohio), and James McDougall (California), General John Logan, New York businessman James Beekman, New York politician Thurlow Weed, and editor of the *New York Herald* James Gordon Bennett were among the objects of Romero's incessant lobbying activity in 1865. Romero also maintained his contacts with past and current cabinet members Montgomery Blair, Postmaster General William Dennison, and Attorney General James Speed. Finally, Romero retained contacts in the State Department who alerted him on foreign relations activity.

A major new force with whom Romero established links in 1865 was General Grant. Grant and Romero discovered their shared views in April and May 1865, forming an alliance that worked effectively over the next several years and a friendship that remained close until Grant's death in 1885. Grant agreed with Romero that the U.S. Civil War and the Liberal struggle against the French-Austrian invasion were parts of one general contest. The two worked closely to create a force of former U.S. and Confederate soldiers to enter Mexican republican service to help drive the French out. They selected from a small list of candidates consisting of Generals William T. Sherman, Philip H. Sheridan, John M. Schofield, and Francis P. Blair, Jr. After

Sherman revealed a lack of interest and Sheridan was judged of greater service in command of the Union forces along the Mexican-Texas border, from where he could funnel supplies, advice, and recruits to the Mexican Liberal forces, Schofield was tapped for the mission. Johnson, Grant, Schofield, and Romero worked out the terms of Schofield's contract and the size of his force. But they were outmaneuvered when Seward persuaded Schofield to accept a diplomatic mission to visit Napoleon to extract a promise that he would depart from Mexico. Seward knew that Napoleon was not likely to allow Schofield to talk with him privately, but Schofield went to Paris and never commanded the forces on the border. Other generals, Lewis Wallace, Francis P. Blair, Jr., and Joseph E. Johnston, were supposed to raise the troops and prepare the operation pending Schofield's return. Eventually, Wallace and others moved some volunteers to the frontier, and apparently several hundred, perhaps several thousand individual volunteers ultimately joined Juárez's forces. But the massive, organized bodies of troops envisioned by Romero and Grant did not join the Mexican Liberals. Still, U.S. arms, funds, and other forms of aid became much more accessible for Juárez's army, indicating a level of success for Romero, the determination of Johnson to aid in the ouster of Maximilian, or both.

JANUARY 10 [Montgomery Blair] told me last night that, while reflecting upon how to terminate the present difficulties of the United States, he had encountered an easily realizable method suited to both Mexican and United States interests.

This reciprocally advantageous arrangement consisted of the following: When the Southern cause should be deemed hopeless, which Blair judged would occur within a month, Confederate President Jefferson Davis should be invited to lead an army of 20,000 men of all three arms to the Mexican Republic to throw the French out and, in this manner, to revindicate himself before his fellow citizens. This army ought to consist of two divisions, each division of three brigades, and each brigade of four regiments. The force's commanding officers, subordinate officers, and men should be drawn in equal proportion from the Confederate and the Union armies. For example, Robert E. Lee could command one division and William T. Sherman the other. Only skeletal regiments would be organized in the United States, which would be raised to full force upon arrival in Mexico.

Once this arrangement is made, with the knowledge and support of the president of the United States, of course, the army would march to Texas. This army would carry sufficient arms to raise a considerable force in Mexico and provisions adequate for several months. Passing to Mexican territory via Matamoros, for example, this force would place itself at the orders of the supreme government. It would serve as the nucleus of the force that would throw the French from our territory.

To implement the plan, Blair claimed, it would be indispensable for the supreme government to authorize me to name Jefferson Davis, General Lee, or whoever circumstances appropriately indicated as general in chief. Alternatively, the supreme government could send me a blank form to fill in the corresponding name here. The general in chief ought to name the two divisional commanders, the six brigadier generals, the twenty-four colonels, and the other officers necessary to organize the force, all with the consent and approbation of a person designated by the supreme government for that purpose.

According to the plan, the supreme government does not even have to spend a cent in the organization of this force, in its transportation to the Republic, or in sustaining it during the time between its arrival in Mexican territory and the occupation of Mexico City. Mexico will recognize all the expenses made with the approval of the designated agent, paying either with unoccupied land or with property confiscated from the traitors (Mexican conservatives). The principal drawback to this arrangement exists in the danger to our independence of having such a considerable force of foreigners, which could prevail over our army anywhere in our territory, beyond the supreme government's authority. This army would have an open road to acquire more [control] and could rebel after occupying the country, proclaiming [Mexico's] annexation to the United States. However, maintaining the equilibrium in the forces sent between the officers and soldiers from the North and South and taking other precautions would reduce this danger.

If we must choose between the aid offered us by this government and by private persons who are willing to bring forces to our country, evidently we ought to prefer this government because it is more responsible than the private individuals whom we could make use of. In addition, we can obtain effective guarantees for our security and independence from this government. Since we are not faced with a situation that would allow us to accept the one and reject the other, I believe we ought to extract the best possible deal out of what is proposed to us. Moreover, I have assurances that once this project begins to develop in the suggested form, the United States will necessarily be drawn into a war with France. In this case, the United States would conveniently sign an alliance with us, thus presenting us the opportunity to solicit and obtain the necessary guarantees. . . . Communicate President Juárez's instructions on this important matter as soon as possible.   [5:4-5]

JANUARY 14 This past December 15, I gave a dinner in this city attended by Senator Wade of Ohio and Representative Winter Davis. Davis mentioned to Wade that the House had passed the appropriation bill for the diplomatic service that day. When it is presented for approval in the Senate, Davis continued, it would be desirable to modify it to read "the Republic of Mexico" where it now reads that certain monies are destined to "pay the appropriate expenses of legations in London, Paris, Mexico, etc." By this step, Davis said, Congress would decide the question of recognizing Maximilian, by denying funds for the president to send a minister to the archduke. In addition, the Senate's decision to accredit only a legation sent to the Mexican republican government would decide the question of recognition because, in Davis's opinion, even should the executive desire otherwise, he would not dare to recognize Maximilian against the Senate's wishes.

Wade accepted the suggestion. Yesterday, while the Senate was discussing the appropriation bill, Davis went to the chamber to remind Wade of the amendment. Wade proposed the amendment, which was accepted unanimously. Although some senators, desiring not to provoke the suspicions or indignation of the French government, were opposed to the amendment, Wade proposed it in such a clever way that no one had the courage to oppose it.

We have obtained a triumph of considerable importance through that decision. Not only does it decide the question of recognition against Maximilian, but it will also make clear to the French public and to all of Europe how illusory Napoleon's assertions are that this government is nearly ready to recognize that puppet regime. It will also produce good results in Mexico City by frightening Maximilian, perhaps contributing to his early retirement from our country.

Davis told me today that he had asked Senator Sumner to offer this amendment in his character as chairman of the Senate Foreign Relations Committee. Sumner refused for fear of arousing the suspicions of the French government. Once the amendment was proposed by Wade, however, Sumner did not dare vote against it.

This is further proof of the great popularity of our cause in this country. [5:7-9]

FEBRUARY 4 On January 10 . . . I received a letter from Montgomery Blair relative to the sending of forces from this country to Mexico. . . . The principal objective of that letter appears to have been to persuade me of the urgent necessity of asking the supreme government either for a blank check for whoever will go as commander in chief of said force or for authorization to name him here. On the evening of the 11th I went with [Juan] Zambrano to see Blair. His conversation focused almost exclusively upon recommending that we immediately request the aforementioned authorization. Once we have the authorization in our hands, he explained, Jefferson Davis and General Lee could be induced to conclude peace with the North and to enter into the undertaking. If the blank check or the authorization to name the general in chief here was so important, I then told Blair, I would send a

special agent to Chihuahua to bring it back if the supreme government decided to issue it. Blair replied that I could not make a better move.

I took care that Zambrano accompanied me during these discussions so
that, if the negotiations had taken an undesirable turn, which could have
developed with this government over our attempting to send armed expeditions to Mexico, the responsibility would fall on him alone [thus protect-
ing Mexico's official relations, via Romero, with Washington].

Afterward, speaking with Zambrano about this, I indicated that he
would go to Chihuahua to inform the supreme government verbally and in
detail of all aspects of this matter and return with its decision and instructions. So that he might carry something tangible, we agreed to present some
proposals to Blair which we believed the supreme government would be
disposed to make. Thus, if they were accepted here, Zambrano could carry
them with him and make clear in Chihuahua what one is disposed to do
here. . . .

The 12th we returned to see Blair to read these proposals to him. They
seemed good to him. He said that they would be approved here. Only the
first item would be difficult to accede to, he judged, because it would involve the United States government in the arrangement. Although this government will be informed of, approve, and support what is being done,
nevertheless, desiring to avoid war with France if possible, it does not wish
to be openly compromised. The 13th Zambrano went to New York to prepare for his trip to Chihuahua. Soon he fell ill and has not returned here,
nor have I heard of him.

The 15th [Francis P.] Blair [Sr.] returned from Richmond. Supposedly
his mission failed. I no longer considered it necessary to send a special agent
with the correspondence relative to this matter. On the 24th I mailed the
correspondence. Since then, however, everything has changed. Now the
probability that the North and South might make peace on the basis of
sustaining the Monroe Doctrine . . . has convinced me anew that it might
be easy for them to make an arrangement such as Blair proposed. Last night
I went to visit Blair. He told me all was going well. Before long peace will
be concluded, he assured me, because our conversations on this matter
were known in Richmond. Peace would be made, Blair claimed, either on
the bases we had discussed or upon other substantially similar bases.

[5:42-43]

APRIL 20   The new president received the diplomatic corps today. . . .

Fifteen minutes before the specified hour, I went with the secretary of
the legation to the State Department, where the diplomatic corps would
gather to be accompanied by [William] Hunter to see the president. . . .
[Prussian minister] Baron [Friedrich von] Gerolt read a speech of which I

had no prior notice in the name of the diplomatic corps. Hunter read an appropriate reply in the president's name. Naturally, both speeches contained only generalities and commonplaces.

After the two speeches, the dean of the diplomatic corps departed, followed by the other members of the diplomatic corps. As I took leave of the president, he said that he was happy to have made my acquaintance and desired to see me at greater length. Shortly before, I had spoken with Preston King, ex-senator from New York and currently perhaps Johnson's most intimate friend. King asked me to visit him tonight at his hotel. Through his intervention, King implied, I would obtain a confidential interview with the president in order to speak with him concerning our affairs.   [5:237-38]

APRIL 24   On April 21 . . . I expressed my desire [to Preston King] for an interview with the president to present some facts relative to the affairs of my country. Desiring to do this confidentially, I preferred not to solicit an interview through the State Department. . . . I entreated him to bring my desires to the president's attention and to advise me when an interview would be granted. King was pleased to do me this favor.

On April 22, King came to my house to inform me that the president would receive me today at 10 a.m. . . .

Today, then, at the designated hour, I went to the Treasury Department. I was conducted to the president's office at once, where I encountered the president with King. After exchanging greetings, King offered to leave us alone so that I could speak to the president with greater liberty. He then withdrew, leaving only the president's private secretary writing at a table a considerable distance away in the room with us.

The president received me very cordially. I began by offering apologies, because of the importance of the matter, for having requested, on short notice, an interview that would distract him from his more pressing matters. He replied that excuses were not necessary. Then he inquired if I had spoken with the secretary of state about the matter I proposed to relate to him. I had brought it repeatedly to Seward's attention, I told him, and now I desired only to communicate these same reports to the president in detail. I considered it necessary to commence my account by informing him of the Mexican parties, their tendencies and aspirations, and the state at which they have presently arrived. I hoped to make clear to him that we [the Liberals] defend the interests of the masses against the privileged classes. The president had used class privileges as a theme in various of his recent speeches responding to the congratulatory messages received from various societies and corporations. Necessarily, this account had to be quite long. Concerned with tiring him, I attempted to abbreviate my account. Noting my effort, Johnson told me: "I am not in a hurry. What you are relating is very interesting to me, so I entreat you not to omit anything you believe necessary to leave me well informed on the present state of affairs in Mexico." Next I informed him of the goal of the French intervention in Mexico. It was more hostile toward the United States, I carefully indicated, than toward Mexico itself because it was undertaken at the moment when the French knew that the Civil War had broken out. Thus their intervention would aid in the destruction of the Union.

From there I passed on to speak of the Mexican Republic's sympathies for the Union cause. We identified it with our cause because we are fighting in defense of our independence, of our autonomy and the rights of the people, and of the republican form of government and liberal institutions. President Johnson has championed these principles in the aforementioned speeches. The defense of the same principles, we understood, had animated the defenders of the Union.

So far the United States has appeared more interested in aiding France than Mexico because it has permitted the French to export from this country what they need to make war against us—wagons and mules. I then observed that the United States has not permitted us to export the arms we imperatively need to continue the defense of our country and our institutions. It was not my intent to lodge a complaint against this conduct, I explained, or even to request its immediate alteration, because the president would do that, I was satisfied, when he decided to work on this matter with the knowledge of all the circumstances of the case. I did feel obliged, however, to tell him that I had rejoiced with all my heart at his accession to power. The government and people of Mexico certainly were also delighted in the same degree because of his past record in favor of democratic institutions and the interests of the people and especially his views in regard to the Monroe Doctrine. I had read with great interest, I told him, his Nashville speech of July 9, 1864, when he was notified that the Baltimore convention had nominated him as the vice-presidential candidate. Besides accepting without reservation that part of the convention's platform relative to the Monroe Doctrine which the legislatures of various loyal states previously approved, his speech demonstrated full comprehension of the importance and the significance of the French intervention in Mexico and of the American people's unwillingness to tolerate a French presence on the American continent for very long. Johnson could not hide his pleasure upon learning of my report on these matters, nor when I mentioned having sent my government a translation of the section on Mexico, which I understood had been published in the Republic.

I referred immediately to the very profound and open sympathy between the Southern rebels and the traitors in Mexico because of their shared principles and their common political opposition to the Union. I mentioned the possibility already suggested in the newspapers that Jefferson Davis and the other chiefs of the rebellion would go to Mexico if driven from the United States. I noted also the preparations [Achille François] Bazaine, who supposedly had departed for the frontier, was making to receive them. He was fortifying the frontier so that the insurgents could offer resistance to pursuing troops at the frontier.

I also communicated to Johnson the tenor of my conversation with [Montgomery] Blair . . . after informing him of various other things. . . . For the future we desire to identify our political interests with the United States, I explained, to celebrate advantageous commercial treaties so that both nations can draw all the advantages of an intimate union and to imitate the United States's great example, thereby arriving by the same road at the prosperity and magnificence it has achieved.

Johnson listened very attentively and without interrupting me. From time to time he asked minor questions to understand better what I was saying. For example, when speaking of our lack of arms and the difficulty we had in importing them, he inquired if we did not manufacture any in the Republic. He also asked what our population was, what part of our population favored the French, how many soldiers we could raise, the population and area of the state of Chihuahua, the distance between Mexico City and Chihuahua, whether there was an abundance of provisions between these two cities, and similar questions. He called for a map to understand my explanations better.

In turn, his ideas and his work in favor of popular government and popular interests, he told me, were too well known to require repeating. He had not changed his ideas nor would he change them, he added. They would remain his guide when the hour to act arrived. This was the tenor of his reflections, if not his exact words, which covered these concepts more extensively. We were certain, I stated, that he would now develop the same political principles and ideas he had proclaimed and defended with great effort. Referring to this point, I had to smile upon seeing in the *Courrier des Etats-Unis* of New York, I explained, the idea calmly advanced that he could not maintain the same ideas as president which he had defended when seeking high office.

Johnson could not restrain his smile upon hearing this. At the same time he asserted: "I am already too old to change my ideas so easily and above all when they constitute my second nature."

It did not appear desirable to say anything to Johnson that could be taken as a direct complaint against Seward's conduct. Upon recovering he might well return to the State Department, in which case I would be placed in a very false position in regard to him.   [5:259-61]

APRIL 30 Lacking authority to encumber more than the income from federal taxes of the state of Tamaulipas for the purpose of bringing 10,000 volunteers from this country to that state, and, since this guarantee is insufficient to raise the necessary funds to satisfy the expenses consequent to that undertaking, General [José María] Carvajal expressed his hope that he might work in concert with Zambrano, who has authorization to dispose of other income.

We met for this purpose at my house on April 28. I expressed the utility for all people who have similar authorizations from the supreme government to coordinate their work rather than to conflict with and prejudice each other. General Carvajal spoke next, saying in essence what I have just related. With a flimsy pretext, Zambrano excused himself from expressing any opinion. Yesterday he informed me that he did not intend to cooperate with anyone else authorized by the supreme government to carry troops to the Republic, offering arguments I considered worthless. At the bottom of this matter, I believe, lies the jealousy that others will do what he wants to accomplish alone.

In the meeting of the 28th I said that in my judgment we ought to make General Grant our confidant, express our wishes to him, and seek his counsel in fulfilling the supreme government's instruction.

This morning I went to inform Grant of this, but found him with other people, so had to limit myself to generalities. He showed me the greatest cordiality. He reiterated what he had told me on other occasions, namely, that although he is tired of war, his major desire is to fight in Mexico against the French, that the Monroe Doctrine has to be defended at any price, and that France ought to leave Mexico before the United States demands it imperatively. He was glad to know, he also told me, that one of Lincoln's last acts had been to sign an exequatur recognizing José A. Godoy Mexican consul in San Francisco.

Grant shared [Montgomery?] Blair's opinion regarding the probability that Jefferson Davis will go to Mexico. In this case Davis will probably place himself on the side of the supreme government so as to expunge his dishonor. Grant considered this war definitely over. Speaking about Texas, he believes General [Edmund] Kirby Smith, now commanding the Confederate forces west of the Mississippi, will surrender or disband his army. If Smith makes the slightest resistance, however, Grant will send forces to subdue him immediately. Obviously Grant does not intend at present to send an expedition to Texas. . . .

General [Jesús González] Ortega, who has already arrived in New York, apparently has given the impression that he came for the purpose of buying arms and enlisting an armed force.   [5:280]

MAY 8   Last night I saw [General Grant]. He was with the commanding generals of the Departments of Washington and West Virginia. As was natural, when I entered the conversation moved to Mexican affairs. Certainly Napoleon regretted what his minister, [Eugène] Rouher, had expressed to the French Corps Législatif concerning the retirement of French forces from Mexico, General [Winfield S.] Hancock maintained, and Rouher would surely have used another tone if he had known previously about the fall of Richmond and the termination of the Civil War.

Then General Grant said that he was expecting a visit from the French chargé, who had asked to see him soon. Grant proposed to tell him that the United States would pursue the same policy of neutrality and nonintervention in regard to Mexico which France had adopted toward the United States Civil War. Grant claimed that 60,000 veterans from the United States Army would march to Mexico as soon as they were mustered out, and this government would not oppose that action.

This caused the conversation to turn toward the armed emigration that will soon move toward Mexico. All the generals expressed the strongest desire that soldiers of bad conduct and bad antecedents should not go to Mexico, but rather veterans who would not harm the Republic and who would leave the name of America well appreciated. This properly prepared the road for what I had to tell General Grant later.

Immediately after this Generals Hancock and [Christopher C.] Augur departed, leaving me alone with General Grant. Before I could frankly state the object of my visit, as if to prove his decision in favor of the Mexican cause, he spontaneously informed me that when he was only a division commander in charge of a military department, he had visited General Banks on the eve of that general's first expedition to Texas. If he were in Banks's place, Grant told him, he would resign from the army upon arriving at the frontier and cross over to Mexico with all his forces, provisions, and equipment to fight against the French under the orders of the supreme government. Now he could not suggest such things, Grant added, because such an indication from him would be taken as an order and could compromise the government.

Then I told him that it would not displease us to receive some of the more renowned soldiers from this country, as much to serve as a sort of nucleus for our army as to make the sympathies of this people more fruitful for our cause by facilitating our acquisition of the resources needed to terminate the war with the French. I then told him that we considered the immigration of armed citizens of the United States into Mexico a very probable development, which neither we nor the United States government could easily prevent. This being the case, we desired to organize and direct that immigration to obtain reciprocal advantages from it instead of the chaos consequent from the march of disorganized parties of filibusters. With full confidence in his experience, patriotism, and good intentions, we desired to consult him, I also suggested, in all cases on which he considered himself free to offer his opinion. Should his official responsibilities impose the necessity of total reserve, however, he need only tell us so immediately, with the understanding that his decision would not offend us. He responded at once that he would not hesitate to present his opinion frankly over any point we solicited.

Then, starting from the indicated assumptions, we considered the regulation of immigration as advantageous to Mexican interests as to those of the United States. With this objective we desired to give the command to a [United States] general of recognized merit and ability, in whom we could have complete trust and whose name would suffice to attract brave men, give credence to the undertaking, and secure material means for us from this country. For example, we aspired, I added, for either Sherman or Sheridan, the generals in whom General Grant has the most confidence, to place himself at the head of the immigration. Either choice would greatly please General Grant. We could not find anyone better, he claimed, although he doubted whether Sherman would be inclined to accept.

We arrived at a difficult point in the conversation. It was necessary to pause. I wanted him to know that he was the most appropriate person successfully to conclude this undertaking aimed at assuring Mexican independence, not only against French intervention, but also against the artifices of American filibusters. Fortunately, his genuine desire to see the affair succeed was such that he opened the road for me, informing me that his wife earnestly wished him to go to Mexico. "Nothing would please us more," I answered him, "than your decision to go because your name would fill a vacuum which no one else in this country, nor in Europe, could fill." "You could go," I added, "as a United States citizen or as a Mexican citizen, as you wished. In the first case, you could request leave from your government. Supposedly leave would be conceded to you and also to the other officers who would accompany you, since I see no reason why the United States would not follow the custom of European nations to grant peacetime leave for their officers to participate in foreign wars." General Grant shared my opinion regarding this matter. He proposed to consult with the secretary of war with regard to the freedom discharged citizens ought to have to emigrate where they wish.   [5:296-98]

MAY 16   On the 9th Grant came with six people from his staff to dine with me. During the meal he and his aides appeared to enjoy themselves and manifested considerable cordiality. It was not the proper occasion to continue the conversation commenced with the general on the 8th, so I limited myself to speaking of general news, which, in our interest, should have come to his attention.

Afterward I had no chance to see him alone. To achieve this purpose, I decided to go to Philadelphia, where he also had to go at the end of last week. Grant had invited my sister to visit Mrs. Grant in that city. Unfortunately, my sister could not go, but I offered to accompany him if he would advise me on which train he was leaving. He graciously sent me word that he would go on Saturday the 13th on the 11:15 a.m. train. I arranged my trip and met him on that train. He traveled quite indisposed. Because he rested during most of the way, I could not speak to him during the trip.

Upon our arrival in Philadelphia, he invited me to stay at his house. I accepted. . . . Although the general was quite indisposed a large part of the time we were there, I had more than ample opportunity to tell him what I wished. His indisposition actually favored me, permitting me to spend almost all my time with him. Otherwise, receiving the people who wanted to see him, I would scarcely have seen him alone in his own house.

My principal objective was to learn if he had decided to go to Mexico. Since I last wrote you on this matter, the idea has occurred to me that it is perhaps more desirable for him to remain here because his elevated position will present him many opportunities to help us. With regard to whoever goes to the Republic, especially in view of what will have to be done there, we can find others who would serve us with equal advantage. I did not find it desirable, then, to insist much upon his decision to go to Mexico. At the same time I discovered that he did not believe his going [to Mexico] was necessary to throw the French out of the Republic.

The danger that this note might fall into our enemies' hands, plus the little to be achieved by referring in minute detail to the terror of my conversations with Grant, prompt me to deviate on this occasion from my custom of reporting to the supreme government every little step I take here to promote the interests of the Republic.

The success of the plan formed here will depend in large part on the secrecy maintained regarding its details. This consideration, no less than my desire not to compromise our best friends, forces me to limit myself to informing you that all goes well here according to our wishes. Soon we will be able to obtain all the assistance we need from this country.

The notes 106, 107, and 108 of this ministry . . . contain all the authorizations and instructions from the supreme government which I could desire regarding this affair, including authorization to contract with the U.S. government for U.S. officers and a cadre to fight in Mexico to expel the French. [5:315-16]

MAY 20   Since the Philadelphia trip, Grant has told me that soon General Sheridan will leave here to command an expedition composed of close to 50,000 veterans. . . . This force will move with Sheridan over Shreveport, Louisiana, where General Kirby Smith, who commands the Confederate forces west of the Mississippi, presently has his headquarters. At the same time nearly 25,000 men who assisted in the capture of Mobile are embarking there to go to the Rio Grande under General [Frederick] Steele's command. Sheridan will be the commander in chief of all these forces and of the Military Department of Texas.

Last night I visited Grant to show him Kirby Smith's proclamation and General [John B.] Magruder's speech. . . . Both items stated very clearly that they expect the aid of France and Maximilian. While I was with Grant he called for Sheridan so that we could converse a while about Mexican affairs. . . .

This afternoon I returned to see Grant in his Georgetown house. He showed me a letter referring to the declarations of Smith and Magruder, which he received from Carvajal, who is now in New York. If the Confederates passed into Mexico, Carvajal's letter said, as governor of Tamaulipas, he would not be opposed if United States forces entered our territory to pursue them. Although I agree with this idea and believe the supreme government will not disapprove it, I found it strange for Carvajal to express it, even representing himself as disposed to make an agreement for this purpose without first having placed himself in agreement with me. He probably does not have authorization for his course.

We probably would not oppose the passage of United States forces into our territory, I told Grant, if it occurred with permission of the local authorities. We would consider it then as a very effective step toward initiating the war between France and the United States, which must break out sooner or later.

Speaking on this same point, I mentioned to Grant how desirable it would be for the United States to throw the French from Mexico before mustering out its army. In the first place, it can do this quickly and with little effort. Because the United States already possesses an abundance of arms, munitions, provisions, transport, and all types of war material, a war with France would cost financially only the soldiers' pay for a six- or eight-month campaign. The United States could very easily prevent the landing of French reinforcements in Mexico. It could finish with those troops now in the Republic in a few days. Since the United States did not possess a merchant marine because either the Confederate raiders had destroyed it or it had passed into English hands, U.S. commerce would not suffer in a foreign war. Victorious in a war with France, the prime military nation of Europe, the United States would assume the most prominent position among the great nations of the globe and would have punished the pride and audacity of the French tyranny. I have managed to express these same considerations to other influential people. If the Confederates in Texas seek refuge in Mexico, the rupture between France and the United States will be very nearly precipitated. Because of some of Grant's words and other signs, apparently this is precisely what is desired here, and this government is preparing for a war with France.

Moreover, Grant informed me that he had received a note the State Department sent to the War Department, which forwarded it to his office. The note inquires whether to concede permission to a French officer serving with Maximilian to visit the United States Army and its hospitals. Because Maximilian is hostile toward the United States, Grant expressed his opinion that permission should not be granted.

From what Grant has told me on several occasions, this government does not intend to permit France to send reinforcements to Mexico. Such a step would be considered here, I infer, as a movement hostile to the United States.

I have succeeded in persuading Grant of the need to construct a railroad from Brazos de Santiago to Brownsville without delay. This railroad will be of the greatest importance in our subsequent operations. [5:327-28]

MAY 21 Yesterday John Conness, senator from California, saw me. He was among those who believed that while the Civil War lasted the United States should not even speak of Mexican affairs. About to depart for San Francisco and having a matter to communicate to me, he desired an interview with me today. I agreed to visit him this morning at his house. . . .

His sympathies for our cause were no less than any other person's, Conness told me at once. The Civil War here having already terminated, he considered himself at full liberty to express his sympathies and to speak out in favor of them. He intended to inaugurate his new policy to this effect at the end of the month, alluding to Mexico in a speech in New York during the presentation of a sword of honor sent from California to General [Joseph] Hooker. This presentation will occur before a large crowd on a solemn occasion in the local club of the New York City Union League.

Conness read the part of his speech referring to our affairs. It consisted of a few but very opportune and energetic sentences. Moreover, he had sent a copy of his speech to Hooker, he told me, to give him time to prepare a suitable reply, while calling Hooker's very special attention to the part referring to Mexico.

Conness's change is very significant and important because of his elevated political position. Moreover, like him, many people of no less influence have experienced similar changes since the war ended in this country, promising the happiest results for our cause.   [5:328-29]

MAY 30   When I informed Grant of the conversation I had with Sherman regarding Mexican affairs [on May 25 Sherman indicated he had no interest in Mexican affairs] . . . Grant told me that after Generals Sherman and Sheridan, he considered General [John] Schofield, now commanding the Department of North Carolina, as the most meritorious general produced by the Civil War. From the political point of view and as a man of talent, Grant classified him superior to Sheridan.

Schofield is currently absent on a commission for his government, which would not permit him to leave the service. Therefore, before choosing from among the generals who have expressed their desire to go to Mexico to supervise the military emigration that will probably be directed to the Republic, I thought it best to verify if Schofield, who has a more elevated position and who is more qualified, would be disposed to assume charge of the enterprise.

Because my presence in this city is absolutely necessary now and not wishing to attract public attention or prematurely reveal our plans . . . I determined to send [Ignacio] Mariscal, secretary of the legation, to Raleigh, capital of North Carolina. . . . I arranged a pass and a letter of introduction from Grant to Schofield. . . .

If Schofield thinks like Sherman, I will have to revert to General [Frank] Blair. Sharing the opinion of our friends, he is the most appropriate among those expressing a desire to serve in Mexico.

Last night his brother, Montgomery Blair, who ardently wishes for his brother to go to Mexico, visited me. He informed me that his friends were working to have the president name his brother secretary of war. This nomination probably would be made, he added, in which case we will have a good friend in this important ministry. If his brother is not named to this position, he will remain free to go to Mexico.

The forces that have orders to go to the Rio Grande and that have already departed for this destination, Grant informed me in our last interview, consisted of General Steele's troops (8,000 white men) and the 23rd Corps, composed solely of Negroes, for a total of 24,000 men. After learning of the surrender of the Texas forces, Grant informed me, he had queried Sheridan by telegram whether he could send the 4th Corps to the Rio Grande. Sheridan had replied that he would do what he could. This will raise the total force on the frontier to 35,000 men, a circumstance that cannot help being significant after the surrender of all the remaining Confederate forces in that region.   [5:343-44]

JUNE 5 Last night I had another important conversation with General Grant. . . . Previously on various occasions, he told me, he had spoken with Lincoln about Mexican affairs and was well acquainted with his manner of thinking and his policy. Grant observed, however, that he had not been able to speak with the new president on this subject. Yesterday, Grant visited the president at his house, finding him alone. . . . He told the president that he did not consider the Civil War completely terminated while the French remained in Mexico. All the discontented Southerners and the people most hostile to the United States, Grant added, would take refuge in Mexico to organize themselves in the shadows of the French, while continuing their intrigues against the United States. For these reasons, Grant informed the president, he had considered it desirable to locate a sizable force along the Rio Grande frontier, where he would soon have more than 40,000 men.

At the same time, General Grant expressed his view that the United States ought to make clear to the French that, if the Mexican people really supported Maximilian, the national forces could sustain him, and, if these forces were not sufficient, the Mexicans should be allowed to decide their own fate.

The president heard these ideas and viewpoints with pleasure. He had not had sufficient time to consider the Mexican question, he responded, but he shared fully in Grant's opinion.

General Grant had previously communicated these ideas and facts to the secretary of war, who had heard them without indicating if he approved or not.

All appearances indicated to me that the United States wants a war with France. Very few troops have been mustered out, and a very considerable force has been gathered on the frontier.

According to Grant, on May 28 the first expedition left City Point for Brazos de Santiago. United States forces occupy the frontier from Brownsville to Rome, Texas. Everything gives the impression that these forces are our most decided friends.

General Carvajal went with me to see General Grant, although Carvajal did not hear the conversation referred to above. At my direction he asked Grant for a letter of introduction to General Sheridan, which Grant offered to send to him. . . . The secretary of the legation left Washington on May 31 to see Schofield. . . . I am very pleased with the extent to which my frequent, long, and cordial conversations with Grant have profited our cause. His [continental] Americanism, good judgment, good intentions, and love of justice have made him realize immediately the importance of the Mexican question and its latent consequences, of benefit to both Mexico and the United States. I have made every effort to present the matter to him with the greatest clarity. In his conversations with other people, I have had the satisfaction of hearing him express as his own various concepts favorable to our cause, whose justice and necessity I have managed with persistence to demonstrate for him. We can, I believe, already count upon him as one of our country's best friends.

Last night I also told Grant that I planned for General Schofield, or the person who would head the migration movement to Mexico, to arrive privately at an understanding with this government in order to know very precisely what he would be allowed to do. Thus he could proceed without any obstacles. With Grant's help and the confidence this country will have in our triumph when it sees a person of recognized merit assuming leadership of our movement, we will obtain ample resources to purchase all the necessary war material and to pay our troops. Our general's influence and his good relations with the most influential members of this government will permit him to buy arms, munitions, and other used army material at a relatively low price. Then everything will move according to our desires.

[5:360-61]

JUNE 18   On the evening of Thursday the 15th I saw Grant in his house. . . . I informed him of what had come to my notice regarding the policy Seward intends to follow with relation to Mexico. . . . On that very day, Grant told me, he had had another conversation with the president on Mexican affairs, and his ideas in that regard were entirely in agreement with Johnson's. Grant also informed me that he had issued an order peremptorily demanding that the French return the cannons and other arms which the Confederates at Brownsville sold to the traitors in Matamoros shortly before surrendering to the United States forces. In this respect, it would be desirable, I indicated to him, if the State Department did not intervene in this matter. If this negotiation is made diplomatic and passed on to Seward, I ventured, Grant's orders will remain unfulfilled.

I reminded him of his offer of a letter of recommendation to Sheridan for Carvajal. . . . Soon I received the letter written by Grant personally. . . . We could not desire a more satisfactory note. . . .

[The following] information came to my attention in an entirely trustworthy manner. The friend who confided it to me, however, specially requested me not to mention his name.

The recent conversations between Grant and President Johnson over Mexico have apparently prompted Johnson to fix his attention seriously on these affairs to sustain or revoke the measures which Grant, as general in chief of the United States Army, already has taken without having consulted any cabinet member. These measures were extremely serious. The president believed that such measures should be discussed in cabinet meetings. He invited Grant to attend the discussion. The cabinet meeting on the 16th was concerned exclusively with this matter. Explaining his conduct and ideas, Grant contended that the French intervention in Mexico had been undertaken in open hostility to the United States. Since all Southern discontents would go to the French area to reorganize themselves and to prepare another war against the United States with European aid, Grant argued, the Civil War should not be considered completely ended while the French remain in Mexico. Now, while the United States was ready and armed, Grant wanted to cut the root cause of the war. Throwing the French from Mexico at this time would involve very little effort and would not even necessitate declaring war on France, Grant added, for it would suffice to give arms to us and to permit us to recruit 10,000 men to serve as the nucleus of our army. Meanwhile, the United States would observe in all this the same neutrality that England and France had observed toward it during the Civil War. He informed the cabinet of the troops he had sent to the border and of his instructions demanding the return of the cannons sold to the Mexican traitors.

Seward took the floor at once, ably refuting Grant's ideas and making his own policy prevail, which is exactly the same one followed during the Lincoln administration. The United States must require the French to abandon Mexico, Seward agreed. He appeared to differ only in the means to be used to obtain that result. Grant's proposals would produce precisely the opposite result, Seward insisted, because they would wound French pride and produce a war with France. With his policy, Seward assured them, there would not be a single foreign bayonet in Mexico within six months. In respect to the demand for the cannons which [General Tomás] Mejía purchased, Seward claimed he would obtain their immediate return via the diplomatic route without complications. Seward maintained that Grant's idea to ask France to retire its forces from Mexico would also lead to war, and therefore he did not consider it.

The other cabinet members made no opposition to Grant's ideas. All, including the president, entirely agree that the French should not remain in Mexico. The president said nothing to indicate his inclination to one policy or the other, only requesting Grant to present his plan in writing so it could be taken into consideration at the next cabinet meeting on June 20.

You will see from the preceding that the Mexican question is in open crisis here. The president has two policies before him. Perhaps before the end of this week, he will have decided on one or the other. Should he decide for Grant's policy, there will be war between the United States and France, if Napoleon has not ordered his forces out of Mexico before the end of the year. Then we will have at our disposition in this country abundant sources of money, arms, war material, and even men. If Johnson decides for Seward's policy, however, we will remain in the same situation as during the darkest days of the Lincoln administration. We will be unable to acquire a dollar, a rifle, or a man here. In fact, we would be reduced to what we can do with our own resources while Seward's preponderance lasts.

Undoubtedly the president's sympathies are decidedly in our favor, but I greatly fear Seward's efforts. He is a man accustomed to parliamentary maneuver and blessed with very excellent qualities, which produce fear of him as an enemy in a cabinet discussion. His qualities will triumph over an opponent's simple and straightforward arguments and over Grant's good faith and simplicity. Above all, this seems likely when I consider that some of Seward's colleagues will support him in the cabinet.

Given the importance of these moments you will comprehend why I have considered it my principal obligation to give Grant any information in my reach so that he can vigorously sustain his policy and influence the president's thought in any conceivable manner. I intended to prepare the president to favor Grant's view by making him realize that Seward's neutrality would be hostile to Mexico to the point of humiliating the United States. I have already taken various steps in this direction, but I will take any additional steps I can in the time remaining until next Tuesday. The nature of these efforts, the desirability of not mentioning the names of the people associated with me, and the little to be achieved through acquainting the supreme government of my efforts in detail lead me to abstain from mentioning these steps in this note. . . .

Returning now to my interview with Grant last night, I must tell you that, being aware of these details, I had a very interesting conversation with him. My purpose was to make Grant aware of what Seward's neutrality leads to and to explain to Grant the very great advantages I really believe the United States and Mexico will reap from adopting his policy. I informed him of several developments so that his plan might appear more solidly founded in fact. This morning I brought him an English copy of Napoleon's letter to General Forey of July 3, 1862, which explained Napoleon's objectives in regard to his Mexican intervention. I spoke of the colonization contract concluded between Maximilian and Gwin, which Colonel [Ignacio] Mejía claims is a political plan to seduce all Southern insurgents to Mexico.

Grant also told me that he had mentioned to the secretary of war my idea of sending an officer of the United States Army to the Republic. Grant related that the secretary immediately expressed a favorable disposition to grant the necessary permission to that officer.

A person enjoying Grant's confidence, I have learned, wrote to General Steele, commanding along the Rio Bravo, telling him that Grant's official advice to Steele to observe neutrality in Mexico's war with France meant the type of neutrality France pursued toward the United States in its Civil

War. In this light, one should not hinder the crossing of arms and war material, nor even armed men, provided of course they were not rebels.

Confidentially and quite reliably, I also know that this government's purpose in sending the 25th Army Corps, composed only of colored soldiers, to the Rio Grande was to offer them the opportunity to cross over to us. Supposedly, large numbers will do this because of the advantages they will enjoy in Mexico, where the Negro race is not the victim of prejudice.

Likewise, the objective of this government, I have learned, in ordering that soldiers mustered out could retain their arms, cartridge belts, and equipment upon payment of a nominal price of only 6 dollars was to facilitate their going into Mexico armed and equipped. Moreover, upon learning that General [Joseph A.] Mower, who commanded the 20th Army Corps under Sherman, wished to fight against the French in Mexico, this government assigned him command of the 25th Corps already on the Rio Grande after his corps was mustered out.

I am well aware that the steps I have taken and will continue to take in this delicate matter could compromise my personal relations with Seward. However, convinced he will never consent to this government taking any decisive measures in our favor, regardless of the demonstrations of his personal appreciation shown me, we stand to lose absolutely nothing if he should become personally ill-disposed toward me. I have not hesitated to risk the slight vexations this enmity might cause me when my conduct may achieve great advantage for my country. [5:390-93]

JUNE 24 Recently I received the triplicate of a letter from General [Plácido] Vega dated in San Francisco, May 13, in which he writes among other things, the following:

General [Irvin] McDowell left yesterday for Los Angeles, informing me that in spite of his repeated messages to Washington, he has not directly received the order, which has been published in the newspapers and which you have confirmed to me, permitting the exportation of arms. Thus we can do nothing in that respect. Mexico will not receive arms-export permission, I really fear, and thus the officials will not return my deposits. My fear is reinforced when, at this very moment, I see a message in which President Johnson categorically asserts that he will not deviate in any way from the policy which the immortal President Lincoln pursued in respect to neutrality in Mexican affairs. Johnson will respect Seward's policy. Meanwhile, he refers to some leaders who are attempting to engage the government in the Mexican question, even though he privately expresses regard for the Monroe Doctrine. What do we say, when yesterday a boat loaded with potatoes and other provisions for the French departed because the order for free exportation had been communicated directly to the customs office? Meanwhile, General McDowell has requested instructions which he claims have not been sent to him. If you have not been able by tomorrow partially to answer my note of May 10 relative to this matter, which I repeat today in case the previous note has gone astray, I will assume that your efforts have been fruitless this time, which I will increasingly regret.

Thus, as of May 13 it appears that the arms had not been returned to Vega although they ought to have been returned in conformity with the president's orders of May 4. If I informed the president of these facts, some of our friends thought he could not fail to see that his subordinates are mocking his orders. Furthermore, he would proceed to ensure that his orders were fulfilled. In the existing circumstances, our friends surmised, my information might produce advantageous changes in the cabinet. . . . On the way to the White House, the possibility occurred to me that the arms could have been returned to us after May 13 even though General Vega had not been able to inform me of that. In this case I would be taking a false step by complaining of the failure to comply with an order that, as I could have verified, had been obeyed. It seemed then that I should proceed more prudently. My complaint would have an irresistible force if I knew, as I could easily learn, that the arms had not yet been returned to us. On the 19th then, I telegraphed General Vega asking him if the arms had been returned and requested a reply. Still without an answer, I have just sent another telegram with the same objective. I am extremely interested in receiving his reply before my next visit with the president. Meanwhile, I had decided not to speak of this matter until a response arrives. Nevertheless, scheduled to see the president this coming Monday on another matter, I will mention this incident then anyway for fear of not having a better opportunity.

When I was in New York, I saw Colonel Mejía, who showed me five letters, two from [William] Gwin, one from Gwin's son, and two more from the correspondent of the *New York Daily News* in Mexico, all concerned with Gwin's Mexican colonization project. The letters were so important that I immediately decided to show them to Grant and the president. Colonel Mejía suggested that he had other papers of no less importance which he has not shown me. In addition, he claimed to know various things which it would be to our advantage for Grant and the president to hear of. For that purpose I requested him to come to Washington. Since Grant would not be in Washington between this past Thursday and Sunday evening, I told the colonel that his arrival on Monday morning would be timely. He agreed to that. Meanwhile, he entrusted me with the five letters. . . .

Early today I went to see the president. Although about 100 people were waiting their turn to see him, among them various senators and high-ranking civil officials, the president's private secretary announced me immediately and the president had me enter at once. I disclosed that I had obtained documents of the greatest importance, which revealed Gwin's plans to colonize in Mexico Southerners who were opposed to the United States government. The documents also revealed what support Gwin had from Napoleon, what he expected from Maximilian, and that some American citizens were apparently involved in his plans. I carried some of these documents with me, I continued, and I would have the others next Monday, when the person who had intercepted them would come to Washington. Furthermore, this person knew other important details regarding the plan. I asked him if he desired me to convey the documents I carried to him, which I would do with pleasure. I thought it would be better, however, to await the arrival of the other material. I added that I had come only to inquire when he desired to see everything.

The president expressed great interest in these documents, suggesting that he would be pleased to see me Monday at 11 A.M.

I had taken the liberty to carry the documents directly to him, I explained next, because their importance seemed to justify my taking this step. Had I limited myself to taking them to the State Department, I supposed, the president would not have seen them, and their contents would perhaps have received little attention from Seward, who had assured me some time ago that Gwin did not enjoy the French government's protection. Seward has perhaps always given more credit to assurances, which I observed have been in this case, as in others, contradicted by the facts. Johnson said he would gladly see me whenever I had something to communicate to him. This authorization will protect me from whatever difficulty I might encounter from Seward on this matter. . . .

When I left the president, I telegraphed Colonel Mejía to come without fail Monday morning. . . . Of course, in the present state of affairs, these documents and the others that will arrive on Monday could decide the question . . . in our favor. [5:401-3]

JUNE 27 On June 25, Colonel [William M.] Wherry, Schofield's chief of staff . . . indicated that the general would prefer to meet in the evening, so as not to attract attention. . . . [I offered] to receive Schofield at nine that evening. At that hour Schofield arrived with Lieutenant-Colonel Ford of his staff. Receiving him very cordially, I asked if he wanted us to enter into the matter. He had come only to get acquainted, he said, and to pay his respects. Not having spoken with Grant, who was absent at that time, he did not think it proper to begin negotiations. Early tomorrow, he added, he would see Grant and then, in the evening, he could return to occupy himself with this matter without reserve. We parted then, agreeing he should return at eight last night. . . .

He came at the appointed hour. He stayed more than two hours, and our conversation was frank and friendly. I began by asking him if he had spoken with Grant. They had had a long conversation, he replied, and had had the pleasure of learning that they shared identical ideas in regard to Mexico. He was disposed to listen to what I would be kind enough to tell him. Then . . . I described the present condition of our affairs, commencing with the beginning of the present difficulties. I also related my conversation with Blair, my instructions on this matter from the supreme government, and our plans for the future. I pointed out our desire to make the sympathy of this people productive for our cause, not only to terminate our war with France in a prompt and satisfactory manner but also to provide for the development of the economic potential of Mexico after the intervention. . . .

Schofield listened attentively, exhibiting approval of what I was saying. His questions on distinct points revealed that he had contemplated undertaking this matter and that he viewed it in a favorable, even attractive, light. Sharing Grant's opinion, he would have decided on the spot to accept the position I offered him had he been an independent person. Because he belongs to the army of this country, he could not accept without his government's approval. Tomorrow, Schofield said, he would accompany Grant to see the president to inform him of everything. If Johnson approved the idea, he would immediately decide for it. We agreed to meet today at nine p.m. because I desired to speak with Grant before that hour.

If the president should approve the project [for a U.S. military figure to attract aid for Mexico], as he probably will do, it will greatly facilitate the plan and we will have nothing more to desire. . . .

Schofield appeared a man of good judgment and sound ideas. If the opinion of Grant, who knows him well and never exaggerates, is well founded, then he is among the premier military men and statesmen of this country. His antecedents are very honorable, his military position in the army is very high, and his reputation among his fellow citizens is very elevated.   [5:424-25]

JUNE 28 Coming at the appointed hour, General Schofield informed me then of everything. Since the president has been indisposed since Monday, Grant and Schofield were unable to see him yesterday. Grant remained charged with seeing the president and expressing Schofield's favorable disposition to accept the commission I have offered him, provided the president is not opposed and is prepared to assist him indirectly. Meanwhile, Schofield left this morning for New York to visit his family, which he had not seen for a long time. He intended to be absent a month unless needed earlier. A telegram will recall him. . . .

Schofield knows that it will be impossible to do anything with the current cabinet. Ultimately the president will decide to accept Grant's policy, he believes, which will require cabinet changes. Schofield favors these changes, offering incontestable reasons that will surely make a strong impression on the president's mind when Grant submits them. I will mention one reason below, primarily to give you an idea of his solidly reasoned good judgment and his elevated manner of seeing things.

The end of the Civil War and the abolition of slavery have destroyed the differences of opinion and political principles that divided this country. Now new principles must be sought, which will serve to organize the parties. Apparently Negro suffrage will be the first. A large majority in the North favor the concession of this right to colored people with some restrictions, although the president does not appear disposed to adopt this policy. His administration will become unpopular then, and the parties will be established upon principles that will profoundly, but equally, divide this people. If the government makes Mexican affairs the principal question, however, it will serve as the basis for reorganizing the parties. Furthermore, the people will almost unanimously follow and support the government with everything proceeding in a satisfactory manner.

Unfortunately, Schofield could not remain here a bit longer to express his ideas to the president. The uncertainty regarding when he could see Johnson and his willingness to return to Washington as soon as necessary to work exclusively in this matter led him to hasten his departure, leaving Grant in charge of everything.

Schofield has already considered the people he will take with him. As is natural, he wishes only those of the most elevated social position and best antecedents to accompany him. . . . Everything merits my complete approval. If his plans are realized, they will produce the best results for the well-being and future development of our country. He expects to commence his movements about August 1. When working without restraint and when this country realizes who heads the expedition, he assumes everything will move so rapidly that the troops could arrive in Mexico at the same time or even before the reports of their organization, thereby preventing the concentration of the French forces or the arrival of French reinforcements.

Schofield thought the loan could be obtained very easily then, whereas currently negotiations would be difficult. Therefore, I will abstain from taking any step toward the loan until the desired conditions exist. I gave him a copy of the conditions we are disposed to accept so that he could examine them and speak to his friends among the New York capitalists, thus preparing the ground for when we will want to act.

The current situation is so attractive that most certainly we will soon have realized all our desires and expectations for victory and for Mexico's future prosperity.

When Schofield and his companions appear at the head of the under-taking, the momentum here will be so unparalleled that it will be irresist-able. . . .

The more I deal with Schofield, the better I realize that Grant's praise of him was not exaggerated.   [5:426-27]

JUNE 29 Last night Grant told me that today he would show me his letter to the president on Mexican affairs. This letter had not been read at the cabinet meeting on the 20th, he informed me, certainly because Seward had been unable to attend because of his wife's grave illness. The letter had been read at the next cabinet meeting on the 23rd, however, and then, by agreement, left pending until Seward's return to learn his opinion after he becomes acquainted with the affair, which is pertinent to his depart-ment. . . .

Today I went to Grant's office to see the above-mentioned letter. . . .

I read the letter hastily in his office while he was speaking with other people. Therefore, I am unable to supply you a complete extract. Dated June 18, first it explained that the grave situation with its great importance for the United States compelled him to direct himself officially to the presi-dent. The United States, he explained at once, should quickly take a decisive position against the establishment of a monarchy in Mexico so as to avoid worse evils. Grant's letter insisted that this conduct was justified for the following reasons. First, the French have established a monarchy in open hostility to the United States, while it was engaged in its Civil War. France and the other European nations, excepting only Russia, wanted to aid the South. Second, Maximilian's hostility to the United States is also apparent from Gwin's project, which is aimed at attracting all the discontents of this country to Mexico to organize them there and from the fact that Maximilian permitted the South to provision itself with necessities and to export its cotton via Matamoros. Additionally, the letter also mentioned that the French have fired upon United States forces, according to a letter published in a Nashville periodical by an officer who had been in Brazos de Santiago. Grant's letter also cited the sale to the traitors in Matamoros of Confederate cannons and arms that really belonged to the United States. Therefore, either the United States should protest energetically against the establish-ment of a monarchy in Mexico in terms that will make France desist in its enterprise without causing a war with the United States, or, Grant pro-posed, the United States should declare itself neutral toward the contending factions, but not a neutrality favorable to the French, but rather one equally permitting both parties to export arms and men to Mexico. He had a great deal to say on these points, Grant indicated, but for lack of time and not being well versed in the details, he merely outlined them. The pages Grant gave me did not contain the end of the letter. Then came another letter dated June 19 to the secretary of war. In this letter Grant stated that Mexico would not resist a decent settlement with France and would concede France's just requests. If the United States lent Mexico some aid, he made clear, it will have to make sure the loan is repaid.

Clearly this latter letter did not leave me completely satisfied. Nevertheless, under the circumstances, it is the best we can expect, and we must recognize Grant's frankness in showing it to me. This is new proof of his good disposition toward us. Certainly when speaking officially, he does not feel free to express the ideas he holds privately.   [5:427-28]

JULY 8   I have visited the White House regularly to inquire about the president's health and to learn when I could see him. . . . Although he was receiving only a very few people, I was announced to him and he sent word that he was waiting. . . .

The importance of the matter I had to communicate to him, I told him, seemed sufficient excuse to trouble him even before he had completely recovered.

He asked me about the nature of this business. I said it involved intercepted documents going to Gwin and others that clarified what the enemies of the United States proposed to do in Mexico with official French approval. He inquired how I had obtained these documents. They had fallen accidentally into the hands of a Mexican colonel, who brought them to me, I replied. Desiring this person to communicate to the president how he had acquired them and what information he had from Mexico regarding this same matter, I had asked him to come here. He had remained a week awaiting the president's recovery. Unable to see the president soon, however, and having urgent business in New York, he had departed on July 1, leaving a letter to explain what I had wished him to reveal personally to the president. I immediately read the letter of Colonel Mejía. . . .

After this, I told the president that it seemed desirable to read him such important intercepted documents. Unfortunately, he was somewhat distracted, as if another important matter preoccupied him. As I began to read, he asked how much time I needed to read them. I said about fifteen minutes or less. . . . I added that, if he preferred, I could summarize their contents in a few words because I had read them various times and knew them well. He expressed his complete confidence in my recapitulation. . . .

When I ended my review, the president observed that these plans could not be fulfilled because Maximilian would not last much longer in Mexico. I took advantage of this opportunity to suggest that Maximilian would probably last sufficiently long to cause great problems for Mexico and for the United States if this government continued to observe the past administration's policy toward Mexico. The past policy had convinced the French government and people that the United States would not oppose in any way the consolidation of an Austro-French empire in Mexico. The French were already so interested in the question, I added, that instead of considering retiring, they intended to send 10,000 more men, according to a letter from Paris dated June 16, published in the *New York Herald* on July 2. These reinforcements, I explained, were being sent because the United States had recently assured the French government that the last administration's policy would be continued. In the early June debate in the Corps Législatif on Mexican affairs, I observed, the spokesmen of the French government had decidedly asserted that their forces would not be retired until Maximilian was firmly in place. In reply to a request for immediate retirement of troops, because some French deputies alleged the danger of complications with the United States, Napoleon's spokesmen denied the slightest basis for such fears. As proof of that, Minister of State Rouher in a speech made on June 9 claimed that the United States minister had assured France that "without doubt we are not pleased to see a monarchy established in Mexico. We certainly favor republican institutions. Respecting the will of peoples and nations, however, we understand that Mexico desires to return to a monarchy under which it was previously governed for a long time. Above all, we will not go to war over the question of the form of government." These words appeared in print to attest to United States acknowledgment that the changes taking place in Mexico were the product of popular will. The president listened attentively, though silently.

These remarks were clearly aimed principally at Seward's policy, with which I know the president was acquainted. My awkward position did not permit me to be more explicit. Before leaving this matter, I must inform you that [Montgomery] Blair copied [John] Bigelow's assurances to use them in a speech he will give in Hagerstown on the 12th of this month . . . in which Blair will severely censure Seward's policy. . . .

At the termination of this matter, I told the president that I had another grave matter to complain of. His order revoking the prohibition to export arms apparently had not been complied with in California. I informed him of what General Vega had written in his letter of May 13. . . . After that date, I understood, the arms seized from the Mexican agent had been returned. Desiring to verify this, however, I had sent three telegrams of inquiry to San Francisco. For some incomprehensible reason I had not received a response. If the reply is unsatisfactory, I said, I would take the liberty of returning to entreat him to have his order complied with. My understanding was that removing the prohibition on arms exportations meant that arms could be shipped to Mexico the same as anywhere else, thereby correcting the great injustice of the past administration, which had deprived us of arms. If abandoning the clearest rights of the United States was considered necessary to conciliate France during Lincoln's administration at the height of the Civil War and when France was openly threatening to aid the South, then that policy had its excuse. Now, with the war ended, however, the United States should not equivocate in that manner.

The president most amply assured me that his orders on arms exportation would be strictly complied with, without odious and unjust exceptions.

Then I told Johnson that I had still another matter to complain of. The Texas rebels approached General [Miguel] Negrete at Matamoros in open aid to the enemies of my government. I mentioned Negrete's communication to me of May 2, reading Johnson various fragments of General [James E.] Slaughter's correspondence. . . . My purpose at this time, I observed, was only to make clear the connivance between the Texas rebels and the French and Mexican traitors in Matamoros so that Johnson would know who his enemies were. Such information could also guide his conduct in the future. Collusion between the French and American traitors, he replied, is a well-established fact, which he indicated would be remedied within a short time.

Returning to the arms business, I told Johnson we were not asking favors of the United States, nor were we attempting to maneuver his government into a war with France; Johnson knew his own intentions regarding war with France. In defense of our own independence against a common enemy and in a cause identified with the United States, however, the least we could demand, we believed, was to be treated justly. The law of the land and the express orders of the president should be observed with regard to us, we thought, even if that should displease and create difficulties with France. I expressed this in such a way that he could understand our need to take money and even people from here besides arms and our hope not to encounter obstacles if we acted without violating United States law. The president appeared to understand my idea very well, answering me with a meaningful smile, while assuring me that he would not injure us in any way.

I asked him if he wished to retain the letters of Gwin and Massey. Since they would be very useful soon, he told me to send them to the State Department. I also sent Seward a copy of Colonel Mejía's letter, suppressing the last paragraph and modifying the first so that it would not appear intended for the president. . . .

I am very satisfied with the conference. The president's manner, more than his words, and many other indications, convince me that he will not approve Seward's policy. Seward will then either have to change his conduct, submitting to Johnson's ideas, which will doubtless be a complete defense of the Monroe Doctrine, or he will have to leave the cabinet.

From the president's house I went to see Grant to inform him of the interview. . . . I found him very contented with an interview he had had with the president while I was in the reception room of the White House. The president thought exactly as he did on Mexican affairs, he assured me, meaning the president favored a complete vindication of the Monroe Doctrine.

Grant informed the president that I had charged him with designating a commander from the United States Army who would command the citizens of this country who would emigrate to Mexico. He had selected one already, he informed Johnson, and would appoint this person, provided the government would grant the leader selected permission to leave the United States. The president not only expressed his willing disposition to grant permission but welcomed the idea. Johnson immediately asked Grant if he would tell him the name of the general selected.

In today's conference Grant asked the president to instruct Seward to notify France and England that the United States would not consent to the establishment of a monarchy in Mexico and that, if the French desisted in this undertaking and retired their troops, everything would end satisfactorily. If France insisted on sustaining Maximilian, however, the United States would forcibly throw the French army out of Mexico. This was the substance of Grant's proposal. He claimed that Seward can give it a suitable diplomatic form so that it does not appear insolent. Grant did not want any change in the basics. If the president really shares our ideas, this plan probably would be adopted. Then there is nothing else we will desire.

Additionally, he had received a communication from General Sheridan . . . Grant informed me, which stated that, only eight miles from Matamoros, [Juan N.] Cortina had cut the communication between that port and Boca del Río and had captured a Confederate steamer, which . . . he had turned over to the United States forces. If the French are as arrogant toward the United States as they are toward us, they ought to demand the return of the vessel, threatening to seize it forcibly if it is not handed over to them at once. Still, I seriously doubt they will adopt this course.

Regarding the cannons which the Confederates at Brownsville sold to the traitors at Matamoros, Sheridan communicated that, responding to Sheridan's claim, Mejía stated that he had forwarded the note to Maximilian and he would communicate the response to Sheridan when received.

Yesterday's *Courrier des Etats-Unis* published an article certainly written or suggested by [French minister Charles François Frédéric de] Montholon after visiting Grant on July 2. Although the United States government has given the amplest assurances to France that it will remain neutral in the Mexican question, the article claimed there are some people close to the government who are hostile to France. Without mentioning names, the article indicated that Grant was the principal one. The sending of a considerable force to Texas was hostile to France, the article implied, and Grant had inspired General Wallace's letter, or at least expressed such ideas. The rest of the article was written in such an insolent tone toward the United States, and especially toward Grant, that it appeared desirable to show it to him. Thus I left the newspaper in his office today, suggesting he take it home and read the article carefully. [5:455-58]

JULY 12 The last time I saw Grant, I understood that he wanted me to speak to President Johnson about our wish for a distinguished leader from the United States to assume command of the emigrants from this country who would go to help defend Mexico's cause. Until then I thought this matter would be arranged through the mediation of Grant and the designated leader without my direct intervention. . . . I agreed to speak generally to the president about our desire, without explaining what we had already done regarding General Schofield. If the president approved my ideas, I would request him to indicate this agreement directly to Schofield or through General Grant. . . . Grant could visit Johnson immediately afterward and take any additional necessary steps.

I will arrange a friendly interview rather than a business meeting with the president this time to explain my ideas to him on this delicate matter more freely and in greater detail. [5:465]

JULY 18 On July 14 I visited the president. . . . Unfortunately, shortly after my arrival, Senator [Edwin D.] Morgan of New York entered the room where we were talking. Combined with the president's uneasiness relative to some matters that seemed to preoccupy him, Senator Morgan's presence did not permit me to tell the president what I wanted to with appropriate calmness and deliberation. . . .

I commenced by explaining that, guided by suggestions from my friends in elevated positions in the Mexican government, I had come to inform him of what my government would like to accomplish in the United States toward promoting the cause of Mexican independence. Thus if the United States government does not oppose these suggestions, we would accomplish them without obstacle. In the contrary case, we will modify our plans to avoid the opposition of this government. Johnson asked me what these plans were. . . .

With our own resources and aided by the patriotism of our people, we have managed to prolong the war against the French for four years. We believe we can prolong it until the French are obliged to leave Mexico, even if only through their exhaustion. If we had arms and financial resources, we could forcibly throw them out of the Republic in a short time. Without adequate resources, however, and if the battle must continue with the disproportionate resources of the past, at best we could expect the French to depart because of exhaustion. Since our fortune is identified with that of the United States to a certain point, and since the United States public has so much sympathy for our cause, we considered it our duty to take effective advantage of the sympathy to extract from the United States the material necessary to terminate the war in a few months; otherwise it would last years. In this undertaking, I told Johnson, we propose to reach agreements with private parties without requesting anything of the government, which will no doubt do what is most convenient for itself.

After this explanation, I disclosed our plan. In the first place, I observed, it consisted of appointing a leader for the inevitable and continual emigration of United States citizens to Mexico. This leader ought to be one of the most distinguished generals of the United States Army, who has acquired the best reputation during the last war and in whom the American people have the utmost confidence. If possible, we would like the president and Grant to assist us in naming this general. Once named, he and the other officers whom he wishes to bring with him must, of course, receive temporary leave from the United States Army to enter our service.

We also wish, I added, that United States citizens desiring to emigrate to Mexico without violating any United States law should not face any obstacles regardless of whatever complaints the French government might make. We want to export freely arms purchased in this country in spite of French complaints. We trust we will not face any obstacles when we float a loan to obtain the funds necessary to realize our plan.

The president asked if I had spoken about this with Seward. I replied in the negative because his illness had prevented me from doing so. Additionally, I did not wish to give an official character to this matter. I intended to regulate affairs through our friends in this country without my official intervention. Since Seward opposed all measures of this kind, I intimated in the most delicate way I could that not proposing it to the secretary of state was wholly excusable. Moreover, I explained that I had spoken about this matter several times with Grant. The general had approved my ideas, proposing that I should submit them directly to the president.

In any event, I must speak with Seward, Johnson claimed, adding that I could return to see him early next week. From his manner of informing me that I should speak with Seward, I knew he had perfectly comprehended my fear that the plan would encounter the secretary of state's open opposition. In fact, Johnson emphatically repeated two or three times that "it will do no harm."

That very night I visited Grant to communicate what had occurred. The

next day, the general told me he would see the president to speak in favor
of this business.   [5:475-76]

JULY 19   After I saw the president on the 14th and proposed to name a
commander from the United States Army to take command of the North
American forces that would enter service in the Republic, you will recall
Grant intended to go the following day to support that idea. He did so on
the 15th. Already aware of the plan and without indicating any displeasure,
the president asked Grant to put the proposal in writing to submit it to the
cabinet. "If the cabinet approves," Johnson said, "good, and if not, we will
see what can be done to carry it into effect." Grant wrote the note relative
to the plan on the same day. Not only should a commander be designated
and given temporary leave from United States service, but Grant also added
that, in his judgment, the government ought to make arms available to
Mexico without demanding immediate payment.

This morning at his office, Grant informed me that his letter had been
read in yesterday's cabinet meeting, provoking some discussion. Finally, the
cabinet agreed to send it to the secretary of war to be worked out as he
might see fit. Already that morning he had seen [Edwin M.] Stanton, who
told him there would be no difficulty in giving Schofield leave for a year. Of
course, this government must not appear to know that Schofield was considering entering our service or what his intentions were. Concerning the
arms, Stanton did not see how the United States could sell them to us and
not demand their price without appearing to ally openly with us. He admitted, however, that he still had not considered this carefully. Since Stanton works entirely in agreement with Seward, we should not expect much
from the secretary of war. . . .

He had been notified, Grant also mentioned, that on July 7 the cannons
and other war material, which the Confederates sold to the traitors after the
surrender of Texas, had been returned to Brownsville. Likewise, a few days
ago, he told me, he ordered Sheridan to concentrate the major part of his
forces on the banks of the Rio Grande, to establish his headquarters there,
and to direct operations in person. The developments are highly significant.

Before Grant visited me, another person of very good judgment had
visited me, stating that if the people should learn Grant's opinion on the
Monroe Doctrine, there would be a truly irresistible pressure in our favor
because Grant is now the most popular idol. We discussed how to make the
general's ideas public. When Grant arrived, I mentioned what had just
passed, explaining the desirability of his ideas becoming generally known.
He would not be embarrassed if his ideas were made public, and, he stated,
he would take advantage of the first opportunity for this purpose. Perhaps

he might write a letter to his father-in-law and authorize him to publish it. In his recently completed official report on the Richmond campaign, Grant mentioned he has stated his judgment that the Civil War in this country is not over while the French remained in Mexico. Unfortunately, this important report will not be published for a month. . . .

For my part, I will arrange for a demonstration in our favor in New York, or for Grant to receive an invitation that will allow him to express his ideas in respect to Mexico.   [5:479-80]

JULY 19   Some time ago, Doctor A. Gregg, a person of very good judgment and some influence and a former delegate from Tennessee to the Baltimore convention, which chose Lincoln and Johnson as candidates, sought me out. He wanted to contribute an emigration or other kind of project that would favor our cause and demonstrate a decided partisanship for the Monroe Doctrine. On another occasion, he offered to put me in contact with [Horace] Maynard, a distinguished citizen of Tennessee, one of Johnson's friends, and a man of political importance, who had also been a member of the Baltimore convention. Unfortunately, not having penetrated the Mexican question in its significance for the United States, Maynard was inclined then toward Lincoln's policy in Mexican affairs. Finally, during an interview with Maynard, I related the reasons for favoring a change in this policy and for adopting another course more energetic and more in conformity with popular opinion.

In a later interview, Dr. Gregg assured me that Maynard had begun to alter his opinion. . . . Maynard wrote me . . . what the president wished to do with respect to our affairs and in favor of our cause. . . .

The third paragraph of the letter indicates the indirect means by which we will be given volunteers from among the very soldiers of the United States Army. This important and serious indication agrees with another made a few days ago by a no less reliable source. . . .

Yesterday I sent for Dr. Gregg, who repeated the same idea verbally . . . suggesting that with a little more effort Maynard would support our cause. I will do what I can to obtain such a valuable acquisition.   [5:481]

JULY 20   Yesterday, Grant told me, he had seen the president, who authorized him, if he judged it desirable, to proceed on his own account without consulting or arranging prior approval for his actions. The president demonstrated great interest in Mexican affairs, Grant assured me, holding the best views toward us.

The general appears to have adopted his line of conduct already. As I understand it, Grant's course contains a contingency that could produce an open and immediate rupture with France, which he most ardently desires.

Grant will see Schofield in West Point early this week. Grant will order him to Washington to finish making arrangements. The rest I do not believe convenient to mention at this time.

Grant wants to see General Carvajal to urge him to go to the border area as soon as possible. Evidently, this new situation allows me to avoid the necessity of reaching an agreement directly with the president, which could not be avoided much longer. I will arrange, nevertheless, to see him whenever desirable.

Then I saw Secretary of the Interior [James] Harlan. I congratulated him on his speech of the 14th. . . . I mentioned it would be desirable for United States public opinion on the Monroe Doctrine to become known in Europe and particularly in France. Harlan mentioned that Seward had been surprised to see Bigelow's words cited in Blair's speech. . . . Seward has instructed Bigelow to retract them. If this is true, and I see no reason not to believe it, evidently either Bigelow's assurances were without authorization from his government, or he did not comply aptly with his instructions. These two options appear, nevertheless, very improbable.   [5:491-92]

JULY 30   On the evening of July 27 Schofield arrived in this city. He saw me at once and told me what Grant had already communicated to me, namely, that at West Point Schofield had accepted Grant's offer to go to the Texas frontier in the character of inspector of the United States Army to avoid rousing suspicions. Schofield would examine the state of affairs first-hand and be able to determine the surest means of arranging the business he will direct. At the same time, he will have permission from this government to separate himself from the United States military service for a year and leave the country, with authorization to use this permission when he finds it convenient.

Moreover, Grant gave him a letter of recommendation to General Sheridan, who, as you know, now commands the Military Division of the Gulf. Sheridan assumed immediate command of the United States Army on the Rio Grande. Schofield read me this letter, the contents of which I will endeavor to recollect and summarize here. After informing Sheridan of the motives and goals of Schofield's trip and telling him that all will depend upon what could be definitively arranged in this city, Grant recommended especially two points: (1) Sheridan should not send the surplus war material accumulated in that region to Washington, whether captured from the Confederates or originating from here, unless he is expressly ordered to do so; rather, everything should be prepared so that Schofield might take advantage of this war material; and (2) the units of the army selected to enter Mexican service will be mustered out in Texas under orders from Washington and the soldiers will conserve their arms and equipment under the arrangement ordered by the president. Moreover, the president is determined to revindicate the Monroe Doctrine, the letter asserted, which he would like to do while avoiding a war with France. If war cannot be avoided, however, preferably events should be arranged to make the French government appear the aggressor, thus making the war more popular in this country. Meanwhile, Sheridan could observe a neutrality toward Mexico, Grant recommended, similar to that which France followed in respect to the United States during the Civil War.

The very important arrangements in this city which Grant referred to are apparently those being made with me, since there is no doubt of the president's determination regarding them.

Last, Schofield told me that he was going to see the president and the secretary of war at once, not having spoken yet with either about this matter. In the evening, he continued, he would return to communicate the results of his interviews, if he obtained them.

Thus Schofield acted. On his second visit, he informed me, he had had a long, frank conversation with the president. Although Johnson viewed the project with much favor, Schofield reported, he believed it undesirable to reveal it for now and even less desirable for the government to appear to be supporting it. For that very reason this government might not sustain Schofield, who could be exposed to penalties very serious for his position and his future, which do make the project quite risky in its present form.

This preliminary statement preceded Schofield's principal proposal, which I must enter into in some detail.

In a previous interview with Schofield, I read him . . . the instructions controlling me in the organization and dispatch of this force. As you will recall, the ninth article of these instructions conceded the premium of $100,000 to the general in chief commanding the force.

Schofield asked me then, or a little later, if he and the other officers in his position could anticipate a part of the premium. In his own case, being poor, he hoped to arrange the future subsistence of his family before embarking on this undertaking. All this would be arranged to his satisfaction, I replied, because it seemed to me a very just request.

On the second visit he asked if I had contemplated this matter and what sum I considered myself authorized to advance. Estimating the campaign would last a year, I would be disposed to advance him ten thousand dollars from his bonus, I replied, to provide amply a year's subsistence for his family. Then, speaking frankly, he told me, he would not go for anything less than the hundred thousand dollars because he would completely lose his position as soldier and as statesman in this country if he came out badly in Mexico. Without taking into consideration his well-founded expectations of future betterment, he pointed out that his current position would produce an income of seven thousand dollars annually, which represented the return on one hundred thousand dollars. He believed the least he could do in fulfilling his duty to his family was to assure them that income, because he was risking on his part his priceless reputation.

These were the principal reasons he offered to sustain his request. He emphasized that our acceptance of them was an absolutely indispensable condition for his joining the undertaking. Without pretending to give him a definite reply, I told him that the supreme government had promised very liberal bonuses to officers and soldiers who came to aid us in the war against the French, but with the intention of paying them at the end of the war and then principally in real estate. If the government advanced him all his bonus, I continued, other officers would also want advances, but our limited resources would not permit us to satisfy their desires.

Responding to these considerations, Schofield found no need to publicize the advance payment of his bonus. Moreover, Schofield suggested it was not necessary to do the same for other officers except in cases of positive necessity. In any case, he believed the sum invested in this form would not exceed five hundred thousand dollars, including his hundred thousand.

Then Schofield read a memorandum of the conditions he demanded prior to going to Mexico. . . . I made some minor reflections regarding it, requesting him to leave a copy for more detailed examination. I promised him a definite reply on the next day.

It is necessary, I believe, to examine each article of his memorandum, explaining why I decided to accept each article or to propose its modification.

In the first article Schofield requested not only the supreme command of the forces to be organized from United States immigrants but also of all Mexican forces detailed to operate in union with them. On the 29th I explained to Schofield that this did not conform with the Mexican government's instructions. If Mexico had a more capable general, he contended, then his trip would not be necessary. If he was considered the most able general in the Republic, he argued, all the forces within the Republic ought to be placed under his orders. Without entering into the question of whether there were or were not more able generals than he, we desired his services, I replied, not only to take advantage of his military talent, but also for the political and even financial advantages we expected from his departure for Mexico.

In our interview on the 28th, I told him that because none of our generals had his experience in commanding large armies, the government, which seeks only the triumph of our cause, would probably give him command over any Mexican forces cooperating with his troops. It seemed undesirable, however, to stipulate this expressly, so as not to wound the pride of the Mexican people. Maximilian had agreed with Napoleon, I observed, that whenever Mexican and French forces were united, the French commander would also command the Mexican forces, regardless of rank. Since we sought propaganda advantage by presenting this stipulation as a humiliation to the Republic, which we really considered it to be, we ought not to agree to a similar thing which our enemies could use against us. Therefore, either this stipulation must be entirely suppressed, I proposed, or be changed to read, for example, that all forces detailed to him by the government will remain under his command. Persuaded of the desirability of making this change, Schofield accepted it at once.

According to Schofield's explanation, the army corps, composed of four divisions which he will organize under the terms of the second clause, will total forty thousand men more or less at full force. Schofield diverged from the supreme government's instructions in this matter because he knew that generally one can count on only half the muster roll strength for a campaign. Thus an army corps of forty thousand men has only twenty thousand effective troops. Since this article leaves the number of troops to be raised subject to Mexico's needs, I accepted the change, provided he would raise only twenty thousand men immediately. In agreement with the supreme government, he would raise the rest only if necessary after his arrival in the Republic.

It seemed convenient to accept the third article, even diverging from the supreme government's instructions. Since we do not know the antecedents of the officers of this army, and since we ought to have full confidence in the commanding general to whom we entrust the organization of the army to be formed from citizens of this country, our restrictions on naming his subordinates will only produce embarrassment and difficulties. We can have a direct interest only in the appointments to general of division. Schofield would not give these generalships to the two persons who have attracted his attention until now without consulting me, as he has been doing.

Regarding article five, heeding the interests of the Republic, I proposed to Schofield that the army be paid in United States treasury notes or their equivalent in Mexican money. He assented at once. This will reduce the loss we suffer in those notes through negotiating our loan here. I must also observe that Mexican law permits subordinate officers very poor pay compared with that enjoyed in this country. The supreme government may have to increase this pay to satisfy the subordinates who Schofield brings because people accustomed to some comfort cannot live with so little.

Article 6 caused me very long deliberation, after which I decided to accept it, with the understanding that the total expenditure for advance bonuses would not exceed five hundred thousand dollars. I must indicate why I determined to accept it.

Advancing the commanding general all of his bonus suggests that he might not retain a great interest in the enterprise's success, particularly since he had made this point a condition, sine qua non. Nevertheless, his good name and reputation, which will depend on the success of the undertaking, are sufficient motives to assure us that his interest will not diminish after having received his expected financial reward.

It has been suggested, for example, that we could give him a quarter of the money at once and leave the rest deposited in a bank at his disposition when the war is terminated. This method would not augment his financial interest in the success of the campaign because the money would already be his. It would, however, offer proof of our distrust, which could cool his ardor or cause his indisposition toward us. When we exhibit almost unlimited confidence in him by placing the fate of our Republic in his hands, I find it undesirable to distrust him over the small sum of money we have offered him.

If the enterprise has great success, as seems highly probable, contributing not only toward terminating our war with France but also to Mexico's development and future prosperity, this sum is truly a bagatelle. Thus, since the government had decided to spend it, we ought not to permit the terms of payment to occasion difficulties in the arrangement of the principal business. This is especially so when the business is already very advanced and on the eve of being realized in a very satisfactory manner.

If, as it currently appears, we will not have to pay the transportation costs of the soldiers, the five hundred thousand dollars in advance payments to the officers will be a relatively modest sum.

The 7th article was clearly acceptable. Schofield told me that he would add the bonuses conceded in the decree of August 11, 1864, to it.

Regarding article 8, I proposed making the enlistment for three years or for the duration of the war as was done here. The soldiers would not likely want to enlist for more than three years, he explained, besides which, the war would probably not last that long. According to Schofield's explanation, the commanding general's authority to muster out soldiers ought to embrace the wounded and incapacitated, with the right to disband or muster out the whole or a considerable part of the army reserved exclusively to the president.

Before showing me his memorandum, Schofield asked me if we had people in New York charged with purchasing the necessary materials. After I replied in the negative, he observed that skilled and market-wise officers of his staff could make the purchases advantageously. I approved his suggestion, which is included as the ninth article of the memorandum. Afterward, I indicated to him my preference for the intervention of a Mexican agent in these purchases because a very considerable sum would be expended in New York for arms, munitions, and provisions and because abuses prejudicial to the national treasury could be committed in purchasing these items. He accepted this suggestion immediately.

Schofield had accepted my invitation to go together to Silver Spring on the afternoon of the 28th, where General [Frank] Blair, [Jr.], is currently passing several days with his father. Unfortunately, on that afternoon I began to feel quite ill from the sickness that has been keeping me in bed since. I could neither go with him nor even speak to him about the details of the memorandum with the desired patience.

When Schofield came for me, he mentioned having had another fully satisfactory interview with the president. He had just finished seeing the secretary of war, who was wrongly indifferent toward us. Although convinced the Mexican people were not capable of vindicating their liberties or of reconquering their independence, the secretary of war indicated his support for the project. Certainly he offered support because he knows the project has the approval of the president and General Grant. The secretary of war offered his cooperation and told Schofield that all the United States surplus war material in the military division of the Gulf will be placed on the market as soon as Schofield is ready to purchase it.

So far, Schofield has decided on two of the generals to command divisions. General [Frank] Blair is one, and the other is Confederate General Joseph Johnston. It is hoped that Johnston will favorably attract Southern sympathy for the enterprise and help enlistment of people from that region. An offer will be made to Johnston soon. His acceptance would be a major gain. Without dispute, he is one of the best generals of the South, many believe superior to Lee himself.

Blair will probably accept Schofield's offer provided the president does not name him secretary of war, as he apparently still expects. In the latter case, he will lend us more effective service than by going to the Republic.

Yesterday afternoon Schofield came to see me again to inform me that he had returned to visit the president. The president wanted the purpose of his trip to the frontier made public. If it can be done, he remarked, it would greatly favor the immediate development of the plan under the best auspices.

For the purpose of resolving this, Schofield said, he wanted to reveal the plan to Seward and obtain his cooperation. The president told Schofield that he probably would obtain it. Thus if the plan is presented in a suitable manner, Schofield believes Seward cannot help but approve it, partly because of the confidence demonstrated by consulting him and partly because Seward would not likely wish to be placed in opposition to the president. If Seward approves, no obstacle to the development of the plan will remain.

Last night Schofield went to Cape May, where Seward is currently staying, to speak with him on this matter. Schofield will remain with Seward as long as necessary. Afterward he will go to New York to see General Carvajal. . . .

Montgomery Blair, General Frank Blair's brother, warned Schofield that he could not accept any office from the supreme government or sign the contract . . . without violating the laws of the United States. This left Schofield somewhat undecided. He does not wish to compromise himself with an open violation of the laws of his country. In effect, if strictly complied with, the law of April 20, 1818, which is still in force, would completely prevent our implementing this plan. Its very rigor will probably lead in the present case to its being neglected or to its interpretation in a manner favorable to us. . . . Agreement celebrated today, the ———— of ————, 1865, by the government of the Mexican Republic, through its minister in Washington, and Major General J. M. Schofield of the United States Army.

I. General Schofield accepts the position of general of division in the Mexican army with the character of commanding general of all the forces that are raised under the terms of this agreement and of all other troops the government of Mexico orders to operate in union with Schofield's forces.

II. At convenient points on Mexican territory, General Schofield will organize an army corps to be composed of emigrants from the United States. This corps will consist of three infantry divisions, nine batteries of artillery, and a division of cavalry. This corps will consist either of that part of this force which it is possible to raise or which the necessities of the Republic demand.

III. It is desired that the organization of this army corps will follow the provisions of the laws of the United States.

IV. All the officers of the army corps will be named by the commanding general.

V. The pay of the soldiers and officers will be that prescribed by the corresponding rank in the Mexican army.

VI. The following bonuses will be paid to the general and officers of the staff upon accepting their position, to wit:

commanding general————	Commissary general (lieutenant colonel)————
4 generals of division, to each————	Adjutant-general (lieutenant colonel————
12 generals of brigade————	Paymaster general (major)————
Chief of the general staff (brigadier general)————	
Chief of engineers (colonel)————	
Chief of the medical corps (lieutenant colonel)————	

VII. This army corps will form part of the Mexican army, and all of its officers and soldiers will have the right, from the date of their entry into service, to all the considerations and privileges of citizenship in the Republic of Mexico.

VIII. The officers as well as the soldiers will enlist in the service for three years, but the president of Mexico or the commanding general may muster them out before this time.

IX. Funds will be obtained for the payment of the troops and for the purchase of all classes of provisions by means of a loan which the Mexican government will negotiate in the United States. All disbursement from the account of the army corps described here will be made only by the respective staff officers and by order of the commanding general or of the employee designated by him for this purpose.

All disbursements will be made by means of documents drawn in the form prescribed by the laws and regulations observed in the United States Army.   [5:513-19]

AUGUST 4 Schofield told me that he had seen Seward at Cape May this past Monday. Schofield said he explained to Seward what our plans were and what the president's disposition toward them was. Seward looked with favor on the project, Schofield claimed, but at the same time, he wished to take another step which would contribute to the fuller success of the enterprise. Schofield should go to the French emperor as the confidential agent of this government and explain to him the existing danger of a rupture between France and the United States if Napoleon would not withdraw his forces from Mexico. Schofield told me that he had not definitely replied to this offer before speaking with me.

Evidently Seward desires to undo the arrangement by flattering Schofield with a mission to France, which would separate Schofield from the undertaking, and then, by presenting delays, allow enough time to transpire to abort the project or to allow Seward's other plans to mature. This is confirmed by keeping in mind Seward's desire for Schofield to go first to the Rio Grande to see the state of things so that he can talk with more direct knowledge. If Seward desires a general to undertake this mission, why didn't he use one of the many who are capable of undertaking it?

Unfortunately, Schofield does not recognize Seward's real purpose in the present case. The idea of going to France with a special commission from this government has captivated Schofield. No disadvantage would occur from accepting Seward's proposal, Schofield is convinced, not even the loss of time, because his agents will continue actively recruiting during his absence. Thus everything will be ready for his return. He believes many advantages will occur from accepting it. Among the principal advantages would be attracting Seward's support and having him decidedly in our favor in case Napoleon refused to withdraw his forces, or, at least, learning Seward's objective. With this attitude, Schofield had already decided to accept Seward's mission. He asked my opinion on the matter only as a personal favor.

If Seward in fact was proceeding in good faith, I told him, he would return from France within one to two months. The mission might produce very important advantages, I observed, but if it were only a scheme to undo the plan, accepting it placed him on very shaky ground and left him entirely in Seward's hands. In a certain sense, I added, accepting Seward's mission meant he renounced the idea of carrying our plan to completion. Since Grant had assumed such a large role in this matter, I proposed that before deciding to take such a delicate step, he should consult Grant. Schofield was absolutely certain that Grant would approve Seward's proposal gladly and without hesitation.

During his absence, Schofield told me, Generals Blair and Johnston would be organizing two divisions from the forces already at the border. To cover the preliminary expenses of the organization, he explained also, some funds would be required. I replied that he should make an estimate of these. General Johnston should arrive here shortly. I will see him at once to interest him in the undertaking.

I am very sorry that Schofield's good faith in prevailing on Seward could so easily upset an affair which I considered already entirely concluded and with the best prospects. After meditating at length on this disagreeable incident, I have concluded that we should not oppose Schofield's acceptance of the mission. Even the fact that his mission will go to France represents a gain for our cause. While he is absent we will finish preparations and the loan negotiation. Meanwhile, the supreme government can cover urgent needs with funds which Carvajal has indicated he has placed or is going to place at its disposal. They will also have Carvajal's organized force, which he claims will exceed ten thousand men.

If I can manage it, I will arrange for Schofield not to promise to visit Rio Grande before going to France. The visit would produce nothing more than the loss of a month or more without any desirable results. I will also try to pursuade him not to pursue his mission to France for more than two months after acceptance. Should two months elapse without his return, I will consult with Grant about naming another person. [5:530-31]

AUGUST 19 On August 17 . . . I accompanied James W. Beekman to spend a day at his country house. I was pleased to discover that his prior ardent sympathy for our cause had not diminished. Not being a friend of Seward's, he favors the popular demonstrations sympathetic to us. However, these are more difficult to organize now than before, he recognizes, because Seward's prestige, which had always been strong in this city, has augmented greatly since he was the victim of the assassination attempt this past April. Nevertheless, he believes, it will be possible to celebrate a great meeting here in our favor this coming autumn.

Beekman asked me with great interest when the constitutional period of President Juárez, for whom he has great admiration, terminates and who ought to succeed him. Since I was talking with one of our best and most disinterested friends in this country, I replied with the appropriate frankness. I explained the present condition of this question. I expected the supreme government to solve this problem by declaring that since it cannot hold elections now and since the present case was foreseen in the constitution, all the top, popularly elected officials ought to continue exercising their constitutional functions until new elections are possible.

Expressing the opinion of the thinking men of this country, the interests of our cause required, Beekman maintained, that no change in the personnel of our government should occur while the French are making war on us. Since the French strove to bring down Juárez's government, he contended, our national honor demanded that this same president terminate the war and reestablish peace in the Republic. Though in a very difficult position, Beekman added, the United States understood its Civil War in this manner. It recognized the need to reelect Lincoln, and this reelection produced the termination of the Civil War, just as the election of another candidate inevitably would have produced Southern independence.

Beekman's philosophical observations assume much greater importance in light of local opinion about General González Ortega's intention to go to Chihuahua on November 30 to ask for the government which in his opinion belongs to him. Should the president refuse to transfer power, González Ortega will either protest in writing only and retire to private life or continue fighting in defense of the national cause. Lately, he has allegedly changed his mind. If the presidency is not turned over to him, he intends to establish his government at some point in the Republic, calling it the constitutional one. He will consider Juárez's government a usurper.

When I communicated these facts to Beekman, I indicated their potentially dangerous character. At the same time, certainly González Ortega's patriotism suggests that he will not pursue the advice of evil-intentioned people. He would not create any new difficulties for his country, I added, which might produce considerable gain for our invaders. Beekman recognized at once the misfortune which González Ortega's conduct would be for our cause. Beekman proposed various plans to dissuade Ortega from taking such a false step, which would cause such great difficulties. Although Ortega would not succeed in dividing the Mexican patriots, Beekman believed his conduct would create a great scandal among foreign countries, and, in consequence, our cause would suffer in proportion.

Doubting his ability to give good advice in such a grave matter, Beekman proposed that I should also converse informally with Thurlow Weed, one of this country's ablest statesmen. Although Weed has never occupied public office, he has advised various governments, managed many victorious election campaigns, and exercised a decisive influence in this nation's, and very especially in New York State's, destiny. Since his youth, Weed has been Seward's intimate friend and political associate. Supposedly Weed is advising him now. Weed has always lived in Albany, capital of this state, where he exercised a dominant influence. Recently, however, he moved to New York City and assumed editorship of the *Daily Times*.

Although I doubted whether Weed could tell me more than Beekman had already told me on this matter, I accepted Beekman's suggestion so as to establish cordial personal relations with Weed. . . . Moreover, if I could capture his sympathies for our cause, apparently we would gain a great deal. In this case, I could at least learn his ideas regarding Mexico, which might permit me to understand Seward's plans and policy better.

This morning I met with Weed. I knew him already, having dined with him at Seward's house. He received me very cordially. I mentioned the uncertainty that existed, or seemed to exist, regarding the constitutional term of the Mexican president. I asked his opinion on this point. Without hesitation he responded that the present functionaries ought to continue discharging the offices for which they were popularly elected until new elections could be held. . . .

I will arrange to inform myself better of Ortega's intentions. If he really contemplates doing what is attributed to him, I will attempt to dissuade him from taking this step, explaining to him, among other things, that the United States would not recognize his government. On this point, I can cite Weed's opinion, which is similar to Seward's, and even put Ortega in contact with Weed. . . .

I request the supreme government please to determine as soon as possible what course to follow with respect to Ortega. Thus we will avoid complications and difficulties that could result in General Ortega being considered the so-called president of the Republic next November 30. [5:572-73]

SEPTEMBER 18 The president expressed the same interest as always for our cause. From the beginning, I told him, I had believed that if the United States had asked France to withdraw its forces from Mexico shortly after Johnston's surrender, they would have obtained this objective easily. The president had had to yield to his cabinet's opinion, however, which was opposed to taking that step then. I have just received a letter from Grant, recommending very specially that I should not allow this matter to lie dormant. The news of the occupation of Chihuahua certainly alarmed Grant. The president listened with interest as Schofield explained what we are doing. We should not desist in our course, Johnson recommended; rather, we should continue working. He assured us that this government will sustain us. . . . During the conversation other incidents also revealed his interest in our cause and his desire to honor the arrangements Grant made with his approval.

Seward informed Schofield that he had received a very immoderate reply to his note to the French government accompanying the correspondence intercepted from Gwin. He responded in energetic terms, Seward also told Schofield, clearly expressing the United States government's views with respect to the Mexican question. . . . The French reply to his communication ought to initiate the negotiation, Seward stated, or the crisis that will produce an agreement between France and the United States. In the meanwhile it did not seem desirable for Schofield to go to France because, if the French government replies on hostile terms, his trip will be unnecessary. Seward also read Schofield a note from Bigelow, United States minister in Paris, communicating a conversation with the attaché to Maximilian's legation in Paris, who, upon receiving orders to return to Mexico, ridiculed the order. From this conduct Bigelow infers that Maximilian's own agents and subordinates despise him.

All these inducements have augmented Schofield's desire to go to the [Mexican?] Republic. Meanwhile, we shall see if there are funds at our disposal for this venture.   [5:632-33]

SEPTEMBER 18   Yesterday I visited [James Gordon] Bennett, editor and proprietor of the *New York Herald* . . . to communicate some information regarding our affairs, which I hoped might help encourage his defense of our cause as he has consistently done. He was somewhat indisposed. . . . I agreed to see him later. . . .

I do not believe I can give you better proof of the *Herald*'s influence in this country than to note that the French minister attempts to gain its support. For this purpose he has used means which very few people would adopt. [Three lines of the original memorandum are here omitted from Romero's edition.] Montholon has brought his wife to visit Mrs. Bennett. He has invited Mrs. Bennett to spend a few days with them in Washington. But because Mrs. Bennett does not enjoy traveling for fear of railroad accidents, which have occurred very frequently recently, Montholon offered a French war vessel to bring her to Washington. [Between two and three lines omitted.]

Since Mrs. Bennett has considerable influence on her husband, and the Montholon family's attentions toward her could not have failed to please her, quite possibly the *Herald*, previously a very good friend of our cause, would cool off a little at least. Nevertheless, many reasons indicate that it will easily resume the position it has held until now.

Bennett told me that Montholon had assured him that Napoleon was disgusted with his expedition to Mexico, desiring to withdraw his forces as soon as possible. If the United States did not disturb Napoleon, Montholon claimed, he would withdraw them before long. If this government should become insistent, however, war would be inevitable. Bennett expressed his opposition to this eventuality because he considered war unnecessary. Whether this is true or not, until now Montholon has continued to use the same weapon to contain this government's action. [5:633-34]

OCTOBER 2 This morning I conversed at length with Montgomery Blair. . . .

If Seward continues in the cabinet, Blair maintained, nothing will be done favoring Mexico. If the Republican party, Seward's party, wins the next election in New York, he contended, not even Congress will be able to occupy itself with the Mexican question because its sessions will be fully occupied discussing Reconstruction. In Blair's opinion, the New York elections are going to decide this difficult question. If the election favors the Democratic party, Congress will have to approve the president's Reconstruction policy, and nothing will prevent it from considering the Mexican question. On the contrary, however, if the Republicans win, the president will receive a blow from which he will recover with difficulty. Then everything achieved in [presidential] Reconstruction will be lost and Congress will not be able to concern itself with anything but Reconstruction. This view of things seems well based in reason to me. Moreover, another reason currently to desire a Democratic party victory is that their platform plank referring to the Monroe Doctrine is much more explicit than the Republican convention's plank.

The president will recognize the necessity for allying himself with the Democratic party, Blair believes, and before the elections he will reorganize his cabinet by accepting Seward's resignation. But this does not seem very likely to me.

Moreover, Seward has informed the president, Blair told me, that Napoleon wishes to retire his forces from Mexico, which will take place soon if the United States does not disturb him. Blair has this information from Postmaster General [William] Dennison. I went immediately to see Dennison, who during the last three months has shared Blair's ideas on Mexican affairs. We had a frank conversation. Dennison told me he believed and *always had believed* that Napoleon would not leave Mexico unless the United States compelled him to. He mentioned also that the president had convinced him that the French would have already retired from Mexico by this date. I explained that on the whole the French are thinking less about withdrawing. In confirmation of that assertion I cited their ultimate movements in Mexico and read him [Luis] Maneyro's letter, which I had received recently from Paris. . . .

The acquisition of Dennison's sympathy and friendship is a great gain for our cause. He is a man of talent, of very good reputation in the United States, and on very good terms with the president.   [5:662-63]

OCTOBER 7   I had a long, important conversation with Grant.

A month ago, Grant told me, he wrote the president expressing the urgency of taking some action regarding Mexico. Yesterday the president informed him that this letter had been read at a cabinet meeting. When Grant arrived, he conferred with the president about our affairs. Johnson mentioned what we were doing, which he knew about from Generals Schofield and Wallace. Grant said Johnson was very satisfied with our course, believing our efforts would soon produce good results.

Grant informed me that Sheridan was very disgusted with the conduct of General [Frederick] Steele, who recently has commanded the United States forces on the Rio Grande. Despite verbal or written instructions given this general to take advantage of the least pretext to break relations with the traitors and the French, he conducted himself very differently. He has entered into friendly relations with the traitors. Allegedly he has attended their dances and dinners, even on one occasion toasting Maximilian, although Grant is not certain of this act. Sent to Matamoras to captivate Steele, [Maximilian agent] Luis Robles has already returned to Mexico. With the general already in such a good attitude, Robles was definitely convinced that his presence in that port was unnecessary.

Upon returning to this city, Grant's first concern was to obtain the president's agreement to remove Steele from that command. As he told me today, he had telegraphed Sheridan the order for Steele's removal yesterday. This will indicate to you more clearly than anything else the dispositions of the president and Grant.

Completely sharing the ideas and desires of his chief, Sheridan has sent agents to various parts of the Republic to inform himself of the condition of things, of the number and distribution of French forces, of our people's disposition toward the French, of the facilities for obtaining food, fodder, horses, and mules, and of various other details, with the intention of delivering a sure blow when the occasion arrives to attack the French. Grant was going to read me a private letter from Sheridan on this matter, which he had received yesterday, but then the arrival of a committee from Kentucky was announced. We had to interrupt our conversation. Nevertheless, what he told me was sufficient for me to understand his plans. Their realization awaits Steele's removal.

Sheridan had not mustered out any part of his army, Grant also informed me, nor would he before Schofield is ready to take advantage of that process.

Grant explained to me why he had changed his mind regarding the publication of his ideas on the Mexican question. He maintained it was so as not to prejudice our cause. From what he had heard from people of all political leanings on his recent trips through the whole country, he was satisfied that public opinion is unanimously favorable. Yet if we begin a debate over this, a great danger exists that it might turn into a partisan question, in which case a large part of this country's citizens would oppose us.

Then I communicated to Grant what he should know. I insisted very especially upon the idea that, far from contemplating retiring his forces from Mexico, Napoleon is sending reinforcements and making a major effort to consolidate Maximilian and to throw the national government out of the Republic. When the United States finally intervenes, Napoleon hopes to be able to inform them that no other government exists in Mexico but Maximilian's, which has already established its authority throughout the whole country. Napoleon hopes to accomplish this without disturbing the United States in its belief that he would retire if left time to develop his plans and complete his arrangements.   [5:675-76]

OCTOBER 9   Recently General [R. Delevan] Mussey, presently military secretary to the president, expressed his desire to go to the Republic to fight against the French and his wish to speak with me in more detail on this matter. . . .

Mussey's official position permits him knowledge of our different arrangements with Schofield and Wallace. From this information he generated his own no less satisfactory plan. He is colonel of a Negro regiment now stationed in Tennessee, but he could arrange for it to be ordered to reunite with its corps. Meanwhile, Mussey believes that the authorities in Arizona will request forces to protect them against Indian attack. The governor of Tennessee, for his part, wants the government to remove the Negro troops from that state. In Mussey's opinion, the secretary of war will order a brigade to march from Nashville to Arizona. Upon arriving in Arizona, Mussey will inform his superiors that all is quiet and there is nothing to fear from the Indians. Then the government will order the mustering out of these troops, already on the border. Once mustered out, they will follow their inclination to cross into Mexico and enter our service in Sonora. Nevertheless, Mussey's plan is obviously subject to many contingencies.

Previously Mussey indicated to Grant his desire to enter our service. Cordially approving this desire, the lieutenant general offered to give him permission to leave the country for that purpose. When Grant returns, Mussey will submit his complete plan. Conceivably it might be approved and put into immediate execution.

Mussey assured me that the president is as much a friend of our cause as Grant. However, the next session of Congress being already so near, the question being so serious, and being occupied meanwhile with reconstructing the Union, the president has not wanted to precipitate action on the Mexican question. Rather, he has preferred to settle Reconstruction first, leaving the initiative in United States policy regarding Mexican affairs to Congress.   [5:677-78]

OCTOBER 14 Yesterday . . . I saw Grant at his house in the evening. Although several people were with him, he approached me. That very day he had received two letters from Sheridan, he whispered, communicating to him that the supporters of Mexican independence had united a considerable force on the frontier and that our situation presented a better outlook now than in any other epoch. The country was tired of Maximilian, Sheridan's letters claimed, and ready to rise against him when supported. Now it was more necessary than ever, Sheridan contended, for this government not to give the usurper any hope of recognition. The French and the traitors confidently claim, he observed, that they have nothing to fear from the United States. They even believe that this government will soon recognize Maximilian. In conclusion, Sheridan recommended, even very earnestly entreated, that the United States should not take this step if it does not wish to be an accomplice in Napoleon's crime and to his intrigues against the American Union.

Moreover, Grant informed me that he had sent the originals of both letters to the president to acquaint him with their contents. Johnson would certainly never recognize Maximilian, Grant maintained, regardless of Seward's desires of his assurances to the contrary.

I showed Grant the memorandum, explaining the United States's rights in accordance with international law to intervene diplomatically in our affairs. . . . He read it closely and told me that it appeared very good to him.

In the presence of the people who were there it did not seem desirable to ask Grant to read it to the president. Believing I could persuade Mussey to read the memorandum to the president, I saw Mussey today. If Grant presented the memorandum, Mussey thought, it would have a better effect upon the president. Immediately, I conversed at length with Dennison on this matter. I read him the memorandum and explained that the Department of State circular of this past July 2 . . .[the so-called Romero circular forbidding foreign diplomats to see the president without going through the secretary of state] left me no liberty to see the president without Seward's intervention. Since I could not present the president with the memorandum, I did not know who I could employ to show it to him. Dennison offered to communicate its contents to the president but suggested that Grant would be the most appropriate person for this purpose. Tomorrow I will see Grant about this and other matters.

In addition to Dennison and Grant, I have read the memorandum to Secretary of the Interior Harlan and have given copies to Montgomery Blair for use in a forthcoming speech in New York, to George Wilkes, editor of a newspaper that has always defended our cause, and to Sumner, chairman of the Senate Foreign Relations Committee. [5:695-96]

OCTOBER 20   Last night I had a conversation with [James] Speed, attorney general of the United States. I mentioned Maximilian's decree reestablishing slavery in Mexico and the plans of French agents to bring all the Southern leaders who still oppose United States authority to Mexico. Speed appeared to agree entirely with me on these points. Only yesterday, he told me, he had finished his report on the matter, submitting it to Seward. . . . He had emphatically declared Maximilian's September 5 decree the equivalent to the reestablishment of slavery in Mexico. [5:715]

OCTOBER 23   Yesterday evening . . . I read Grant the letters of Mr. P. [Edward Lee Plumb?]. . . . After listening to them with interest, he agreed that Clarence A. Seward would not likely have taken part in the Imperial Express Company without his [William Seward's?] approval. He also advised me to take advantage of Seward's absence to visit the president and complain of the aforementioned situation. . . .

Various dispatches from Sheridan [had] arrived which the general could read only recently. The two principal letters, which address United States recognition of Maximilian and the Mexican political situation, were submitted directly to the president. . . . Grant's reply entirely approved Sheridan's conduct. Since, as communicated to Grant in their last meeting, the president very strongly expressed his desires for Mexico to prolong its resistance to the French a while longer, Grant believed that Sheridan's conduct also merited the president's most complete approval. Thus when the time arrives for the United States to intervene, which will surely be when Congress reconvenes, if not before, a foothold to begin from and a center of national support will exist. Therefore, Grant recommended, the patriots on the frontier should be encouraged and aided to prolong their resistance as long as possible. He wished his opinion regarding Secretary Seward were mistaken, Grant notified Sheridan, but he feared his judgment was absolutely correct; Seward was no friend of our cause.

Regardless of Seward's opinions and sympathies and whatever his commitments to France, Grant also assured me, the president would never permit the recognition of Maximilian or Seward to become an obstacle to the development of our plans. Under different conditions, Grant added, the president would not listen to Seward's opinions without contradicting them. Finally, he had had various conversations, which included discussion of Mexican affairs with the secretary of state, Grant told me, but he had always remained unsatisfied with the tenor of the conversations.

Next we spoke generally of our affairs. Grant expressed little confidence in General [Lew] Wallace, fearing failure and discredit with whatever he undertakes. As on other occasions, Grant manifested the fullest confidence in General Schofield's aptitude, character, sound judgment, and military knowledge. I told him what I believed ought to be done and would attempt to have done is the following.

Because Wallace claims that his people are ready and it is impossible to get rid of him without openly breaking with General Carvajal, thereby causing a major scandal here, it is best to permit Wallace to depart with his followers. Schofield will have to leave simultaneously for the Rio Grande, as inspector or in some other character, to make the necessary arrangement to purchase arms. Once Wallace's forces have crossed the river, Schofield will assume command of them. Attracting whatever additional forces he can from the other side of the river, Schofield will then organize the largest possible number of Mexican troops.

This plan appeared satisfactory to Grant. I strongly recommend that the supreme government adopt the plan in total if it wishes to use the forces of foreigners who would go to the Republic and those to be organized in its shadows on our soil. This plan will probably produce a rupture with Carvajal, but the disadvantages resulting from not accepting it would be much greater.

Speaking of Wallace, Grant mentioned that Wallace wanted this government to construct a railroad from Punta Isabel to Brownsville so he could move his people without arousing suspicion. Considering this suggestion absurd, Grant contended that no pretext was necessary to transport United States citizens from one point to another within the country.

Before visiting Grant, I met with General Mussey . . . who returned last night from Philadelphia. I read him the aforementioned letters of Mr. P. [Plumb?]. It would be worthwhile to verify the date of Clarence A. Seward's resignation from the Department of State, Mussey thought, because he believed it was after the Maximilian concession was received here. Undoubtedly, Mussey will inform the president of these facts.

The *New York Herald* has not published the letters from Mexico and Paris which . . . I had sent. Since each day of delay makes their publication more difficult, yesterday I sent them to the *Washington National Intelligencer*. . . . The first one was published today. The principal goal of this letter was to impress the public with two ideas: (1) neither the French nor Maximilian considers leaving Mexico, and (2) Maximilian has reestablished slavery in Mexico. This morning I sent Mussey a copy of the *National Intelligencer* with a note attesting this information's authenticity and requesting him to have the president read the letter.

Today I visited Dennison at his office to show him the letters of Mr. P. Finding him very busy, however, I left him the letters to read at his convenience.   [5:721-23]

OCTOBER 27 I had a long, frank conversation with Welles about Maximilian's intrigues to form a faction in this country and his success until now. I read him [Plumb's?] letters, just as I had done for the secretaries of the treasury and interior. I showed him the prospectus of the "Express" company and gave him all the other convenient explanations. Apparently Welles already knew of this, or at least expected it, especially concerning Seward. He did not reveal the surprise I had observed in the other cabinet members. On the contrary, these intrigues contained nothing unusual, he told me, because Seward was and had been no big friend of ours.

I inquired regarding the desirability of bringing these facts to the president's attention and of my difficulty in communicating them. I asked him if he would be inconvenienced in doing so. He would do it with pleasure, he said, but it seemed more appropriate and desirable to our interests for someone who is not in the cabinet to communicate this.

I asked him who he thought could do it. Without hesitation, he mentioned Blair, who is our friend and who knows Seward's policy well. . . . As soon as Blair returns from New York I will speak to him about this matter.

Welles's manner of expressing himself indicated that he seemed to consider Seward entirely favorable to our enemies and working in their behalf.   [5:734-35]

OCTOBER 28 Yesterday afternoon I visited Grant to learn the results of the interview he and Schofield had that morning with the president. . . . Grant told me the conversation had been long and interesting, but the only good result was the president's suspension of an order to muster out some units of Sheridan's army. He also told me that the president had received the suggestion to send a first-class minister to the Mexican Republic very well.

In the evening Schofield came to see me, as we had agreed. He knew what had occurred at the interview. The president was already well aware of Clarence A. Seward's participation in Maximilian's Express Company. He expressed interest and concern with respect to our affairs, but concerning Seward, Johnson was disposed to await the development of his policy. Finding Johnson so disposed, Schofield did not think it suitable to tell the president everything he wished to regarding the secretary of state. Grant was more explicit but also did not achieve much. The president charged him with speaking to Seward about our affairs.

In Schofield's opinion, because Seward has convinced the president that his note to Bigelow of this past September 6 . . . demanded that the French government retire its invading forces from Mexico and he now daily awaits Drouyn de L'Huys's reply, it seemed undesirable to disapprove Seward's conduct while the consequences were unclear. Moreover, Seward is indisputably the most influential man in this country. Since his influence increased very considerably after the attempt to assassinate him, Johnson cannot dismiss him, even if he wanted to, except for reasons which the conscience of the North American people would deem justifiable.

Doubtless, then, he will continue in the State Department for some time longer. While he remains in the cabinet, policy will not change. In addition, none of his colleagues can oppose him successfully. He is sufficiently skillful to obtain his objective, even in opposition to the president's desires and will.

The president had received the idea of sending a minister to El Paso very favorably, Schofield related also, but this probably would not be done while Seward remains in the cabinet.

Although the secretary of state's ideas, wishes, and policy appear indecipherable for those of us who view them from near, Schofield judged that Seward has deceived himself about two things: first, the president's [Juárez] departure from the [Mexican] Republic and the subsequent dissolution of our forces, and second, the French army's withdrawal after the president's departure. In Schofield's judgment, Seward has been expecting the first event for a long time and still awaits it because only that fact could explain his policy.   [5:741-42]

OCTOBER 31   Yesterday, after I thought that Grant had already visited Seward, I went to see the general at his office to learn what had been the outcome of the interview. I also wanted to show Grant the . . . clipping from the . . . *Herald,* which reported that the Austrian emperor had signed an agreement with Maximilian to permit him to recruit 2,000 men per year in the Austrian Empire.

The general had in fact already spoken with Seward, but finding several people present, he had been somewhat reserved. Grant related only Seward's explanation that he had nothing to do with the Express Company business in which his nephew was involved. If Grant or other persons would write him asking if his nephew was working with his consent, Seward would respond in a satisfactory manner and make his reply public. Grant also reported that Seward already spoke about our affairs in a manner very distinct from just a short time ago. In this sense a great improvement was observable.

In the evening Schofield came to see me. Since Grant had been very explicit with him, he gave me more details about Grant's conversation with Seward. Apparently Seward disclosed his plans or indicated he had a well-matured plan that could not fail and ought to compel the French army to depart from Mexico. Schofield feared that, with his recognized ability, Seward might have deceived Grant solely for the purpose of avoiding Grant's opposition. Schofield also believes that the chief consequence of that conversation will be his mission to Europe, with the purpose as originally designed. Seward intimated to Grant that he would act on the idea of sending a minister to El Paso entirely as Grant thought best.

Things have arrived at a point where Seward will have to perform or give very powerful weapons to his opponents. His continued abuse of Grant's good faith would soon be clear to the general's acknowledged good sense. Then Seward will have Grant as an open opponent. . . .

Yesterday I read to Generals Grant and Schofield and to Dennison a letter which Mr. P. [Plumb] of New York wrote me on October 28, advising me of Clarence A. Seward's departure for New Orleans, Texas, Havana, and Mexico.

Believing it very desirable for us if Grant were the one to complain to Seward about the proceedings of his nephew, last night I requested Schofield to arrange this in the shortest possible time. I offered to send him the two letters [Eugène] de Courcillon has published in the *Herald* and the article on the same matter published in the *Courrier des Etats-Unis* on October 24. In the second letter, de Courcillon removed his mask and openly favored Maximilian. [5:747-48]

NOVEMBER 4 This morning Schofield . . . informed me that he had already received his instructions to go to Paris on a confidential mission. He is instructed to ascertain if the French government is disposed to retire from Mexico and, in the affirmative case, under what conditions. This he will ascertain by means of the United States minister in Paris. Upon obtaining a reply, he will return to communicate the results to the president. Schofield will assert the United States's disposition to accept some financial responsibility to obtain the retirement of the French forces from the Republic.

He has authorization to remain in New York as long as he considers necessary to aid us in the negotiation of a loan. He said that Grant would come next week for the same purpose.

He also informed me that the cabinet had already agreed to send a first-class minister to the residence of the supreme government. The person nominated should be a general, they decided, requesting the secretary of war to propose a suitable person. Schofield suspects this nomination will go to General [Daniel] Sickles, who was sent recently on a special mission to Bogotá.

Then I brought Schofield to the financial agency issuing our bonds where we conversed at length with [Jonathan] Tifft, who informed us of the present state of negotiations. Since our principal difficulty now is the lack of confidence that this government would take any part in the question with France, Schofield offered privately to visit several bank presidents in this city to communicate confidentially the determination of this government and thus obtain their cooperation in the sale of the bonds.   [5:754]

NOVEMBER 14 Schofield and I . . . had an interesting conversation with Grant. He told us that he had countermanded McDowell's order concerning the exportation of arms over the borders of California and Arizona [McDowell's order prohibited arms exports]. . . .

Schofield asked Grant if he could remain another week in this city without great inconvenience. It was of the utmost importance, Grant replied, that Schofield not detain himself one day longer. Therefore, his departure for Europe remained definitely fixed for tomorrow. Grant told me that Seward had changed very noticeably concerning Mexican affairs. Seward now claimed that his whole purpose is to avoid a general war over this question.

Grant also informed me that General Steele, recently arrived in Washington, has given very good reports on the state of things on the frontier and he now claims a great sympathy for our cause. . . . Steele had called at my house, expressing a great desire to see me to give me some important news. Grant also indicated to me that General [John A.] Logan would probably be nominated United States minister to the supreme government. . . .

Today I presented Grant to [James] Beekman. Previously I had arranged with Beekman for the New York Union League Club of which Beekman is vice-president to invite Grant to a reception. In the speech welcoming Grant to the club some allusion would be made to Mexican affairs. . . .

Then Schofield mentioned Tifft's desire for Grant to subscribe to the

Mexican loan or to write a letter expressing his desire to subscribe. Grant said that he would have to consult the president before deciding to do either. [5:785-86]

NOVEMBER 19 A distinguished citizen of this country, Robert Dale Owen, has entered into service for John W. Corlies and Company to aid them in marketing our bonds. He is a person of very sound judgment who can lend valuable service. He has spoken already with several capitalists to persuade them to buy our bonds. Discovering that one of the principal objections is the belief that our loan is in opposition to Johnson's policy, Owen . . . had an interview with his old friend Johnson to clarify this and other important points and thus to be able to answer any of the objections he encounters. . . . He wrote down what happened in the interview in a concise memorandum containing the most important and significant points. . . .

Memorandum of a conference held with President Johnson on the morning of Thursday, November 9, 1865. I initiated the conversation by explaining to the president that some weeks ago Mr. Tifft, associate of the firm John W. Corlies and Company, financial agents for the Mexican Republic, asked me to assist in offering the Mexican loan, which was about to enter the market. Upon questioning Tifft about what attitude our government had in respect to said loan, he mentioned having had an interview with the president and with Seward. The United States government had expressed itself generally favorable toward the loan in the interview, he could assure me, hoping it might be marketed without any difficulties. I told the president that in light of this assertion I had agreed to assist the loan agency. Without this assurance I would not have accepted the proposal. Moreover, the agency has already sent ads to hundreds of newspapermen in all parts of the country, I told him, offering each of them Mexican bonds valued at $50 by subscription for the price of $30, an offer which 9 out of 10 editors have accepted. The editors accompany the ads with favorable editorials and frequently with an enthusiastic letter of recommendation, all of which clearly indicate the state of public sentiment. Regarding the Mexican question, at this point I added: "Upon speaking of the matter with New York capitalists and mentioning my reasons for believing the government favors this loan and desires its success, they have raised this question: 'Mr. Owen, do you have authority from the president to say either that Maximilian will not be recognized during his presidency, or that if he should obtain recognition the subscribers of this loan will be protected in any case?'" To this I could only answer that I lacked such authorization, not having spoken of the matter with the president. I proceeded to tell Johnson that my trip to Washington had no other purpose than to visit him. Therefore, I hoped he would not mind confiding in me, authorizing me to give an assurance, not in public but only in private, to the capitalists to whom I would offer the loan, either that our government will not recognize Maximilian, or, in the event of recognition, the holders of Mexican bonds would be guaranteed against any loss.

He could not conceive, the president replied, that in the remaining three years and few months [of his administration?], any possible circumstances would arise in which this government would recognize Maximilian. Even admitting for a moment the possibility of that eventuality, however, a treaty would guarantee all the rights of our citizens with respect to Mexico. Included among the rights would be those relative to the Mexican loan, assuming that its subscribers had acted in good faith to aid a Republic which we recognized then as the legitimate Mexican government and with which we maintained friendly relations, as the continuation of the Mexican minister Romero in this country and our refusal to receive any minister from Maximilian testify to.

I asked Johnson if he would express these same ideas to a small committee of New York capitalists. He paused for a moment to consider the request and finally responded: "In the current circumstances, I believe it will be better not to give this matter too serious or official a character, but rather that you should communicate these facts confidentially to the private individuals in my name and with my authorization. This will be done, of course, only when necessary to market the loan [from the business point of view]. I believe that will be sufficient and satisfactory. It is better that no more people than are necessary should know of it."

In the course of the conversation, the president concurred in the opinion that this loan could well be the peaceful solution to the Mexican difficulties.

After some observations regarding the great danger to our Pacific possessions from a powerful neighbor like Maximilian, the conversation moved to matters of general policy.

Based on notes made as soon as I returned to my hotel. Robert Dale Owen. Washington, November 9, 1865. . . . I give this copy to Romero in confidence and in secrecy. November 19, 1865. Robert Dale Owen.   [5:811-12]

NOVEMBER 24 Today I took General [Gaspar] Sánchez Ochoa to see Lieutenant General Grant. When we entered his office, Grant gave me an important private letter from Sheridan to read, dated in New Orleans on November 5. . . . Everything he had communicated to Grant privately about Maximilian's unpopularity has been confirmed, Sheridan declared, claiming 95 percent of the Mexican population opposed Maximilian. Sheridan continued, the Liberals are besieging the cities occupied by Maximilian's forces and sustained through levies [conscripted soldiers, money, or both]. Referring to the emigration of United States citizens to enlarge our army, Sheridan wrote Grant, it is necessary to work with much discretion in everything because there are no supplies on the frontier. The North Americans, Sheridan added, could not subsist on tortillas and frijoles as the Mexican soldier does. To avoid the potential disgust among those who go expecting a great deal, yet encounter very little, he contended, it would be better to discard the idea of carrying United States citizens and limit ourselves to organizing the Mexicans. In his opinion, they need only one person to organize and lead them to triumph over the invaders. If the United States government wished to intervene in the matter, Sheridan also wrote, he would promise to settle the affair, if given only six thousand cavalry, which could be taken from fort Duncan. The distances on the frontier are very great, Sheridan noted, the country is sparsely populated, and there are neither supplies nor foodstuffs. For these very reasons, he maintained, the

French army could not concentrate on the frontier. If it attempted to, it could be starved into submission with six thousand cavalry. Moreover, this cavalry force would raise the public spirit in Mexico, permitting the organization of sufficient troops to throw the French out. The Southern insurgents were still, Sheridan asserted, conniving with the French and Mexican traitors, as they undoubtedly had been before the end of the American Civil War. Sheridan believed Napoleon went to Mexico to aid the South. Because of excessive timidity, however, he had lost the opportunity to consummate the South's independence, and now the United States must not follow his example by deferring its intervention in Mexico until it is too late.

Upon receiving this letter, Grant sent it to President Johnson. . . . When Grant showed it to me, Johnson had just returned it. We did not have adequate time to discuss this and other matters because some people interrupted us. . . .

Grant added that he had telegraphed Logan asking him not to make a decision about his nomination as minister to Mexico until after visiting this city.   [5:820-21]

NOVEMBER 26 I have had several conferences recently with [Schuyler] Colfax, who was Speaker of the House of Representatives in the last Congress and probably will be in the next, and [Thaddeus] Stevens, who has been chairman of the Committee on Ways and Means for many years and is generally recognized as a person with great influence in the House. Colfax has always been one of our best friends. Nevertheless, in these recent encounters he appeared somewhat cool. He told me that he was tired of wars and did not wish to provoke another. In his judgment the United States government ought to concede all its moral support to our cause but not go beyond that. He would approve General Logan's nomination for minister to Mexico, but he favored no greater action. Colfax expresses the opinion of a large part of this country.

I saw Colfax primarily to entreat him not to name Henry J. Raymond chairman of the House Foreign Relations Committee. Here the Speaker of the House appoints the chairman. Since, unfortunately for us, Henry Winter Davis is not a member of the next Congress, Colfax will have to name another chairman. Raymond's background and reputation, no less than his good relationship with the secretary of state, might very well lead to his selection. In my judgment, this would be the worst thing that could happen for our cause. Wishing to avoid this, I spoke at length with Colfax about the chairmanship. I mentioned that what Raymond had written in his newspaper, the *New York Times,* as well as what he had said to Grant at a dinner which I attended in New York on November 19, had led to my suspicion, indeed almost certainty, that Raymond was a supporter of Napoleon and

Maximilian. Colfax assured me that Raymond would not receive the chairmanship of that committee. I indicated to Colfax that perhaps General Banks, recently elected to the House, would be the most appropriate person for that post. This suggestion appeared to please him.

[Thaddeus] Stevens from Pennsylvania belongs to the most radical faction of the Republican party. He has been in Congress for many years and is one of its most able and experienced members. He has always been Seward's antagonist. He asked me for information about Mexican affairs with considerable interest. Because, in his view, the House ought to spend a great part of its session in discussing these affairs, Stevens wished to be kept current on developments. I could not have been presented a better opportunity to interest Stevens in our affairs. . . . I have conversed with him at length about the condition of our affairs, about the extent to which I understand this government's policy, and what I judge will result from all this. I gave him ample details of the so-called Mexican Imperial Express Company, of the colonization projects of Gwin and [Matthew] Maury, of Maximilian's decree reestablishing slavery in Mexico, and of various other items. He listened with considerable attention and no doubt will take the initiative in our favor when the time comes. We cannot expect a better champion. As soon as Senator [Benjamin] Wade of Ohio arrives, I will make a similar approach to him. I will obtain representatives and senators from other factions of the Republican and the Democratic parties to act in our favor, so Mexican affairs will not become a question of party politics.   [5:831-32]

DECEMBER 7   I want Congress to request the correspondence from the president on several points to which it is necessary to call public attention in this country. For this purpose, I had written some resolutions which I intended to have presented in the House as well as the Senate. One of these resolutions requests the general correspondence on the present state of Mexican affairs. The others call for the correspondence on Maximilian's so-called decree ordering the summary execution of Mexican patriots who defend the national independence, on the so-called decree that attempts to reestablish slavery in the Republic, on the colonizing plans of [William] Gwin and Maury, and finally on Maximilian's attempts to obtain recognition from this government.

The day before yesterday I carried several of these resolutions to Congress. The arrival of a presidential message, however, permitted me only to entrust Ohio Congressman [James] Garfield with one referring to the pretended reestablishment of slavery in the Republic. . . .

Garfield modified the resolution insubstantially and presented it at yesterday's session. . . .

Connecticut Congressman [Henry C.] Deming opposed this resolution's

admission without debate, therefore it remains pending until the next
session.   [5:872-73]

DECEMBER 10   Yesterday, Major General [Alexander M.] McCook, distinguished citizen of Ohio, came to me with the request for certified English
copies of the following documents: Napoleon's letter to General Forey of
July 3, 1862, Maximilian's decree of September 13, 1865, which pretends
to establish slavery in Mexico, and Maximilian's decree of October 3, 1865,
which declared war to the death against the Mexican Republic. McCook
told me that Senators [Zachariah] Chandler and Wade contemplated offering some resolutions in favor of the Monroe Doctrine in the Senate. To have
a proper foundation, they needed all these documents. I gave him copies. . . .

I went at once to see Senator Wade and mentioned what had occurred.
He had agreed in effect with Chandler to present these resolutions, and they
would ask me for the facts to support them. He would be very glad, he
added, for any suggestions I thought useful. He asked if I would make a
preliminary draft of the resolutions, which I agreed to do. After failing to
locate Wade, I carried it to Chandler. He invited me to a meeting today at 2
p.m. to discuss my proposal with him, Wade, and McCook.

In drafting this proposal I reviewed and succeeded in mentioning all
the acts of Napoleon and Maximilian that would make them odious to this
nation. I took the resolutions from a draft proposal presented to me several
days ago by Samuel S. Cox, Ohio congressman in the last Congress.

We met today at the agreed hour. First, I read my proposal. Wade immediately asked for the facts that justified my assertions. Then McCook read
the three documents previously mentioned while I supplied the necessary
explanations regarding points not embraced in those documents. Then
Wade suggested adopting my proposed preamble, but reducing it to the
fewest possible number of words. Wade thought that having said sufficient
in the preamble, it would be best to express the resolution in the following
words: "Be it resolved to recommend to the president the vindication of the
well-known doctrine and the honor of the United States." Chandler approved this idea, asserting that any other more explicit wording would expose the resolution to defeat. If it were not sufficiently explicit, I mentioned,
Seward could very easily evade the issue. Once the resolution was adopted,
Wade countered, Congress could then adopt other, more adequate resolutions. That very evening then, McCook would draft the preamble and the
resolution in the manner we agreed upon and tomorrow at nine a.m. we
would get together again to discuss them and to make the final arrangements for their presentation. Regarding the manner of presenting the resolution in Congress, Chandler suggested using the previous question proce-

dure in the House of Representatives to eliminate all discussion and produce an immediate vote. Once unanimously or overwhelmingly approved, it would pass to the Senate, where the chairman of the corresponding committee would probably report unfavorably on the resolution, or he would attempt to delay it indefinitely.

I proposed then to have it presented in both houses on the same day. . . . Wade seconded the idea and all approved it. Thus the public will witness concerted action in the two houses on this point.

Once this was agreed to, we considered the selection of the person to present the resolution in the House. I recommended either Stevens of Pennsylvania, [Elihu] Washburne of Illinois, or [Robert C.] Schenck of Ohio. The first is the ablest member of the House, the second is Grant's spokesman, and the third is a candidate for the Senate in his state, who would gladly present the resolution. We agreed that McCook would visit Schenck that night and I would call upon Washburne. I looked but did not find him.

Possibly, the resolution will be presented tomorrow in both houses. It must be done soon because if delayed, and if it becomes known that the resolution will be offered, every possible means will be used to prevent it from reaching the floor. Then presenting the resolution will become very difficult and obtaining approval even more difficult.   [5:883-84]

DECEMBER 11 I went to Chandler's residence at nine this morning. Wade and McCook arrived shortly thereafter. McCook read his draft resolution, which Chandler and Wade found excellent.

I thought the preamble omitted some important points, but to avoid making it longer as well as to avoid losing more time, I did not insist that they be added. We agreed then that today Wade would present the resolutions in the Senate and Schenck in the House. Both did so in fact, but apparently Schenck did not call for the previous question, or, if he did, the House did not concede it. In both houses the resolutions were passed to the Foreign Relations Committee. . . .

General Banks was named chairman of the Foreign Relations Committee, and, unfortunately, Raymond will be vice-chairman of that committee. The others on this committee are not objectionable to us. Surely Colfax could not resist Seward's influence for placing Raymond on that committee, and he gave him one of the most elevated positions in the committee. In the Senate we have Wade as 4th ranking member of their [Foreign Relations] committee. Schenck has been named chairman of the House Committee on Military Affairs.

This morning I asked Chandler to present to the Senate the previously prepared resolutions requesting the president for the correspondence relative to Maximilian's bloody decree of October 3, 1865, declaring a war to the death. I want Congress to have this topic before it and Seward to state, if possible, what he has done in regard to this decree. Supposedly he wrote a note to the French government complaining of the decree. Chandler gladly offered to present the resolution, which he did without altering a single word in my draft. Fortunately, it passed in the Senate without opposition. . . .

Senator [Jacob] Howard of Michigan, a colleague of Chandler, presented another resolution in today's session . . . which was approved in the same manner. This resolution requested from the president all the correspondence, not yet officially published, which has been exchanged between this government and France concerning the French army's occupation of the Mexican Republic and the establishment of a monarchy there. I had nothing to do with this resolution. I believe it was the spontaneous inspiration of Howard, who is a decided partisan of the Monroe Doctrine.

The House of Representatives is no less occupied with our affairs than the Senate. Besides Schenck's resolutions, [Robert T.] Van Horn of Missouri presented others no less interesting. . . . He moved to pass them by calling the previous question, but Stevens of Pennsylvania opposed their passage in this manner. . . . The House voted in favor of Stevens's motion. Just like Schenck's resolution, then, these resolutions will pass to the Foreign Relations Committee.

Desiring my resolution requesting the government for the general correspondence on Mexican affairs to be presented by a member of respectability, whom Seward would not be able to refuse, I asked Stevens to present it. He did so today. It was approved without opposition. He presented the resolution exactly as I had given it to him. . . . I included a request for the correspondence of the French minister as much to learn what he has said, which might be of interest, as to avoid giving Seward the pretext of refusing to send my correspondence alone, because he could not present only one side of the question and thereby fail in the impartiality which neutrals ought to observe.

Finally, Garfield succeeded today in passing his resolution concerning Maximilian's decree pretending to reestablish slavery in Mexico. . . .

Today, then, both houses of Congress occupied themselves to a great extent, if not exclusively, with our affairs. This will produce an impression in this country and in Europe which cannot fail to be highly favorable to our cause. . . .

I still have four important resolutions relative to our affairs which I will give to four other congressmen. I did not use these resolutions previously to avoid clustering all at one time, thereby exhausting the material and leaving us with nothing for the future.   [5:887-88]

DECEMBER 14 The day before yesterday I learned in a completely confidential manner that General Logan had refused the nomination as United States minister to Mexico. Last night he dined with me. In the course of the conversation I mentioned having learned that he had refused the nomination. He was very surprised that I knew of this. Although he did not affirm my knowledge, I know that if he has not refused the post, he has no intention of going. Perhaps the likelihood that he will be chosen senator contributed to this.

Logan clearly does not wish to see the Mexican question reduced to the efforts or caprice of a single man. If the government was not disposed to face and treat the issue as it merits, he added, the minister who attempted to follow his own judgment would appear ridiculous. . . . Logan has spoken with Seward, but the secretary of state's views have not satisfied him.

Henry Roy de la Reintrie is striving to be named minister to Mexico. He is among our most decided friends in this country, but, unfortunately, he does not have the elevated social position of Logan or of many others who want the post.

De la Reintrie wishes my aid to obtain the nomination. In the end I will probably decide to help him. I have been assured that Grant has another candidate, General [Fred] Dent, his brother-in-law.   [5:891-92]

DECEMBER 19 Besides the resolutions regarding our affairs . . . I gave one to Washburne, which referred to the Mexican Imperial Express Company. There was correspondence from Grant on this matter, I indicated, which should be made public. Before presenting the resolution, he deemed it necessary to consult with Grant. . . . Grant [had] no [objection so] Washburne agreed to present it.

Since Washburne is Grant's personal friend and his voice in the House, people will believe that the request emenates from the general. This fact will allow me to avoid further unpleasantness with Seward.

Yesterday I spoke to Senator [John] Conness of California about the Gwin letters in the State Department. I suggested the desirability of requesting these letters. I gave him a memorandum so that he might present a resolution to this effect. He indicated that first he was going to speak with Seward about this matter.

Today I gave Senator [James] McDougall another resolution requesting information about General [Irvin] McDowell's order relative to the exportation of arms over the frontier. . . .

Early last week, I gave Congressman [Godlove] Orth of Indiana another resolution requesting information about the steps taken by Maximilian and the French to receive recognition from this government. . . . My objective was to expose [Thomas] Corwin's efforts and the French minister's intrigues. Nevertheless, Orth thought it necessary to change the wording of the resolution. Happily, Orth followed his wishes because Corwin suffered an attack of a fatal illness on Friday night and died yesterday afternoon. Thus no reason exists now to reveal his labor in favor of Maximilian, nor would it appear noble to do so.

Yesterday Orth presented his resolution . . .[which] was unanimously approved and sent to the president today. Seward will probably enclose the correspondence requested by the resolution, if he decides to send Montholon's note of November 28, in which the French officially solicited recognition for Maximilian, and the secretary of state's response.   [5:907]

DECEMBER 20   Yesterday I went to Grant's office and found him preparing to leave. I inquired if he had sent instructions to Sheridan. He replied that he had sent a very succinct telegram. However, that very day, he added, he would write Sheridan a private letter covering all the necessary details. Even if the president has great interest for our cause, Grant noted, he cannot openly take sides in the question while the United States remains neutral. He was going to recommend the best course to Sheridan, he continued, which would be for Sheridan to proceed as he best saw fit without awaiting instructions, but rather considering consummated facts.   [5:912-13]

1866

For some time, Secretary of State William Seward had been convinced that the French could be persuaded to withdraw from Mexico. President Andrew Johnson apparently came to accept Seward's view so that by early or mid-1866 he became convinced that a military assault on the French position was dangerous and unnecessary. The alienation between Romero and Grant on one hand and the Johnson-Seward team on the other grew during 1866. Seward objected to Romero's confidential meetings with Johnson. To end this practice, he issued what became known as the Romero circular in mid-1865, publicly denying foreign diplomats access to the president except through his office. Of course, Seward knew when he issued the circular that he had in effect won the contest between himself and Grant and Romero for the aid of the president. Romero salvaged what he could. Although Johnson and Seward were not inclined to follow the sharp, confrontational course toward which Grant and Romero hoped to steer the United States, they still maintained a public image of uncompromising opposition to the French intervention in Mexico and the puppet Maximilian empire. Seward and Johnson were patient because they did not view the French intervention as related to the Civil War, and thus they did not view it as an assault upon U.S. sovereignty. Grant and Romero were impatient because they considered the French intervention an extension of the Confederacy's direct challenge to U.S. sovereignty and to the liberalism and nationalism that combined to form the laissez-faire social system.

Johnson and Grant moved further away from each other as 1866 wore on. Grant resented Johnson's effort to use Romero and himself to support Johnson's popularity on his "swing around the circle." Johnson and Seward converted an ostensibly nonpolitical trip to dedicate a statue of Stephen Douglas in Chicago into a political campaign. The trip became an attempt to show solidarity with Mexico and to use Grant's great popularity to bolster Johnson's sagging image. Grant was presented as a supporter of the administration, and Romero was introduced prominently at each stop in a way that associated him and his goal—ridding Mexico of the French—as linked to the Johnson administration's policy. By the later stages of the trip, both Grant and Romero were trying to avoid the appearance that they supported the administration while still milking the large public turnouts for popular support for getting the French out of Mexico as soon as possible. After the Chicago ceremony, Romero made an excuse not to continue with the Johnson party on its return. Grant also diminished his role. During the return trip, the president increasingly politicized his public appearances by attacking the Radicals.

General Grant also resisted Johnson's efforts to exploit his popularity in another scheme. When the French evacuated Mexico in late 1866, Johnson appointed Ohioan Lewis D. Campbell to serve as U.S. minister to the Republic of Mexico and attempted to send Grant along to reinforce the mission, to give it more public attention, and to create the impression that the Johnson administration was working with Grant to expel the French. Because Grant had disagreed sharply with the Johnson-Seward policy, he angrily and categorically refused to accompany the mission. Johnson had been so determined to hitch Grant to the administration's Mexican policy that he had had Grant's role in the mission and his instructions printed for wider distribution. Stymied by Grant, Johnson was forced to substitute General William T. Sherman—the second most popular U.S. military leader—as his symbol of the strength and correctness of his policy to remove the French. Meanwhile, on the frontier, General Sheridan provided whatever aid he could to the Mexican Liberals.

Romero continued his active lobbying work with members of Congress and business, military, and media figures. Occasionally, his efforts encountered significant problems. With the Civil War over and financial and military aid more available in the United States, the number of Mexican liberal agents multiplied rapidly. Romero wanted to control and supervise the Mexican *caudillos*, Mexican regional military-political strong men, and agents operating in the United States but found that task burdensome and difficult. North American speculators such as popular General John C. Frémont waited like vultures to fall upon gullible or inattentive Mexican weapons purchasers. On the cheerier side, Romero found ever larger numbers of U.S. Congressmen willing to introduce resolutions, make speeches, and cooperate with him in other ways. The lobbying campaign he had launched in 1863 was paying fair dividends by 1866.

Finally, in late 1866 and 1867, Romero played a peripheral but not insignificant role in the impeachment of President Johnson. Beginning in December 1866, Romero was made privy to Radical plans, hopes, and aspirations in regard to removing the Johnson-Seward team and thus altering a hated domestic and foreign policy. The plan presented to Romero in December 1866 involved forcing Senator Lafayette Foster of Connecticut to resign, then electing Senator Benjamin Wade as president pro tempore of the Senate, and finally impeaching Johnson to make Wade president of the United States.

JANUARY 11 I implored Wade to prevail upon the Senate Foreign Relations Committee to release its resolutions and to arrange for the Ohio legislature to approve resolutions in favor of the Monroe Doctrine similar to those of the Indiana assembly. He gladly offered his services for both causes.

Yesterday I saw him in the Senate and asked what he had accomplished. Sumner, chairman of the Senate Foreign Relations Committee, he told me, believed Napoleon was going to announce his decision to withdraw from Mexico. Thus Sumner wanted to avoid any action until Napoleon's speech in the Corps Législatif was received here.

Last night I visited Sumner at his house. I discovered that he believed the French are on the eve of departing from the Republic. Until he is convinced of the contrary, he will not be disposed to take any action in regard to our affairs. Sumner claimed in the aforementioned speech that if Napoleon did not declare his intention to retire from Mexico soon and unconditionally, he would be disposed to concern himself with the question. He indicated that he would favor the resolutions at that time. Certainly, then, nothing can be done in the Senate in respect to this matter until next month.

Perhaps another approach might succeed in the House. Until now I have had only one interview with General Banks, chairman of the House committee. I found him poorly informed on the state of the question.

[7:26]

JANUARY 17   Grant . . . mentioned that Sheridan had written him describing in great detail the French army's violations of neutrality on the border during the United States Civil War. Desiring to make this and several other important communications from Sheridan public, I asked Grant if there would be an inconvenience in Congress requesting them. He said there was none. So I decided to ask Senator Chandler, who has good relations with the secretary of war, to request the communications. Yesterday I saw him in the Senate and presented him a draft of the resolution, which reads as follows:

"Be it resolved: That the president is requested to communicate to the Senate, if in his opinion it is not imcompatible with the public interest, the communications of Major General Sheridan, commander of the Military Division of the Gulf, or of any other commander of the Department of Texas concerning the actual state of affairs on the southeast frontier of the United States and especially those referring to violations of neutrality on the part of the army presently occupying the right bank of the Rio Grande."

Chandler offered to present the preceding resolution today. . . . The Senate approved it, and this evening it will go to the president. I consider it quite difficult for the secretary of war to decide to send the communications requested of him. . . .

Congressman Green Clay Smith . . . offered to present the resolution . . . requesting the correspondence on the decree of the Colombian Congress of this past May 2 in honor of Citizen President Juárez.   [7:42]

JANUARY 27   In a conversation we had today, General Logan mentioned his reasons for not accepting the mission of this country near the supreme government when Johnson offered it to him. While speaking to Seward about Mexican affairs, the secretary of state informed him that his nomination had no significance. Seward claimed that it had been made only to satisfy the demands of public opinion. The United States was not considering sustaining the government of the Republic in any way, and if the French overthrew the Mexican Republic, Logan was to return peacefully to his country.

Logan was not the man to accept such a mission, which he believed would have subjected him to ridicule. Since then he has remained in Washington working actively in our favor. In Logan's opinion, Maximilian and the French must be forcibly thrown out of the Republic.

[Lewis D.] Campbell, nominated minister to Mexico after Logan's refusal, still has not accepted the mission because, as I am informed, he awaits

Senate confirmation of his nomination first. It seems this will raise some difficulties.

Today, Sumner, chairman of the [Senate Foreign Relations] committee, assured a friend of mine that Campbell's nomination would not be confirmed.   [7:73-74]

JANUARY 28   Brigadier General G. W. Schofield . . . gave me a letter from his brother, dated in Paris on January 10. . . .

Since Schofield's letter referred to the explanation his brother would give me, I asked him as many questions as I found necessary to inform myself well of developments. A summary of G. W. Schofield's responses follows:

Upon [John] Schofield's arrival in Paris, it was already known, or at least rumored, that he came on a mission in reference to Mexican affairs. This produced much excitement in France. Believing it unnecessary to nourish the excitement further, Schofield announced that he really came on an official mission. He did what he could to placate the existing inquietude. To this end he even toasted peace at the thanksgiving dinner which the United States citizens residing in Paris gave in December. . . .

The same considerations and the desire not to create difficulties or embarrassments for Napoleon have persuaded Schofield not to request presentation in an extraordinary ceremony. Rather, he will await the reception that generally takes place shortly after the New Year, at which the respective ministers present all distinguished foreigners to Napoleon. . . .

Meanwhile, Bigelow had communicated the state of the question to Schofield in detail, explaining that the French were about to withdraw from Mexico. Although Schofield seemed persuaded of this, he still believed Bigelow has too much confidence in the French government.

As soon as I received this letter, I went to show it to Grant, who I knew had received one. In his letter, Grant said, Schofield described the same things as in mine. Tomorrow he will read his letter to the president.

Schofield referred to a plan he considered the only possible one, namely for the United States to guarantee to France the payment of the interest on Maximilian's debt. This would be abhorrent, I explained to Grant, and undesirable in any form. He seemed to share my opinion. I also asked him to present this sentiment to the president when speaking with him upon this matter tomorrow. He offered to do so. I will reply to Schofield in the same sense on this incident.

The idea that Napoleon is about to retire his forces from Mexico continues to gain much support here. Senator Wade, one of the people who has always believed that Napoleon would not leave Mexico unless forcibly thrown out, mentioned today having spoken with the president about our affairs recently. Trusting in the president's good judgment, Wade believes this rumor must be true now. Unfortunately, I cannot share the same opinion in spite of all of this.

Fortunately, Wade is prepared to insist that his resolutions be passed whatever Napoleon's disposition might be. He only awaited Napoleon's speech because Sumner openly refused to concern himself with this matter before that document arrives.   [7:76-77]

FEBRUARY 11 For some days I have wanted to discuss various matters with Stevens, congressman from Pennsylvania, but succeeded in encountering him only today.

In the first place, I mentioned having heard him express great respect for President Juárez on other occasions. This had prompted me to suggest to him that perhaps the United States Congress would approve a resolution in honor of the citizen president similar to one approved by the Colombian Congress. Moreover, he was the most appropriate person to present such a resolution, I observed, and to obtain its approval. Finally, I gave him a copy of Johnson's speech, which contained the documents relative to the resolution of the Colombian Congress. Stevens did not indicate his intentions in regard to this matter.

Immediately, I mentioned the desirability and necessity of the United States making a loan to us. If it did not, I told him, the danger existed that the French could throw the Mexican Republic's government from the national territory, thereby presenting themselves as, at least, the de facto government and giving a cloak of legality to their usurpation. Stevens appeared persuaded of the necessity of our receiving some assistance. To this end, he told me, he had been attempting for some time to offer a resolution, which he would have presented tomorrow except for the funeral services Congress would celebrate in honor of President Lincoln, thus preventing the House from occupying itself with any other matter. However, he would present his resolution as soon as possible.

Then I asked him if he believed it necessary to present a resolution requesting information from the government about the constitutional period of the president of Mexico. . . . In his judgment, Stevens said, Congress was satisfied on this point. Therefore, he did not believe this information necessary. Senator Wade shares this opinion. Thus for the present I will leave the subject pending.   [7:142-43]

MARCH 20 In my note of January 28, I communicated to you the president's remarks to Senator Wade of Ohio about assurances he considered adequate to convince him of Napoleon's determination to retire his forces from Mexico. At that time I did not tell you, because it did not seem necessary, that these assurances consisted primarily of a letter Governor [Oliver] Morton had written from Paris.

This gentleman is one of this nation's most distinguished men. He was governor of Indiana during the four years of the Civil War and demonstrated qualities that have given him a national reputation. His wartime anxieties produced a dangerous illness that forced him to retire from public life and to travel to Europe for a change of climate and for some rest. Upon arriving in Paris, Morton believed that Napoleon was about to retire from Mexico. He wrote in this sense to the president. Aware of Morton's good judgment and sane critical ability, Johnson considered his opinion adequate assurance that the French would soon retire from Mexico. Neither information from Seward nor reports from [John] Bigelow had convinced Johnson on this matter, I informed Wade, but rather Morton's letter.

A short while ago Morton returned from Europe. Upon arriving in New York, I recently learned, he had stated that, far from contemplating withdrawing his forces from Mexico, Napoleon was striving to declare Mexico a French colony. Considering it to be very desirable for Morton to come to this city to converse with the president and with those who believe Napoleon seriously contemplates retiring from Mexico . . . I obtained my goal through the intervention of a mutual friend. . . .

Yesterday he saw the president and Grant. Today I saw him. Without revealing that I already knew what he had said to these two people, I mentioned that his letter to Johnson upon his arrival in Paris had contributed more than anything else toward convincing the president that the French would retire from Mexico within a short time. He had a duty to himself and to his country, I insinuated, to return to see the president in order to express his current opinion formed with better information and after opportunities for maturer judgment. He had spoken to the president yesterday, Morton told me, retracting what he had said in the aforementioned letter, which he regretted having written. He was now persuaded, he informed President Johnson, that Napoleon was not considering leaving Mexico. Napoleon's current situation is such, he suggested, that he would not do so if threatened. Meanwhile, Napoleon expected the American people to become accustomed to the French presence in Mexico just as they had to the English in Canada. Napoleon dreamed, Morton told the president, that the French could go on creating favorable interest groups in the United States and that the Mexican opposition would disappear. Then, deposing Maximilian under the pretext that the latter has not fulfilled his contractual obligations, Napoleon will assert the need to retain Mexico until it has paid its debt to France. Furthermore, this retention will amount to the establishment of a colonial regime and will end with that step. Finally, the French intervention in Mexico was now unpopular, Morton informed the president, because the

French people saw their money expended and blood spilled exclusively to benefit an Austrian. When Napoleon declares Mexico a French colony, however, the undertaking will become an eminently popular one.

Speaking of Bigelow, the president had [Morton] informed yesterday that Bigelow seemingly places confidence only in confidential innuendos and took these as assurances.

Morton spoke to Grant in the same terms.

I do not believe that anything could have produced better results at this moment than Morton's conversation. . . . We have other projects pending whose success may depend on this conversation. As I was leaving Governor Morton's lodging, General Banks entered to see him. Banks is another who, in our interest, should hear Morton's views. I also managed to see Sumner today. His continued belief in Montholon's sincerity has convinced him that the French will retire sometime from Mexico. . . .

Morton's visit has produced incalculable good.   [7:330-32]

APRIL 6   Yesterday, upon receiving an invitation to visit the president . . . my first impulse was to hide the meeting from Seward just as I did the conversations that prompted the invitation. It seemed injudicious to inform Seward of our course, partly because it seemed inappropriate to reveal what Grant was doing for us and partly because Seward will certainly oppose the objectives I strive for from that interview.

Nevertheless, after mature deliberation, I was persuaded that . . . whatever the outcome, the matter would certainly be brought to the attention of Seward, who would understand what I have done. If I hid the meeting from Seward, he would have the additional ground of indignation to oppose our wishes. He would think that I had solicited conferences with the president behind his back in order to speak against him and to attempt to involve this government in acts that could result in war. . . .

[Informing Seward] might not achieve anything; at the same time it assuredly would not lose anything.

Thus, desiring to speak to Seward, I went to his house last night with the ostensible excuse of making the customary visit after receiving an invitation to a dinner or dance. . . . Shortly after I entered his house, we passed to an adjoining room, where we remained alone for more than an hour. During this time we spoke with complete liberty on Mexican affairs.

First, I mentioned that our situation was very difficult because of the absolute lack of resources, even of the most indispensable war materials such as arms and munitions. As I had informed him on other occasions, this was so critical that some elements of our forces recently have had to capitulate, laying down their arms and submitting to the French for lack of ammunition. By the next steamer, we might well receive notice, I continued, that General [Alejandro] García's forces suffered the same fate because, after the capitulation of General [Ignacio R.] Alatorre, all the enemy forces that had campaigned against Alatorre and other national forces would march on the coast of Sotavento de Veracruz. General García also lacks ammunition, which will probably compel his surrender. Recently, I informed Seward, agents from various parts of Mexico had informed me of the difficult situation, requesting arms and munitions. They assumed we had realized a considerable sum from the Mexican loan placed on the market this past October. One of these commissioners carried a letter from a distinguished officer of the United States Army on the Rio Grande addressed to Seward, which had not been delivered, I added, because I had been advised against it. The leaders who came seeking arms and munitions were very disconsolate upon discovering my inability to supply them, I continued, because they thought we could obtain some supplies from this government. Aware of his friendship for our cause and his frustrated attempts to supply us with war material, several asked to be presented to Grant. I disclosed a plan that, if it merits the approval of this government, could supply us the needed aid without compelling this government to fail in its neutral obligations toward France. I had communicated this plan to Grant, who urged me to submit it to the president. I could not see the president except when accompanied by the secretary of state, which would lend my visit an official character, I had explained to Grant, unless the president would invite me to visit him, in which case I could speak to him informally. Grant had communicated my disposition to Johnson. Today I received an invitation to see Johnson tomorrow morning at 10 a.m. I asked Seward if I should tell him what I intended to tell the president tomorrow, or if, on the contrary, I should abstain from informing him so he would never have official knowledge of the steps I am taking for this objective.

At first Seward said he would accompany me to see the president tomorrow after the cabinet meeting. I observed then that my appointment was for ten, two hours before the cabinet meeting. Finally, he decided that he did not wish to hear what I would say to the president. If it led to something, he continued, he would learn about it later at a cabinet meeting. Thus my exchange with Johnson would be entirely extraofficial. . . .

This induced Seward to speak of the Mexican question itself. Since Napoleon could not maintain his forces in Mexico much longer, even if only because of the expense of the Maximilian experiment, he claimed to have no doubt that within a year the French will have left Mexico. Even if the United States did not take a single action in the question, Seward was fully convinced France would have to abandon Mexico shortly. There were various items which he could not repeat, he added, that sufficed to convince him of the accuracy of his contention. . . . As soon as the Union would be reestablished (he understood this to mean when the representatives of the Southern states are readmitted to Congress), he knew the French would have to withdraw from Mexico without anyone demanding that of them. Napoleon's project was a very clever one if the Union was broken, he observed, but its reestablishment made the idea equally absurd.

In the course of the conversation several times he repeated the idea, firmly fixed in his mind, that it is totally impossible for the French to remain in Mexico and that they will have to leave soon, even if for no other reason than the expense of the undertaking.

On various occasions I explained that, although my opinion regarding the absurdity of the undertaking and the great difficulties that must be overcome to carry it to completion was identical to his, I differed on several of the secondary points such as whether the financial difficulties were sufficient to make Napoleon desist. Having become involved to such a degree in this matter, I stated my conviction that Napoleon would not hesitate to spend twenty or thirty million pesos yearly to preserve the appearance of a government established in Mexico City. In this manner he would not expose his error and bad faith. Because he was a despotic and irresponsible monarch, I continued, he could expend as much money as he wished without great difficulty. Moreover, judging by what he cared to publish regarding the disposition of the French government, I saw no reason to believe he was on the eve of leaving Mexico or that he even had discussed that idea. On the contrary, since his official declarations stated conditions for abandoning Mexico which made it little less than impossible, everything indicated that Napoleon was not considering departing. My disagreement with some of Seward's ideas, I observed, visibly disturbed him even though I had expressed my contrary judgments with great moderation. At one point I asked him what he thought Napoleon would do about the two hundred million pesos he had spent in Mexico. Seward replied without hesitation that he had no recourse but to lose them.

If this government's policy was to be effective, Seward told me, it was indispensable not to detour in the slightest from the high road it has assumed. Any United States conduct that could be interpreted as a desire to substitute itself for the French in Mexico, he observed, would completely justify the French intervention. If the United States should help us now with money or arms, besides failing in its neutral duties, Seward claimed, this course would make a French evacuation much more difficult. Obviously, then, the United States would not be defending its proclaimed principles with reason but would be intriguing surreptitiously in favor of the evacuation.

Seward attempted to explain that it was in Mexico's best interests for the United States to give [Juárez's government] no material aid, but only the moral support it has given up to this point. If a United States army went to Mexico, he claimed it would never return. It was indeed easy to throw the French out of Mexico, he added, but it would be impossible to throw the Yankees out. For each million dollars the United States government lent Mexico now, he surmised, later it would cost us a state, and for each arm in these circumstances, the eventual cost would be an acre of mineral land. This served to confirm my considered opinion that Seward will always oppose this government furnishing us any sort of material assistance.

Throughout the whole conversation, Seward's obvious fervor left no doubt he was expressing his convictions. He also indicated great confidence in his ability to compete triumphantly against Napoleon. In a moment of exaltation, while reminding me that he was ten years older than Napoleon, he made it plain that this age difference gave him a proportional advantage in experience.

Seward also informed me that he did not conceive of any circumstances that would make United States recognition of Maximilian probable. The government of the Mexican Republic would retain recognition, he noted, even if the president had to leave the national territory. . . . The interview ended in a very good manner because Seward appeared satisfied and I had obtained my objective.   [7:382-85]

APRIL 8 At the designated hour [10 A.M.] I arrived and at eleven the president received me in his private library. He began by excusing himself for not having seen me sooner and for having made me wait these last three days. I regretted distracting him from the many problems surrounding him, I responded, but the matter I wished to bring to his attention was no less important.

Not wishing to encourage our enemies, I could not tell him some things officially, I said, but would not find it inconvenient to relate them in an unofficial manner. One must suppose, I explained, that our country was exhausted after our long civil war and, as a consequence of the current war, commerce was paralyzed, agriculture suspended, and all sources of wealth closed. In addition, with the French in possession of the small national income, the totality permitted one to form an exact idea of our situation. Only the patriotism of the Mexican people, I observed, had prolonged the resistance for so long in such an unequal contest. Until now, I acknowledged, the expectation that either Napoleon would cease his effort to conquer Mexico after the United States Civil War or that the United States would intervene in the contest had sustained the patriotism of the Mexican people. These expectations led them to accept sacrifices which they believed would not last much longer. However, neither expectation is being realized. Instead of retiring, Napoleon is making a major drive to reduce all resistance and consolidate Maximilian's position. At the same time, the exhaustion of Mexico has reached a dangerous level. Shortly after receiving this report, I was officially notified that various units of our forces have had to surrender because of complete lack of munitions. Assuming we had realized a considerable sum from our loan, I continued, several commanding officers still in the field have sent agents here to ask for arms and munitions. These commanders have indicated that if we do not send material in time, they will also have to surrender. I had spoken frequently about this matter with Grant, I added, who expressed great interest in giving us some arms, but until now all steps taken toward this objective have failed. On this occasion I limited myself to speaking of our need for arms and how, in my judgment, we could obtain them from this government without causing it to fail in its neutral duties.

I had thought deeply on this matter, I told him then, and there seemed two ways in which we could obtain arms. First, as commanding general of the United States Army, Grant could request a certain number of arms without specifying why he needed them. Given his antecedents, good services, and actual position, they would probably be given him without question. If, unexpectedly, the French should discover that these arms had fallen into our hands and protest, the government could then decide to approve or disapprove Grant's conduct and the matter would not go beyond that.

The second method was more frank and perhaps more decorous for this country. I would request to purchase 50,000 rifles for my country and to pay for them with a long-term note drawn on our treasury or with other acceptable financial obligations. If the French government wanted to buy arms from the United States, I assumed it certainly would be sold any quantity it desired. If this were legitimate treatment for the French, I saw no reason why Mexico should not be treated the same way.

The president told me then, somewhat surprised, that he understood we already had received arms via Grant. I replied in the negative. Although the general had adopted the first plan indicated and was prepared to accept the responsibility that might fall on him for such conduct, the secretary of war had encountered some difficulties that prevented the plan's realization.

He positively desired us to receive arms, the president asserted then, which he would give us if it could be done in a manner honorable for the United States. He would accept in payment what we could offer for them. With the great abundance of arms, he found it strange that some had not already passed into our hands.

Grant, who I saw frequently and who was well aware of our situation, I informed him, had made a special effort on his own responsibility to give us some weapons. Up to this point, however, he had not succeeded. The president asked me then if the secretary of war opposed giving us some. He had objected to Grant's proposal to give some rifles to General [Pedro] Baranda, I replied, which resulted in none being given us. The president asked at once where General Baranda was. Although he had remained here awaiting the arms he believed he could obtain from Grant, but finally losing all hope of obtaining them, I responded, he had made preparations to leave tomorrow for New York. If he obtained the arms now and sent them to his forces, I added, Baranda feared they might arrive too late. We have received word that the French were moving with considerable force on that front, and since there was a total lack of arms and munitions there, the French would probably obtain an easy victory. Johnson desired General Baranda to remain a little longer in this city, either to carry the arms Grant would give him or to buy a larger quantity if this other extreme were adopted and my official character would not permit my intervention in the matter. Since this was the only reason Baranda came to the United States, I told Johnson, he would remain here for whatever time was necessary to arrange the matter, if it could be arranged.

Expanding my remarks regarding our lack of arms and resources a little, I told the president that we had to prepare for a long war because, in my judgment, Napoleon was not considering leaving Mexico soon. Although he certainly ought to be satisfied that the intervention was a big mistake, this expedition so involved his honor and reputation as an able, clever man that he will prefer to continue spending money and spilling blood rather than recognize his error. I had not encountered anything published either by this government or by the French government, I also told Johnson, that could be taken as a real promise of a French withdrawal from Mexico within a reasonable time.

Furthermore, even if the French should learn of the arms to be sold us, I indicated to Johnson, they could not protest against it from a firm foundation because the United States could offer France the purchase of arms on the same terms. In addition, this arms sale would make clear to the French people and government that the United States is not indifferent to Mexico's fate, as they apparently believe at present. Although some declarations from reliable sources indicate the contrary, I observed that the French government can accept only those remarks that emanate from the United States minister in Paris as proceeding from this government. Some of Bigelow's remarks, which both this government and the French published, could only suggest that the United States might contentedly look upon the consolidation of Maximilian's empire. As if my remarks persuaded him, the president interjected then: "You are quite right." Continuing my argument on this matter, I pointed out that although he repeated the important statements from his speech receiving the French minister later in a more solemn manner in his first message to Congress, and although the secretary of state had expressed similar ideas in a speech given in Auburn, the French government considered these remarks offered exclusively to satisfy the populace and without significance.

At once, the president asked me with great interest for my opinion regarding the state of affairs in Mexico. With proper frankness and clarity, I responded that with or without United States assistance, I judged we would ultimately triumph over our invaders, but it would take time. If we continued in our present state, without resources to organize, arm, or sustain armies, I recognized we are at the mercy of the invaders, who could remain in our country as long as they wished. We hoped then to prolong our resistance indefinitely until they are convinced of the impossibility of consolidating Maximilian's position. Finally, after a few years, if they were not forcibly thrown out earlier, fatigue would force them to leave. The time would be long or short, depending upon the will of Napoleon, but our duty was to shorten it as much as we could. It could be shortened considerably if the French at least were not gaining new advantages over us. The successes of garrison after garrison and guerrilla band after guerrilla band falling into their hands, however, would encourage the French to new efforts with the hope of eliminating all resistance and solidifying Maximilian. To shorten their stay, I had hoped that they would not obtain control over another square inch of territory, other than what they already controlled, or receive the surrender of another [Mexican] soldier. Yet the only way to avoid these losses would be, at least, to provide arms to our forces. We could not be more modest, I concluded, than to agree to accept only arms when we had nothing and needed everything.

After the president repeatedly said that he desired us to have arms and that he saw no major difficulty in the United States government supplying us with them, he concluded not to give me a *definite* answer today, bestowing marked emphasis on the word definite. He said that he would talk with Grant tomorrow to see what could be done. Finally, I said that if he desired to see me on another occasion, he need only call for me. . . .

I will make certain that Grant learns the details of this conversation before he sees the president tomorrow.   [7:391-93]

APRIL 11 Even though Grant could not give me much hope in the arms matter, he replied that our affairs generally presented a much more favorable aspect than he had imagined. . . . Since he is reputed to say something only when he is convinced of it, Grant's phrasing immediately aroused great hopes in me. Moreover, things without merit do not easily impress him, nor is he accustomed to exaggerate things. . . .

This morning at nine Grant made a lengthy visit. After his interview yesterday with the president, he told me, Johnson had requested him to attend yesterday's cabinet meeting in which Mexican affairs were discussed. At that meeting, Grant reported, it was resolved that the United States could not sell arms to any belligerent without failing in its neutral obligations. Nevertheless, if arms were sold to private parties, clearly it would not be necessary to examine where the arms might end up, and the belligerents did have the right to take arms from this country, carrying them where they wished.

Grant also explained that he had spoken generally on the [Mexican] question in this cabinet meeting. He did not consider himself at liberty to tell me what had occurred, although he was certainly persuaded that within two months at the latest the question would come to a crisis and before a year the French would have left the Republic. Emanating from Grant, these assurances are very significant and possess great weight.

Because of some of Grant's words and the tone of his conversation, I imagine the following might have passed in the cabinet meeting yesterday. After speaking of the resolution he made last Sunday and seeing it was unacceptable, the president expressed displeasure at the turn the question had taken. He wanted the matter to be given another turn more in harmony with the wishes of this people and the interests of this country. In his note of February 12, Seward would then claim he had prepared the ground to pursue the course the president desired, and he expected the French government's reply to that note any day. Once the reply is received, he would peremptorily insist on the principles indicated in his note, even sending an *ultimatum* demanding the retirement of the French forces from the Republic.

The following reasons argue for considering this presumption well founded. Last night I learned that as of yesterday afternoon the State Department had not received the French reply. . . . Two months should have been more than sufficient for Seward to have sent his *ultimatum*, for the *ultimatum's* reception in Paris, and even for the French government's reply to the *ultimatum* to have arrived in this city.

One of the circumstances that most convinces me that Grant has reason to believe the question will come to a crisis shortly and that he has not been deceived this time as on other occasions is that, when speaking of Seward, Grant's words revealed his judgment to rest on the unvarying determination of the president, not on the secretary of state's opinion. Speaking of the probable departure of the French from Mexico within a year, the president indicated to Grant that they would not do so of their own volition, as Seward assured him, but rather under obligation to the United States.

Thus, thanks to Grant's intervention, my interview with the president produced much better results than I expected. Seward knew already where the storm came from, without having grounds either to be offended or to complain of my conduct. Seward advised me that he intended to have certain meetings with an agent of [Antonio López de] Santa Anna. In response, I mentioned my forthcoming interview with the president. The results will reveal who may have achieved greater advantage from his interview.

In conclusion, Grant told me today that if we locate an American merchant who would buy arms for us, the United States will sell them to him at a nominal price. I asked what he intended to do with those he had sent to locations on the border. He replied that he would order them sold at private sales at nominal prices. Therefore, today I hastened to communicate this information to General [Mariano] Escobedo . . . for his knowledge and subsequent action. . . .

If we have not achieved much in the arms business, which was only an insignificant part of the whole question, General Baranda leaves satisfied that great progress has been made upon the principal point.   [7:406-7]

APRIL 26   A resolution which [Godlove] Orth, a member of the House Foreign Relations Committee, presented . . . authorizes the government to sell arms and contraband of war to the American republics, receiving bonds or other types of obligations in payment. Should this resolution become law, nothing will impede this government from furnishing us with as many arms and munitions as we need.

Because I had a long conversation with Orth on the night of April 22, and because he had not indicated his intention to present the resolution, I assume he had not thought of it then. Perhaps afterward, someone suggested the desirability of doing so.

I am not being too adventuresome, I believe, if I express my opinion that the suggestion might have emanated from President Johnson. [7:446]

APRIL 26   I saw General Grant about Andrés Revino's desire to purchase arms from this government. . . . I asked Grant what he thought of the published correspondence regarding the French departure from Mexico. The correspondence referring to Austria pleased him, he responded, but he was not satisfied with that relating to the French withdrawal. Unquestionably Napoleon intended to delay the departure of his soldiers in the hope, continued Grant, that Maximilian might meanwhile be able to consolidate his position. He considered anything that was not slanted to see Maximilian deposed and to remove his force immediately as unsatisfactory for the United States. . . .

This morning Grant saw President [Johnson] to express his opinion of the unsatisfactory character of that correspondence. Grant stated that Johnson had entreated him to attend tomorrow's cabinet meeting at which they will discuss this question.

I suspect the president, unsatisfied with the response of the French government and seeking more favorable support for his ideas, deferred the discussion of this matter until General Grant returned. Certainly then, the response of this government will be unsatisfactory for Napoleon. It will insist the troops depart quickly and lend no further assistance to Maximilian.

[7:447-48]

APRIL 28   Last night . . . I asked Grant how the cabinet meeting had gone. Very well, he told me, since he was very satisfied with what he had heard there. Because everything said in such a meeting was of a reserved character, he explained, he could not tell me today what took place there, but he had remained very pleased. Our affairs now apparently had a much more satisfactory character than at any other time. His remarks suggested that the United States government will request the French government to reduce the time limit fixed for the evacuation of its forces from Mexico. Furthermore, the United States will interpret the sending of one additional soldier to Mexico as a violation of that binding agreement.

I warned Grant of my fear that now the French would solicit the United States' good offices to obtain an armistice while they removed their troops. He replied that he would not favor such an armistice unless the French would depart immediately. If they thought to remain awhile, he would be happy if, when they are reduced to half strength, we should attack that half, taking advantage of any opportunities presented to us.   [7:452-53]

MAY 6   In the Senate's secret session on the confirmation of Campbell's nomination as United States minister to Mexico, supposedly the question was raised whether this government needed to send a minister to the Republic or not. . . .

Wade told me that some senators had spoken against sending Campbell. His response expressed shame, he said, that they lacked the courage of their ancestors. When the United States was one hundred times weaker than now, Wade observed, it dared to defy all of Europe by proclaiming the Monroe Doctrine. He lamented that now the government lacks the courage even to defend that doctrine. Under no circumstance would France accept a war with the United States, he also explained, so this government was in a position to impose its terms.

Wade's speech was very well received and produced the confirmation of Campbell without any opposing votes. Wade said that he had not realized how many friends we really have in the Senate.

When the question was treated in this way, Campbell's personality was quickly forgotten. . . . Campbell possesses for the Senate the character of the president's personal friend and a partisan of his policy.

Thus the confirmation of Campbell's nomination is equivalent to a new ratification on the Senate's part of the president's policy of continuing to recognize the national government of Mexico and further proof of adherence to the Monroe Doctrine.   [7:487-88]

MAY 11   Grant told me that Seward's decision to remove United States minister [John L.] Motley from Vienna, in case Austrian troops should leave for Mexico, appeared very good to him. This decision had been communicated to the French government, Grant added, as normal procedure and under the assumption that Napoleon neither intended nor considered sending reinforcements to the Republic. According to Grant, Seward believes that the French government will not claim to have the right to send more reinforcements and thus will remain committed not to send any.

Nevertheless, news received yesterday from Havana mentioned new reinforcements sent from France to Veracruz by the steamers from San Nazario. The European news claimed that Maximilian's commissioners in Vienna have concluded an agreement with a steamship line for the transportation of 5,000 Austrians from Trieste to Veracruz. . . .

Grant mentioned receiving a letter from General Schofield which announced his imminent return to the United States. Schofield judged that Napoleon acted in good faith in offering to retire his forces from Mexico. Schofield believed Napoleon would reduce the period fixed for retiring them if the United States demanded it.   [7:516]

MAY 11   On May 8 General [John C.] Frémont came to Washington . . . chiefly to propose that we should not mention the nullification of the contract he had signed with General Sánchez Ochoa in any agreement we reach so that he could validate it later. Frémont was and is convinced the contract is valid and obligatory on the Mexican nation.

In today's interview Frémont began by acknowledging receipt of my note of yesterday, which declared the aforementioned contract null. As soon as he returns to New York, Frémont added, he would speak to Ochoa about this point and then reply to my letter. He claimed he would tell Ochoa that it was not proper to attempt to complete an agreement the Mexican government had disapproved. Not to wound Sánchez Ochoa's pride, however, Frémont desired to avoid any allusion to that contract in the one he would negotiate with me now. I would take this matter into consideration, I told him, consult my instructions, and send him my reply in the afternoon.

We spoke at once of the other points of the contract. After a long discussion, we agreed upon the following: the three million dollars in bonds which I had offered him would be reduced to two; he will expend at least half of this sum in obtaining the guarantee; and this money will be given him only if he obtains the guarantee of fifty million dollars in Mexican bonds during the present session of Congress under terms no more onerous for Mexico than those contained in the resolution presented to the House of Representatives this past March 4. All this was consigned to a draft contract . . . which the secretary of the legation brought to Frémont at once. To satisfy his sentiments of delicacy, I had Mariscal inform Frémont that I would not insist upon inserting a clause in the new contract declaring the Frémont–Sánchez Ochoa contract null. Instructed to assure this point in whatever arrangement might be made with him, however, I could not ignore this point. To conform with my instructions, after having spoken with Sánchez Ochoa, Frémont's acknowledgment of my note of May 9 could recognize the nullity of that contract. Frémont agreed to act in this manner, charging Mariscal to urge me to send the signed contract. But I will not do so until I receive his reply and only then if it is in satisfactory terms. . . .

The Draft Contract between Romero and Frémont.

Matías Romero, representative of the Mexican Republic, and General John C. Frémont have agreed to the following:

(1) Matías Romero will place at General Frémont's disposal two million dollars in bonds guaranteed by the United States, as compensation for his services to the Mexican Republic and also as indemnification for any expenses incurred for such purpose, under the conditions expressed below.

(2) General Frémont binds himself to distribute at least half of the two million in expenses which he judges necessary to obtain the United States guarantee of fifty million dollars in Mexican bonds, without, however, being obliged to render a detailed account of his distributions.

(3) As a necessary condition before General Frémont has a right to the referred to two million or before he could dispose in total or in part of the half assigned to him as a contingency fund, the indicated guarantee for fifty million dollars in Mexican bonds must be obtained in a definite form during the present session of the United States Congress, either in the form proposed by the March 4 resolution of the House of Representatives and sent to its Foreign Affairs Committee, or in another similar form that would be no more onerous for Mexico.

(4) In case conditions onerous to Mexico are amended to the resolution, General Frémont will receive the compensation which Matías Romero judges equitable for his services.   [7:518-19]

JUNE 5 General Schofield came to see me today, having returned recently from Europe. . . . His goal in going to Europe, he maintained, had been to arrange for the United States to insist that Napoleon withdraw his forces from Mexico. He sought either the French government's promise to retire its forces or its expressed refusal to do so, adding that shortly after his arrival he had obtained this objective. Although he had not managed to speak about Mexican affairs with either Napoleon or Drouyn de L'Huys, he observed, he had conversed frankly about Mexican affairs with various persons sent to explore his thoughts. Certainly these intermediaries faithfully reported the tenor of the conversations to the emperor and his minister. He believes that Napoleon will fulfill his promise because he has no other alternative.

In Schofield's judgment, Napoleon is still not disposed to see Maximilian fall and will even arrange to sustain him by helping him secretly with his private resources. Schofield believes Napoleon secretly supplied the funds necessary to pay the passage of the Austrian soldiers who were prepared to depart for Veracruz at the beginning of this past May. He also presumes, however, that the United States can very easily impede the success of such intrigues, as it did in the case of the departure of the Austrian soldiers for Mexico.

Schofield feared greatly that the supreme government would not be able to sustain itself during the year and a half while the French retire from the Republic. He seemed very pleased with my assurances that Mexico could sustain itself as long as necessary to achieve the complete triumph of its cause.

Referring to the proposal for this government to guarantee our bonds, at first Schofield expressed the great fear that a guarantee effectively violated United States neutrality in Mexico's war with France. Later, he indicated that if the sum guaranteed were ten or fifteen million, with the understanding that the money would not be used to make war on France, it would no longer constitute a violation of neutrality.

In the course of the conversation he said "our" cause, "our" people, and "our" government when referring to the Mexican Republic's cause, the people of Mexico, and the supreme government, which convinced me he does not wish to break his relations with us. He has very clearly indicated his intention to continue working for our cause. I will arrange for Tifft to conclude a suitable agreement with him out of the funds destined for this purpose. Through this agreement his services will not become detrimental to the supreme government, while at the same time they might be of great utility.   [7:603]

JUNE 25 Saturday, June 23, Schofield brought me a note from Grant, suggesting I come to his office to see some favorable reports. . . .

In a telegram, Sheridan mentioned just returning from the border, where everything appeared very favorable to our business. Our cause was popular in that part of the Republic, Sheridan asserted, because the imperialists could not count upon more than one in twenty inhabitants, while Santa Anna had no partisans at all because he was considered an agent of some French and English businesses interested in preserving the acts of the intervention.

Today I returned to Grant's office. . . . I found him very content at having received good news from the Republic. He asked for a recent telegram from Sheridan. . . . It confirmed General Escobedo's reported capture of a large supply train. Allegedly his victory took place on the 16th near Camargo. The captured train consisted of 250 wagons, each drawn by twelve mules, with its contents valued at one and a half million dollars. In addition, Sheridan reported that Escobedo captured eleven pieces of artillery with munitions and eight hundred prisoners. In Sheridan's opinion this victory was equivalent to ending the war in the Rio Grande.

I requested a *memorandum* of this telegram from Grant so I could publish it. He ordered that I be given one, charging me with altering the message so that its source would not be recognized. I altered it to appear as if I had received the report from the Mexican consul in New Orleans and sent it at once to the press association and to various other newspapers that do not subscribe to that service.

Grant communicated this telegram, as well as Saturday's, to the president and to the secretary of war.   [7:713-14]

JULY 14   Postmaster General Dennison has resigned his post in Johnson's cabinet. Supposedly Montgomery Blair was to be named postmaster general, but . . . as a necessary condition for his entering the cabinet, Blair told me, he had insisted upon Seward's departure. This condition was not accepted. The president named [Alexander] Randall, the chief subordinate official in the Post Office, to the vacant position.   [8:72]

JULY 17   Last evening I had an important conversation with ex-Postmaster General Dennison, who has just left the cabinet. He quite frankly informed me of various things I did not know. Now, as he no longer was in Johnson's cabinet, he was at liberty to disclose that he had been Mexico's best friend in the cabinet. He had always favored us, he claimed, supporting the immediate vindication of the Monroe Doctrine at any cost and always opposing Seward's policy. In addition, he maintained that Stanton had also been our friend, always agreeing with him. Derived from other sources and supported by the facts, my information persuades me, nevertheless, that Stanton acted in absolute conformity with Seward. Although Harlan seldom spoke in the cabinet and manifested his friendship on few occasions, he had been our friend.

Indirectly Dennison made it clear that Seward was neither a friend of ours nor a partisan of the Monroe Doctrine. I found this very strange because hardly a year ago Dennison had assured me of his great confidence in Seward's policy, entreating me very earnestly not to do anything that would place me in conflict with the secretary of state. Nevertheless, I must believe that he did not consider himself at liberty to tell me everything then and now he is more frank.

Dennison told me also that Seward had used the copies I sent him of Schenck's letter and my reply to brief the cabinet. . . . Seward had personally informed me of this on July 12. In my note to you I did not mention this incident [Seward's briefing the cabinet] because Seward had specifically charged me not to say anything about it, either to my government or to Schenck.

Now learning this story from another source and without a charge of secrecy, however, I consider myself at liberty to communicate the incident to you. Seward told me that he had laid Schenck's letter and my reply before the president. The president considered my reply disrespectful to this government. The cabinet wanted to make this decision known to me. He had gone so far as to write a note on the matter, Seward added, but then considered the matter not worth the trouble. He had decided to tell me informally of the government's concern on the first convenient occasion, suggesting that the incident should not go beyond us two. I was very sorry that my letter to Schenck had not pleased the president, I said then, but it would have appeared disrespectful, almost rude, not to answer, unofficially, a private letter from a distinguished public person of this country. In replying, I had taken special care to say nothing that could be considered disrespectful to this government. Carefully sending [Seward] copies of the letter and my reply, I considered my procedure courteous and in compliance with all my obligations as a gentleman and as a representative of a friendly government. . . . Then Seward told me that the letter contained nothing objectionable. He was displeased because I had responded without consulting him in the first place.

From what Seward told me previously and what Dennison related to me last night, I infer that the following occurred: Seward was immensely disgusted upon receipt of the copies of the letters cited, and he did with them what he has rarely done with my notes, even when they are of interest, namely, he communicated them to the cabinet. He handled this in such a manner that even our own friends believed my conduct in responding to a private letter of a public person was somewhat irregular. Later, if he took this matter seriously, he realized that he ran the risk of being in a weak position in the subsequent discussion, or, at least, with regard to my explanations. He preferred to appear generous, making me believe that he had not fulfilled a cabinet agreement out of consideration for me.

After hearing my explanation, Dennison, who at the beginning of our conversation had viewed my conduct as somewhat irregular, could do no less than tell me that I had acted correctly. If there had been an irregularity, he observed, it had been only on Schenck's part. Dennison also told me that the president had not revealed disgust or displeasure upon hearing my letter read. Seward had attributed his own personal sentiments to the president in assuring me of this.

In spite of all this, I propose to be much more cautious in the future than I have been until now so as not to give Seward even the appearance of a good reason for displeasure. Above all, I wish to avoid offering him any pretext to present us in bad light to the president or to cause us damage in any other manner.

Dennison also revealed something I already knew, namely, that Seward was displeased when his opinions were placed in doubt or when his assertions were discussed. All the secretaries consulted Seward in matters affecting foreign relations, he added, submitting without appeal to his decisions.

[8:76-78]

AUGUST 4 Last night, Banks, chairman of the House Foreign Relations Committee, came to see me and, not finding me at home, returned this morning. He would return to his state tonight, Banks told me, and before departing he wished to explain that he had been and was Mexico's sincere friend. If it had been impossible to do anything for us in the last meeting of Congress, he asserted his expectation to do so in the next meetings. In principle, he told me, he favored United States financial aid to Mexico, but he had not been able to report in favor of this action for two reasons: first, the aid could have given Napoleon a plausible pretext to make his Mexican intervention popular in France and to avoid fulfilling his promise to withdraw his forces from the Republic; and second, with this government's present disposition toward Mexico, this measure would have been ineffective and only discredited the people who wished to help Mexico without any benefit for Mexico.

Moreover, Banks informed me, he had written a bill in favor of the Monroe Doctrine which concluded with three very carefully drafted general resolutions, which he implied had been submitted to the French minister in this city. Banks added that the French minister had found the resolutions satisfactory, claiming they would help Napoleon remove his forces from Mexico because he could take them as the express desires of the American people. Nevertheless, Banks could not arrange for House permission to present his resolutions because many congressmen feared someone would present the loan resolution as an amendment. In Banks's judgment, even the opponents of the loan did not want to be forced to vote against it.

We conversed in general about Mexico's future and about the future of United States policy in relation to us. Banks expressed very judicious and reasonable ideas in all these matters and a great desire to assist our cause and to contribute toward seeing our country in a tranquil and prosperous situation. Everything he told me indirectly contradicted the falsehoods Generals González Ortega and Sánchez Ochoa circulated about him, after they thought they had bought him and persuaded him to declare them the legitimate Mexican government in Congress. Until now the facts have best refuted those claims.

Finally, Banks informed me that Tifft had arranged to offer him three hundred thousand dollars if he would vote for the resolution Tifft proposed. This offer made it impossible for him to vote for the resolution, Banks added, even if he had believed it opportune and necessary. He indicated also that it would be good to separate all classes of interested parties from our cause.   [8:131-32]

SEPTEMBER 2   On August 28, I departed Washington in company of the president of the United States, some members of his cabinet, his family, and his staff, General Grant, Admiral [David] Farragut, and other distinguished persons. After a stop of more than an hour in Baltimore, we arrived at Phildelphia, where we remained that night. Since the local authorities had not arranged a reception for the president, there was no official demonstration. On the other hand, however, the people congregated to see Johnson's arrival and to serenade him in the evening.

On the 29th we left Philadelphia and arrived in New York at midday, where there was a very imposing official reception. In the parade from the City Hall to Johnson's hotel, as well as in the review that followed, I was given a preferential place. In the evening I was invited and assigned a seat of honor at a grand banquet for 250 persons at Delmonico's restaurant. The ministers to Russia and Brazil also attended, the former being present in New York by chance and the latter residing in that city.

The mayor of New York presided at the dinner and proposed four toasts: the first for the president of the United States, the second for his cabinet, the third for the army and navy, and the fourth for those friendly nations who truly wished the United States's peace and prosperity. In this latter toast, I believe he wanted to allude only to Russia and Mexico. The minister of Brazil said nothing. When [the Russian minister, Baron de] Stoeckl finished his response, various guests loudly requested me to speak. I think this greatly displeased Seward, who even wished to avoid it. . . . When I decided to speak, I attempted to avoid anything that could have displeased him. . . .

My reply to the toast was not published in the New York newspapers because the correspondent of the press association was not present at the dinner. I have arranged for the publication in the [New York] papers of any of my succeeding speeches. This arrangement has already commenced operation.

On the morning of the 30th we left New York on board a river steamer. After a short stay at West Point, where the military college of this country is located, we arrived as night fell in Albany, the capital of New York State. In Albany they also gave me a place of honor at an official dinner. Since subsequently this was always done at banquets and receptions, I do not believe it necessary to reiterate this circumstance when describing later occasions.

On the 31st we left Albany and at four in the afternoon arrived in Auburn, the end of the day's journey and Seward's home town. We stopped at various points in transit, but no allusion was made to Mexico at any of them. In Auburn we were taken to a stand placed in the city park, from which the mayor greeted the president on his arrival. Johnson responded to this greeting, and immediately thereafter Seward presented various people from the president's party to the Auburn citizens gathered there. I was among those presented. When presenting me, Seward said: "This gentleman is Señor Romero, minister of the United States of Mexico. For Mexico's benefit and to prevent Mexico's destruction, the president of the United States had given notification that the foreign intervention will have to cease by this coming November."

Regrettably, only some of the correspondents for the New York papers took notice of these words, and others, in doubt about what Seward had said, changed them in a manner to weaken their meaning significantly. . . .

Seward's words apparently did not proceed from a prior considered disposition to make the declaration they contained, but rather they emanated from the heat of the moment. They were spoken without sufficient meditation and without considering that they would be taken for a formal declaration.

From the park in Auburn we went to a dinner the city had prepared for us. First, the mayor toasted the president and then the cabinet, especially Seward. Replying to this toast, the secretary of state proposed another for the United States Army and Navy represented by General Grant and Admiral Farragut. When the general rose to respond to Seward's toast, he said: "I propose to you that we toast the health of Señor Romero, minister of Mexico, and the genuine success of the cause which he represents."

This toast emanating from that particular source could produce no less than the best results. . . . To prevent a recurrence of what happened to the text of my toast in New York, I wrote the text out shortly after having spoken it and placed it in the hands of the press association correspondent. Consequently, all the New York dailies published my reply. . . .

Yesterday morning we left Auburn and arrived in Niagara Falls, N.Y., where we will remain until early tomorrow. I could not accompany the president at the various stops where he left the train because I had become very seriously ill in Auburn and had to remain in bed all day. The frequent receptions and parades on the itinerary have occasioned such excitement that almost everyone accompanying the president is indisposed. In addition to the excitement, we have necessarily had great irregularity in the meals. At times, as in Albany, we have not seated ourselves at the table until ten in the evening. If you add to this the lack of sleep because we must rise early and go to bed late in the midst of the greatest commotion and shouting, you will form an approximate idea of the strain of this journey. In view of what has occurred with relation to Mexico, I am satisfied to have undertaken this strenuous trip. I hold my illnesses and discomfiture well suffered.

This city's population being very small, there was no grand demonstration upon our arrival yesterday. Remaining quiet here today has granted us a complete day of rest. . . .

Tomorrow I expect to be sufficiently rested to continue the tour. The three most arduous days still remain before us. I will attempt to remain with the president until the end of the journey, hoping that this might produce good results for us.

As a result of my part on this trip up to this point, I believe I ought to make two brief observations at once. Perhaps I may return to them on another occasion, after I have had more time for ample reflection. First, Seward's influence over the president is complete. One does not need to be with them for long to observe that Seward understands very well how to gain Johnson's confidence. Therefore in almost all his speeches, Johnson alludes very flatteringly to Seward. Second, General Grant is extremely popular. Quite obviously his receptions contrast significantly with the president's. Everywhere Grant's presence excites the greatest enthusiasm. All those who manage to approach our carriages desire only to see the general.

[8:235-37]

SEPTEMBER 7   Having rested somewhat with the layover day at Niagara Falls, I could continue on the 3rd when President Johnson departed for Cleveland. A great popular reunion awaited us in Buffalo, a city of nearly 100,000 inhabitants, only a short distance from Niagara. Ex-President [Millard] Fillmore received Johnson and presented him to the people, afterward doing the same with Seward. The secretary of state immediately presented me. In doing so, he suggested that the crowd should give three cheers for the Republic of Mexico, which it did with great enthusiasm. If Mexico needed soldiers, someone in the crowd said aloud, the United States would be able to supply us. The newspapers noted and published this remark.

In Dunkirk and various other points of transit, either Seward or the local authorities presented me to the people in the same manner. Everywhere enthusiasm was manifested for the Republic cause, which only compares with the enthusiasm General Grant's presence excites in the people. In one place, where the train halted only long enough to make the presentations and to permit the president to speak to the public, the introductions were made two by two to save time. Seward was presented with General Grant, Secretary of the Navy Welles with Admiral Farragut, and I was presented with Postmaster General Randall.

On the night of the 3rd we arrived in Cleveland, a large city in Ohio. Here I was also presented to a grand multitude gathered at the front of our hotel. Forgetting the decorum of his high position, the president made a speech there which his own friends disliked. He descended to respond to the questions and interjections of individuals whose political views differed from his. Moreover, some of the interjections were highly offensive and insulting.

On the 4th we left Cleveland and arrived in Detroit at dusk. At midday we stopped in Toledo, where I was presented in the midst of the greatest acclamation of popular enthusiasm. The same occurred in Aragula, a village in Ohio. Arriving in Monroe, Michigan, the hometown of General [George A.] Custer, who had accompanied the president from New York and who, on other occasions, had expressed to me his desire to enter into our service, this general presented me to the public and proposed three cheers for the Republic of Mexico. This was carried out with complete spontaneity and unanimity. In Detroit the president and Seward made speeches. The latter's was interrupted by a person who asked if he were disposed to sustain the Monroe Doctrine. The secretary of state replied: "Yes, sir, I will endeavor to sustain it so far as having one jawbone alone permits me to do it," with which he alluded to the internal difficulties of this country.

On the 5th we left Detroit for this city [Chicago]. In transit various presentations occurred. At one stop three enthusiastic cheers were given for the Republic, while the request [for cheers] in honor of the president was given with very little spirit. This disgusted Seward who, speaking immediately thereafter, expressed disbelief that they desired peace for the Mexican Republic more than for their own country.

At 10:30 in the evening we arrived in this city [Chicago], whose inhabitants are largely members of the party in opposition to the president. For this reason the local authorities did not receive him, and his remaining here was somewhat embarrassing. On the night of the 5th, he spoke to the people from his hotel balcony, but with the experience of what occurred to him in Cleveland, his speech was very moderate and brief.

Yesterday there was neither an official nor a popular demonstration in favor of the president. At 10 a.m. we left the hotel to attend the ceremony of laying the cornerstone of the monument to be erected in memory of [Stephen A.] Douglas. The president was only a spectator and did not preside at the function. After General [John A.] Dix concluded the main speech, the president read a short eulogy of Douglas. Seward gave another, and the ceremony ended. In the evening there was a concert in the opera house which the president did not attend.

With his party very considerably reduced, the president left this morning for Springfield, capital of Illinois. In Niagara it was decided to extend his journey to various other principal cities of the West. This will move him further from Washington and separate him from that city for a longer time. For various and powerful reasons, I did not find it convenient to continue in his company.

The president's trip to Chicago was originally announced as without a political character. Undoubtedly Johnson would have been received better everywhere if this program had been carried out, thereby allowing him to travel like the chief magistrate of the country and not like the leader of a party. However, Johnson preferred to convert his trip into an election campaign. In almost all his speeches he has spoken very harshly of Congress and of the people who disagree with him. Directly or indirectly, he has asked his fellow citizens to vote for the candidates of the party supporting him in the next elections. Seward has done the same, although in a more circumspect manner. From the moment this happened, the president's trip has ceased to be a national event, converting itself into a party undertaking. In the former case, far from being an inconvenience, I would have rejoiced greatly to continue the trip until the end. In the latter case, however, it seemed more prudent to abstain from continuing on a trip where my presence could permit harmful interpretations and could perhaps produce the enmity or at least the indifference of one of this country's major parties.

Up to this point, I doubt anyone would attribute to me a desire to mix myself in the domestic matters of the country for having accompanied the president to Chicago. When they announced the trip and invited me, there was no reason to believe the journey would take the turn the president has given it. Having filled the purpose of the invitation, however, already aware of what the president proposes to do and seeing the trip extended without any other apparent object than to visit some cities, my presence among the people who accompany Johnson could give rise, with or without reason, to jealousy and comments, which I believe I ought to avoid. Leaving upon the first appropriate occasion will prove that when I departed Washington I had no intention to mix myself into the domestic business of this people in any way. Later I could refer to my departure should any of our enemies attempt to use this incident to present me in a bad light to the party in opposition to Johnson.

While deciding not to continue with the president, I took special care that no one perceived my motives. To achieve this objective, my health, which has suffered much from the molestations and fatigue consequent to a trip of this type, has greatly aided me. Although I am not physically precluded from continuing, if I would submit the case to a doctor, undoubtedly he would decide I ought not to prolong the strain of travel in the manner I have done until now. Thus, although my health would not detain me from proceeding if any favorable result could be attained, it conveniently presents me with a credible personal excuse for not continuing with the president.

Last night I advised Seward that I could not continue in his company today. I told him that I was very pleased by the good manner in which I had been treated. My only motive for complaint was, I said, that upon leaving, whenever I asked to pay my account in the hotel where we had stopped, they always informed me that it had already been paid. I had wanted to complain to him of this since the first day, but I had believed it would be better not to bother him and to regulate the difficulty with the person charged with paying the accounts. I desired to settle my account by reimbursing him for everything that had been paid for me. Seward responded that we would regulate this in Washington. After I had informed him of my sole motive for not continuing, the bad condition of my health, he stated his deep regret that I had to leave. He would be especially grateful to me, he added, if I should make an effort to continue with the president until Washington. Last night I told him that if I began to feel better this morning, I would go on with them. Early today, I advised him that having passed a bad night, I still felt ill, and I had decided to remain another day in this city to consult a doctor. If I improved tomorrow, I would join them in St. Louis. Otherwise, I would remain here or return to Washington. With this understanding, we took leave of each other.

Before leaving here this afternoon for Washington, I will telegraph Seward that I am unable to continue with them, and I will return to Washington.

The above-mentioned reasons left me little desire to appear in public during the last two days of the trip. I avoided some presentations.

[8:237-40]

SEPTEMBER 7 I desire to inform the supreme government succinctly of some matters related to the president's trip as well as the tenor of some conversations with Seward during this trip.

On the same day we left Washington, the *New York Herald* published an article about the litigation pending between Santa Anna and [Dario] Mazuera. From this correspondence Mazuera apparently had assured Santa Anna that, when he came as commissioner for Santa Anna, Seward had written him a letter informing him that if Santa Anna came to the United

States, the United States government would give him men and a loan of 30 million pesos [peso = dollar] to throw Maximilian out. This story conformed with information that had been given me previously and which I had communicated to Seward a short while ago. When we arrived at Philadelphia, I called Seward's attention to that article. He immediately expressed a desire to read it, so I gave him a copy. He read its contents with interest. In view of this article, surely he again regrets having received Mazuera and will not consider having anything to do with either him or Santa Anna again. This decision will become even firmer when later publications reveal that Santa Anna or his friends attempted to bribe the judge presiding at the suit Montgomery filed against Santa Anna in such a disgraceful and insulting manner that the judge believed it desirable to publish the letter. Luis G. de Vidaly Rivas, an important agent for Santa Anna and his father-in-law, was also apparently charged with and then sentenced to prison for refusing to or being unable to pay $355 owed to the owner of a pension in New York for room and board. In a society like this, such incidents suffice to discredit permanently a person of the most well-established reputation.

During the day we journeyed from New York to Albany, Seward informed me that, after having left New York, he received a visiting card from a president of Mexico with headquarters in New York. By his sarcastic terms, I knew that Seward referred to Jesús González Ortega, who certainly believed Seward would not refuse to receive him if he titled himself president of Mexico. However, Ortega occupies a position even lower than Santa Anna in Seward's opinion.

The day we traveled from Cleveland to Detroit, I conversed at length with Seward. Noting that he did not wish to discuss business, I directed the conversation away from those matters. Nevertheless, we managed to mention Montholon. Not long ago, I observed, an incident occurred that convinced me that this gentleman was a person of judgment who desired peace between the United States and France. Some days ago, in the house of a common friend, I told Seward, I encountered the wife of Mariano Degollado, one of the few Mexicans so identified with the usurper that they heartily desired his triumph. Because previously my relations with this lady had been pleasant, we discussed Mexico's situation. She spoke in the harshest terms against Montholon, attributing Napoleon's decision to retire his forces from Mexico to his false reports and devious work. The French minister sought only to conserve his lucrative employment, she conjectured, because he would lose his position the moment war broke out between his country and the United States. Since she obviously believed that only a war between France and the United States would save Maximilian, she judged that the French minister in Washington had the duty to produce that war at all costs. Montholon was in fact a person of judgment, Seward claimed, who did not delude himself in respect to the Mexican situation and with whom Seward had no difficulty in arriving at an understanding.

During the five days we spent in New York State, where the president has much support, the subsequently marked difference between the popularity of the president and General Grant was scarcely perceptible. Of course, even in New York, General Grant's presence and name excited much more enthusiasm than Johnson's presence and name. Yet this never succeeded in establishing an antagonism between the two, as occurred after we left New York. In Ohio as well as in Michigan and Illinois, the popular demonstrations left no doubt that General Grant has the esteem he merits. Clearly, he was considered the candidate to oppose Johnson or his party for the presidency in the coming elections. Mainly in Chicago, I have had occasion to observe this very markedly. The people have called to General Grant before the president. They have interrupted the president when he has wished to speak and cheered the general to the point of proclaiming him the next president. Naturally, this has caused some cooling off in the relationship between General Grant and Johnson and some jealousy and rivalry between their friends.

On the part of Seward and even of Johnson, there have been attempts to publicize General Grant's support for the president's policy. This has greatly modified the views of the General, who holds to the maxim that soldiers ought not mix themselves in politics. Perhaps Seward intended to place General Grant in a false position so that he might lose some of his prestige and not become the opposing candidate in the next election. This plan has commenced to produce considerable success. The least judicious Republican newspapers, losing confidence in the situation, have, with very little tact, asked General Grant to state frankly which party he had decided for.

Nevertheless, the good judgment of the majority of the party will prevail in the end, I believe, and the party will proclaim Grant its candidate. In this case, I also believe his election is beyond doubt. Nor can I conceive of any event more favorable for our interests than for General Grant to become president of the United States.

This trip has given me a better understanding of President Johnson's character and the state of his relationship with Seward. I do not risk anything, I believe, by affirming that Seward will continue as secretary of state and director of this government's policy as long as Johnson remains in the presidential chair, without anyone being able to force his departure from the cabinet. This observation will help me also to fix a norm for my future conduct with Seward. Insofar as we are concerned, he and only he will remain the United States government for the next two years.

Otherwise, this trip has permitted me to create more cordial and intimate relations with the president, with the cabinet members who accompanied him, and with various public men who have joined the party at different points. Before the president left today, I took leave of him and expressed my regrets for not being able to accompany him further.

[8:240-42]

NOVEMBER 3   Grant began our conversation by inquiring if Seward had communicated Campbell's instructions to me. I responded that he had not. This would be because of the loss [the death of his daughter] which the secretary of state has just suffered, Grant then explained, since he claimed in the cabinet meeting he would communicate them to the French and Mexican ministers.

Yesterday, Grant mentioned next, he had received a telegram from General Sherman in Cincinnati. Sherman wanted me to advise the Mexican president in the quickest way possible that the United States minister accredited to Mexico would leave shortly for Veracruz on the steamship *Susquehanna*. Sherman thought it would be best if the minister were expected in Mexico. Grant sent this telegram to President Johnson. This morning Grant informed Johnson that I would transmit the message Sherman desired to my government. Grant then told President Johnson that he had not felt authorized to communicate to me what had occurred [in the cabinet?], assuming Seward would do so. If the president authorized him, however, he would gladly inform me. Johnson granted this authorization, telling Grant that I ought to be acquainted with everything being done.

Immediately, with a marked display of satisfaction at being the conveyor of this information, Grant told me that the president had wanted him to go to Mexico in company with Campbell as the latter's adviser and to direct measures within his field of competence, as I will make clear later. Since Grant could not leave Washington at this time, it was decided to send Sherman. Sherman had proposed going directly to Veracruz, Grant continued, because, according to the information Seward presented in a cabinet meeting, the whole French army will assuredly have withdrawn from Mexico before the mission arrives at that port, thus leaving open the road to Mexico City where the supreme government would already be established.

Then Grant read me Seward's instructions to Campbell, which were dated October 25 and written in the supposition that Grant would accompany Campbell. . . .

Since the French government offered to retire its forces in three parts under the conditions known to you, the instructions began, at least a part of the invading army will already be en route for France when Campbell arrives in Mexico. Even though some doubt whether the French would fulfill this agreement, the president was satisfied that they will faithfully comply. The French government has not offered more, nor is it obligated to anything more, the instructions continued, than to withdraw its forces from Mexico by November 1867 and to cease to intervene in the Republic at that time. Supposedly they propose to do two things, however, the instructions noted: (1) to make Maximilian leave Mexico before the evacuation, and (2) to implement the withdrawal in one single move in the course of this month. In addition to the factions sustaining Maximilian and President Juárez, the instructions claimed that this government knows other groups exist with various plans for reestablishing order and consolidating peace in Mexico. But the United States government will not recognize any government in Mexico other than President Juárez's. Hence Campbell will not be authorized to recognize any other government, military chief, or combination of people who pretend to exercise authority. In case of necessity, however, he may speak with them, communicating their plans to the State Department with any observations he considers pertinent. The instructions stated that the United States does not propose to acquire any part of Mexican territory or to intervene in any way in our affairs. The United States desires only that we freely establish the government of our own choice. The minister is informed that the president authorized the United States general accompanying him to lend us material aid with land and naval forces if the legitimate authorities in Mexico might require aid and if the general judges aid desirable to reestablish order in some place, especially at locations on the Mexican–United States frontier. Moreover, these instructions contained two other important points: (1) Campbell may not reside in any place under the control of the enemies of the supreme government, and (2) he should not undertake anything that would embarrass the French withdrawal.

As you can see, these instructions were as good as we could hope for even though a person with bad intentions or prejudiced toward us could misinterpret some points, thereby causing grave trouble and difficulty. Without hesitation I told Grant how extremely sorry I was that he had not accepted the commission to go with Campbell. From the positive inclination and the perfect knowledge which his profound study had given him of the Mexican question, I observed, we could expect the best results. With regard to Sherman, however, some danger existed because his slight knowledge of the problem and his tendencies to favor conservative ideas could generate embarrassment and difficulties. Then I paused for a moment to make clear that it might be easy for Sherman, at least, to wish to protect the traitors in Mexico with the same guarantees he had conceded to the Southern insurgents. Grant assured me that danger did not exist. Besides the fact that Sherman could not reside in any place occupied by our enemies, all his communications would have to pass through Grant's hands.

The plan adopted then, as I understand it, consists in Campbell and

Sherman embarking in New York sometime next week on board a United States warship headed for Veracruz. If they discover upon arrival at Veracruz, as Seward privately assured them, that the French had already or were about to withdraw, and that the supreme government was en route to Mexico City, they will proceed to that city to present themselves to the president. If the situation is other than expected, they would move on to Tampico or Matamoros, from whichever city Campbell would travel to the residence of the supreme government. In this case, Sherman will probably not go with him.

Sherman is very confident that upon his arrival at Veracruz the supreme government will have an open road to Mexico City. Hence he wanted the Mexican president to be informed of these matters so that Juárez could move to Mexico City in time for Sherman's arrival there.

The principal point of these instructions was this government's disposition to lend us material aid for the purpose of consolidated order in the Republic. In the hands of a friendly general like Grant or Sheridan, this possibility would be of great utility, although in the wrong hands it could be very dangerous.   [8:530-32]

NOVEMBER 24   A special cabinet meeting took place on the 22nd. Grant attended this meeting, which discussed Mexican affairs and resolved the following matters:

(1) to request explanations from France regarding the reasons for not complying with its agreement with the United States to withdraw a part of its army from Mexico during the current month; and

(2) to approve General Sheridan's decision to prevent Jesús González Ortega from passing into the Republic to promote a mutiny against the supreme government.

Desiring to ascertain immediately what truth might be in this, I went to see Grant today. Without raising any direct question and referring only to the news stories, I guided the conversation to both points. Regarding the first point, Grant asked me if Seward had not communicated this government's decision to me. After my negative reply, he was very surprised to learn that not even Campbell's instructions had been communicated to me yet. He told me there was no reason why I should not be informed about this government's decisions favorable to our cause. Having attended the cabinet meeting on Thursday, he explained at once, he was not at liberty to inform me of what occurred there. He could indeed assure me, however, that everything ought to be very satisfactory for me and that matters were in a very good state. I inferred from this that the newspaper items were essentially correct.

Grant spoke much more frankly regarding the second point, mentioning everything that happened. Upon reporting González Ortega's arrest, he told me, Sheridan claimed this course had produced the best results. González Ortega had no more partisans, Sheridan maintained, than a few French and English merchants in Matamoros and Tampico, who were interested in continuing the disorder in the Republic, and some imperialists, whose intrigues had been stymied by González Ortega's arrest. In view of all this, Sheridan requested government approval of his conduct. Upon receiving Sheridan's telegram, Grant contended that Sheridan deserved the most complete approval. Since neither the president nor the secretary of war presently wished to accept responsibility to approve or disapprove, Grant observed, meanwhile everything remained at Sheridan's discretion. Without delay, Grant telegraphed Sheridan that his conduct merited the most complete approval. This should suffice now so that the arrest order appears sanctioned by this government.   [8:625-26]

DECEMBER 3 Yesterday I visited various of the principal senators and representatives. From our conversations I believe the Radical faction of the Republican party is disposed to impeach the president. They plan to force the resignation of the president pro tempore of the Senate, moderate Republican [Lafayette] Foster [of Connecticut], who has just failed reelection in his state, and to replace him with Radical Republican Senator [Benjamin] Wade of Ohio. They apparently are disposed to act if they can count on the two-thirds of the Senate necessary to impeach the president. In that case Wade would become president until a new election was held.

If the election were held in the fervor of the moment, supposedly Wade would be elected, or perhaps General Grant. . . .

The representatives and senators manifest a great disgust with the president and very especially with Seward, whom they detest intensely. In general, they have credited the rumors that this government has offered to assume payment of the French debt, retaining in exchange some Mexican states. The congressmen and senators are decidedly opposed to this arrangement, which they categorize as undignified and iniquitous. Others believe that the president and Seward wish to provoke a foreign war at any price in order to exit from their present bad situation. These others are disposed to impede the development of the plans [of Johnson and Seward].

Thus you will see that the situation is quite critical. Great prudence will be necessary to prevent blind party spirit from converting this good disposition toward our cause into a basis for hostility.

Yesterday I prepared five resolutions requesting information from the president on different aspects of our affairs, distributing them to our friends among the representatives and senators. Today two of the resolutions were presented. . . .

The resolutions are as follows:

1. a request for the general correspondence on Mexican affairs;
2. a request for the correspondence concerning Napoleon's failure to fulfill his promise to withdraw a part of his forces this past November;
3. a request for the correspondence on the Campbell–Sherman mission to Mexico;
4. a request for information on the plans of Santa Anna and Ortega to overthrow the Mexican national government; and
5. a request for the unpublished correspondence concerning the establishment of a monarchy in Mexico.

The correspondence referred to in the 2nd and 3rd resolutions will be sent this week.   [8:693-94]

December 4 As soon as the Senate opened its session yesterday, Chandler presented unaltered the resolution I had given him the previous day requesting information from the government on the French withdrawal from Mexico. . . . In drafting this resolution I carefully presented the non-withdrawal of the French army, a part of which ought to have left this past November, as an open violation of Napoleon's promises. Its presentation on the very day Congress opened its sessions, and even before the president's message could be read, indicated the Senate's great interest in the question and can only produce good results.

In conformity with Senate rules, Sumner's opposition to the admission of the resolution left it pending for today. In today's session, Sumner finally succeeded in moving the resolution to the Senate Foreign Relations Committee, which he chairs. . . . His committee will certainly not present a report on the resolution . . . but, because all my expected objectives have already been obtained from the resolution, it is best to allow the resolution to sleep in the committee.

Yesterday Congressman MacKee [Samuel McKee] from Kentucky also presented unaltered the resolution I had previously given him, soliciting the general correspondence on Mexican affairs. . . . Since Banks, chairman of the House Foreign Relations Committee, thought that the information requested would be sent with the president's message, he asked to have it passed to that committee. MacKee asked for the suspension of the rules. Since he did not obtain the necessary votes to that end, the resolution remained pending for one day.

Today Orth presented a resolution which I gave him yesterday, requesting information on the efforts of Antonio López de Santa Anna and Jesús

González Ortega to organize armed expeditions in this country to over-throw the Mexican national government. This resolution was approved without opposition. . . . This resolution was carefully drafted so that, if some congressman influenced by Frémont to favor Ortega would have pre-sented a resolution during the proceedings, either it would not have been admitted, or the government could have pointed out that the requested in-formation was being sent in response to this resolution.

Tomorrow I will go to the State Department with the intention of as-suring that all the proper documents are sent. [8:697-98]

1867

U.S. minister to Mexico Lewis D. Campbell's mission—to establish contact with the Juárez government and to observe the French withdrawal—had proved an unmitigated disaster, dragging on into early 1867 before Campbell was forced to resign. Sherman had had the good sense to return to the United States much earlier. Later, the Johnson administration sent Marcus Otterbourg to Mexico as minister. Romero and other observers thought Otterbourg's mission was to prevent the execution of Archduke Maximilian. Romero tried to warn the U.S. government that it should not seek to interfere in Mexican treatment of Maximilian. Above all, Romero cautioned, the U.S. government should not seek a compromise that would have Maximilian "abdicate" because that would imply the legitimacy of his crown, which both the United States and Mexico had denied up to that point. Romero warned Seward and other public figures that any attempt to aid Maximilian would be considered a U.S. effort to meddle in the internal affairs of Mexico. He pointed out that the United States had rejected friendly Russian mediation offers in 1863 with the charge of interference in the internal affairs of the United States. The same applied to Mexico in 1867. Finally, Romero reminded Seward that when Juárez had been threatened with capture by the French in 1864 and 1865, the United States had not seen fit to request the French to treat him with legal and moral respect. Mexico would resent any indication that it needed to be treated in a manner different from the French. Another minor but interesting problem arose in relation to the effort of Seward to offer General Antonio López de Santa Anna as an intermediate option between Juárez and the Mexican conservatives around Maximilian. In any event, Santa Anna was arrested upon his return to Mexico in 1867.

Romero's lobbying efforts remained active and fairly successful as he maintained steady contact with congressional leaders and media sources to urge U.S. action to remove the French and to establish close, sympathetic relations with liberal Mexico. The piper came to be paid, however. Many of those whom Romero had successfully lobbied for support of Juárez's Mexico, such as Nathaniel P. Banks and Thaddeus Stevens, sought repayment in some form. Banks forged an ill-defined link with the Charles Knapp group, which owned Tehuantepec railroad and transportation interests, and Thaddeus Stevens's nephew, Simon Stevens, associated with the Marshall O. Roberts Tehuantepec railroad and transportation interests. Romero felt obligated to both Banks and Stevens and urged the contending factions to come to terms and present a joint proposal. But the profits looked better in one large pile than in two small ones, so the Tehuantepec transit interests remained apart, sniping at each other.

Romero's most loyal and effective personal link—his bond with Grant—remained strong. Grant had lost all influence with Johnson, however. Romero returned to Mexico in late 1867 but returned to complete the claims treaty of 1868. Then he returned again to Mexico until the 1880s, when he ventured north once more to serve for more than fifteen years as Mexico's minister and first ambassador to the United States.

FEBRUARY 23   Last night I encountered Banks at a dance given by [New York Senator Ira] Harris. Banks said he had been to see me two or three times in order to explain the current state of this government's guarantee of our bonds. He assured me that Tifft and his friends were quite deceived with respect to Congress's inclination to approve this measure. Several times some names were mentioned to him; he observed with assurances that these people were disposed to vote in favor of the guarantee. Then, when Banks inquired if this were true, they replied in the negative. One principal difficulty in guaranteeing the loan now, Banks observed, was the fear that most of the money would end up in the hands of speculators, with the supreme government receiving very little. However, he continued, if the negotiation could be presented in another manner, he was almost certain the guarantee could be obtained later. On this point, Banks's opinion agrees with the judgment of many other people, who argue that for the guarantee to be successful, the firm selling our bonds should be one of the best re-garded and most respectable in this country.

Moreover, congressional opinion was growing daily, Banks claimed, that the United States is morally responsible before the world for the estab-lishment of a national government in Mexico and for the consolidation of peace, and that certainly this government should do what is necessary to obtain that goal, either offering its moral support or lending us money. Fi-nally, personally favoring lending any aid to Mexico, he assured me, he would be very happy for an opportunity to prove it.

This is one of the many incidents that persuade me that the guarantee project will pass sooner or later, if we can avoid fresh complications and if circumstances change favorably for our cause, but that it is not likely for now. [9:152-53]

FEBRUARY 24   Today I had a long conversation on Mexican affairs with Grant. Observing the efforts of some speculators from this country to ac-quire more or less considerable portions of our country, he repeated what he had often said, namely, that the masses and the thinking people in this country oppose such acquisition, with only a tiny minority desiring it. This minority subordinates everything in its eagerness for money, Grant ob-served, but it will not be able to influence significantly this government's policy. This government ought to proclaim to the world, he told me, that it would not acquire any foreign territory except under conditions necessary for acquiring property among private individuals, which means acquisition only with the full and free consent of the nation possessing the desired territory.

If the United States followed this course, I expected the entire world's opinion toward it would greatly improve. The United States would also

more easily obtain whatever benefits it sought from the American republics,
I noted, and ultimately the doctrine containing these principles would obtain more notoriety than the Monroe Doctrine. Whereas in the Monroe
Doctrine, a weak nation had declared it would not permit acts of conquest
on the continent, I suggested that in the new doctrine, a powerful nation
would declare its respect for foreign territory and for the rights of the weak.
If the United States president announced this doctrine in one of his annual
messages, I added, his name would become immortal. If Grant becomes
president, which presently appears very probable, he will undoubtedly
make this important declaration at the first available opportunity, perhaps
even in his inaugural address.   [9:155-56]

APRIL 5 Last night Simon Stevens came to see me to explain that Marshall O. Roberts's son, who had been ill, died recently. This misfortune had
prevented Roberts from coming to Washington. Roberts had already written
a prospectus, however, which Stevens read to me. From the prospectus it
appears Roberts is trying to form a new company called "The Railroad and
Steamship Company of New York and Tehuantepec," which will purchase
the rights of the Louisiana Company and of the Transit Company. According
to this prospectus, a treaty between the United States and Mexico must be
negotiated to protect the rights acquired by the new company.

Stevens told me that his uncle, Congressman Thaddeus Stevens from
Pennsylvania, wished to speak with me on this subject tomorrow. . . .
[Romero visited Stevens.] Since I believe Thaddeus Stevens was the treaty's
originator, I stated very clearly my grave doubts regarding whether the supreme government would conclude such a treaty. Certainly it would not
propose negotiations to the United States in any case because then Mexico
would appear to doubt its own good faith and to desire foreign intervention
to compel it to comply with its promises. Apparently convinced by the force
of this reasoning, Stevens said he would advise Roberts to pursue another
course.

Under the present circumstances Seward would most likely refuse to
propose the negotiation of this treaty.   [9:254]

APRIL 17 Senator [Oliver] Morton of Indiana . . . intends to present a
resolution at today's Senate session asking the United States government to
offer its mediation between the belligerents in Mexico. He wished to speak
with me about this. . . .

I went to his hotel at once. He advised me immediately that Senator
Reverdy Johnson of Maryland had presented a resolution yesterday based
upon the correspondence concerning this government's intervention in favor of Maximilian. This resolution prepared the president to offer United

States mediation to the belligerents in Mexico under the condition that Maximilian would abdicate his throne and leave the country. Morton did not believe Senator Johnson had any other motive than compassion for Maximilian, but he desired to hear my opinion in regard to this point. If that resolution were approved, I responded immediately, it would produce very bad effects in Mexico, because after the United States had ignored the traitors up to this point, they would be elevated to the rank of a legal power in the final moment of defeat. This would encourage them to redouble their efforts to prolong the war, or at least to seek conditions unacceptable to us. . . . In addition, Senator Johnson's resolution amounted to direct United States intervention in the internal affairs of Mexico, which, I was almost positive, would be unacceptable to the Mexican government. If the United States expressed a wish for Maximilian to abdicate his throne, it would recognize the character of emperor, which Napoleon had attempted to invest him with, thereby openly contradicting its prior words and actions. Moreover, it appeared improper for the United States, which had not offered mediation when this step could have produced some beneficial result, that is, while the French army was still in Mexico, to offer it now when the French had already departed and when Mexico was about to settle the question without its intervention.

Morton agreed with these ideas, asking me various questions, surely for the purpose of speaking against the resolution in the Senate. The questions inquired who was responsible for the October 3, 1865, decree, since the Austrian minister claimed it was the French, not Maximilian. . . . After placing all the documents he desired into his hands, I reminded him that Russia, a friend of the United States, had its offer of mediation [during the Civil War] abruptly rejected by this government, which considered the offer European meddling in the internal affairs of this country. Then I took leave of him, because the Senate executive session, which was handling this matter, had commenced, and, in conformity with Senate rules, this type of session is always secret.

I doubt very much that the Senate will approve Senator Johnson's absurd resolution, although it would not surprise me if it did. Certainly Sumner will support the resolution.

This government's pretensions to mix in our affairs will continue to augment each day if the supreme government does not firmly reject this intermeddling the first time that it is presented. By acting in this manner, various newspapers will speak out against us for a few days, but it will not go beyond that. Afterward, neither Seward nor Congress will risk being snubbed again.

On April 14 . . . Wade voiced his disapproval of Seward's intervention in favor of Maximilian. Wade expressed the greatest desire for the United

States to aid us financially. This positive disposition is much more valuable because he could become president of the United States some day.

[9:295-96]

APRIL 19   Desiring to learn what had happened with Senator Johnson's resolution . . . I visited Senator Morton at his hotel last night. I found him with some friends, which prevented me from obtaining all the desired details of the discussion. He told me only that the matter had been concluded satisfactorily for our cause today.

To learn the details, I went immediately to see Senator Zachariah Chandler from Michigan. Chandler told me that Senators Johnson and Sumner made speeches in favor of the resolution, which had certainly been prepared and even written out. They spoke quite harshly about us, especially for the shooting of the San Jacinto prisoners. Immediately, Chandler requested the floor to speak against the resolution. The United States government had acted with cowardice and baseness in the Mexican question, Chandler observed, therefore it would be improper to attempt to intervene now and even more improper to intervene in favor of a filibuster, the author of the barbarous decree of October 3, 1865. Because he was unprepared, Chandler said he could not cite the cruel sections of that decree nor support his discourse with citation from official documents. His antagonists denied Maximilian's responsibility for that decree, claiming a European minister (undoubtedly the Austrian minister, he said) had given written assurance that the decree was the work of the French. However, Maximilian's signature at the foot of the decree was sufficient evidence, Chandler countered, so that he and only he was responsible for this savage measure.

Following Chandler, and with all the necessary documents before him, Morton spoke with considerable merit against the resolution, which he labeled direct intervention in Mexican internal affairs in favor of a filibuster and the assassin of the Mexican people, a person unworthy of the interest the United States had shown for him. After refusing to intervene when the French were in Mexico, Morton asserted, this country could not properly intervene now when the war was virtually concluded. He added various other weighty reasons, which produced a notable effect upon his colleagues.

Senator Joseph S. Fowler of Tennessee presented an amendment to the resolution, which stated that, since the United States had not offered mediation in the war while the French were in the Republic when mediation could have produced some beneficial result, and since, demonstrating valor and determination to defend their independence alone, the Mexican people have succeeded in expelling the foreign invader, the Senate believes it is not the time to interfere in Mexican affairs. Fowler's amendment concluded that the American people have complete confidence in the Mexican nation's proper treatment of prisoners of war under international law.

Chandler did not know the outcome of the debate because he had to leave the Senate while the matter was pending. He thought, however, that the matter had been carried over for today. He was certain that Senator Johnson's resolution would be rejected and Fowler's would pass with a large majority.

Since Chandler's information varied somewhat from Morton's regarding the results, I thought it best to visit Wade, president of the Senate, to assure myself on the matter. . . . He verified all the previous information. Satisfied his resolution would not pass, he informed me, Senator Johnson had withdrawn it. This had concluded the whole affair. Moreover, the Foreign Relations Committee, or at least a majority of it, Wade enlightened me, had informally approved Senator Johnson's resolution. The ideas our friends poured out against Austria and France had been so hard, he observed, that, if the speeches were published, they would cause difficulties with those nations. Wade considered the debate's result a great victory for us. If he had not been so pleased with the speeches of our friends, he claimed, he would have stepped down from the chair to speak out strongly against the resolution.

I asked Wade if there would be any difficulty in the Senate's consenting to have the discussion made public. He saw none other than . . . the problems that could be produced with the Austrian and French governments. At his suggestion, then, I returned to request Chandler to propose this step tomorrow.

Since our friends [the dispatch reads "amigos" (friends) but should read "enemigos" (enemies)] could extract great profit from the secret nature of the discussion, thus allowing them to present the affair as unfavorable to us, last night I wrote a detailed report of the matter in terms very favorable to our cause . . .[which] I sent to the correspondent for the press association of New York in this city [Washington]. I saw him yesterday to persuade him to send it unchanged. Today this report appeared in New York's daily newspaper with almost the identical wording of my draft. . . . I planned to create the impression in the public mind that the debate's result had been a vote of censure against any intervention in favor of Maximilian and simultaneously a vote of confidence in Mexico's willingness to treat its prisoners in accordance with international law.

Both Chandler and Wade told me that this gave us still another basis to reject mediation or Seward's supplication in favor of Maximilian because the Senate would quite obviously refuse to sanction such proceedings.

[9:297-99]

APRIL 23   I encountered Senator Chandler on the train to New York. . . .

I asked him immediately what had happened last Saturday in the Senate. The friends of United States intervention in favor of Maximilian, he replied, had wanted it to appear that they had not been defeated and were about to take action. Therefore they had decided to present their resolutions in a public session, but Senate opinion was decidedly against them. A large majority of that body was not only opposed to intervention in favor of Maximilian but also would justify our executing him if we took him prisoner.

Grant shares this opinion. He has mentioned several times that if he were Mexican and Maximilian should fall into his hands, he would probably try him and, after condemning him to die, pardon him so that the Republic could humiliate Maximilian. At the same time, however, if the supreme government should decide to execute Maximilian, which it has a right to do, he would defend this action.   [9:404-5]

APRIL 28   Last night Senator Fowler of Tennessee came to see me. He had presented the amendment in our favor to [Reverdy] Johnson's resolution on mediation. He spoke strongly against this resolution, principally censuring Sumner. He informed me that Sumner had arranged for Johnson to present the resolution in the public session. Seeing this, supposedly Fowler had wanted to present the amendment he had proposed in the secret session in the same way. Unfortunately, however, he could not locate the amendment, and, without time to write another because the Senate was pressed to close its sessions, he lost the opportunity to do so. Supposedly he was determined to present the amendment on the first day of the next session. Since the question will certainly be totally decided by then, I did not comprehend how that could be. Finally, Fowler mentioned speaking at length against the Johnson resolution in secret sessions. Fowler is one of our best friends in the Senate.

I visited Sumner today to learn his ideas on the proposal that his government should grant us financial aid to help reestablish peace in the Republic. As soon as I entered his office, he spoke of his resolution. He maintained that his only objective was to see the civil war in the Republic terminated with the least possible spilling of blood, while obtaining Maximilian's safe and sound departure from his present difficult situation. I responded that we wanted to reestablish peace in our country more than he. We believed, however, that United States mediation at this hour would encourage the enemy to prolong the war and give him false hopes concerning this country's sympathy. Therefore, we were pleased with the Senate's decision.

Sumner expressed a great fear that, animated by a spirit of ignoble vengeance, President [Juárez] would order unnecessary executions, or, at least, would be powerless to prevent executions by his subordinates. I eased his concern on this point by pointing out what he seemed totally to ignore, namely, that the president is a wise, humane, and patriotic man, therefore there is nothing to fear from him. He had always wanted to present his resolution in the public session, he informed me then, believing it would contribute toward moderating our government's desires for vengeance. He assumed that, upon reading about the resolution, the president and the military leaders would know that there are people in the Senate who were watching them and who would censure their excessive conduct. This is the true explanation of Sumner's conduct.

During our conversation Sumner asserted that the United States would be responsible for what occurred in Mexico because it had forged the French retirement. I also had to disagree with Sumner on this point. We believed, I said, that United States's moral influence had been one of several factors compelling Napoleon to withdraw his forces from Mexico. We did not consider it the only one, however, or even the major one. If the United States had remained indifferent to everything, we believed Napoleon perhaps could have postponed the withdrawal of his forces somewhat longer, but in the end they would have left. Although we were grateful to the United States public for their sympathy toward us, we do not believe we owe our success exclusively to that country.

Then I spoke to Sumner about the chief purpose of my visit. If the United States desired to aid the reestablishment and consolidation of peace in Mexico, the best course, I suggested, would be to concede us financial aid. This aid would be the only thing we needed and the only thing we could accept. I spoke about this in detail, indicating all the advantageous reasons in favor of this policy and requesting his opinion regarding financial aid. . . . Sumner claimed to favor financial aid to Mexico. Yet he would place so many restrictions on the aid that his apparent good disposition would be totally futile.

Then we spoke of [Lewis] Campbell, for whom Sumner has no respect. When Seward returns to Washington, Sumner stated, if possible, he would try to prevent Campbell being sent to Mexico.   [9:417-18]

MAY 12 Banks is willing to work toward the goal of this government conceding us economic aid. He believed it could be obtained even against Seward's opposition.

Referring to the Tehuantepec affair, Banks asserted that when he went to New York, he would advise Marshall O. Roberts to join [Charles] Knapp's company, thus combining sides to undertake the enterprise. He asked my opinion whether, once the company was formed and reorganized and had seriously commenced work, the Mexican government might possibly negotiate a commercial treaty with the United States under terms equitable for both countries and with a stipulation guaranteeing the neutrality of the isthmus. In reply, I supposed our government would not propose the negotiation of a treaty for this purpose. If the United States requested such a treaty, however, our government would undoubtedly be favorably disposed to conclude a mutually advantageous agreement.

Seward had told him, Banks mentioned, that if the United States aided our government, or obtained an advantageous treaty from it, either thing could cause the fall, perhaps through violence, of the Mexican government.

Concerning the Tehuantepec business, I am reliably assured that Roberts sent an agent to the supreme government who certainly will propose something on this matter. Roberts has not told me anything about sending the agent, nor has Simon Stevens, who visited me recently; possibly Stevens did not know about it.   [9:446]

JUNE 30 Since our affairs have taken a favorable turn, ending the necessity of seeing Grant frequently, I have ceased going to his office as often as I did before. . . . I have limited myself to visiting him at his home every Sunday. . . . We have the opportunity to speak freely about our affairs and those of this country. My visits have become so regular that when by some accident I cannot go some Sunday, he misses me, sending someone or coming himself to inquire if anything has happened to me.

Since Grant no longer has great influence with the president, and an almost open rupture exists between him and Seward, his ideas and wishes can possess only a future interest for us in case he becomes president of the United States or as a competent authority when he evaluates public opinion in certain contingencies. For this reason, recently I have not reported our many conversations with the care and detail I had before. Today we spoke of several important points. . . . Grant has considered writing a letter of congratulations to President [Juárez] on the triumph of our cause to be sent with Mrs. Juárez. Perhaps he will do so. I stated that the president would be very pleased to receive such a letter.

Regarding [Marcus] Otterbourg's nomination as minister to Mexico, I showed Grant some documents. . . . Even before acquainting himself with these documents, he told me he would rejoice if the president would not receive Otterbourg as United States minister because he had sympathized with the empire. Grant was certain the American people would view this course with satisfaction. Since Otterbourg's nomination was as offensive to the Mexican people as to those in the United States, Grant believed America's respect for President [Juárez] would diminish somewhat if he consented to receive Otterbourg.

Presumably Grant would not be displeased if his opinion on Otterbourg's nomination were published in the terms he has expressed. If you believe we might gain something, publication could be arranged under certain conditions. The publication of the preceding paragraph in this note, omitting only the beginning, could be authorized. . . .

Grant mentioned various indications that the president had in his hands a project concerning the acquisition of the North Mexican states. Moreover, Grant added, although Seward was opposed in principle to more territorial acquisition, the president indeed desired him to work persistently in favor of the project. Grant observed that he had been striving to impede the project's realization. This removed any remaining doubts regarding the correctness of the information communicated in the first of my previous notes. With reference to this matter, Grant also indicated that, if I do return to the Republic this summer, it would be convenient if I would have returned [to the United States] by next December. This suggests that the danger is greater than I had imagined. . . .

Yesterday William E. Dodge, Jr., a person with a very elevated position in New York commercial circles and who therefore obtains his information from very different sources than Grant, and George E. Church wrote me the following:

"Confidential. Today I was informed in a confidential manner that our government is considering an armed occupation of Mexico, and toward this goal is sending war material to the Rio Grande. I hope this is no more than an unfounded rumor." . . .

Grant also suggested that because Seward does not represent the aspirations of this people or of the Congress that governs this country, we ought not worry too much about condemning his announcements. Although this is true, I judge it most prudent to pursue a conciliatory policy toward Seward insofar as possible. [9:644-45]

JULY 9 Senator Chandler of Michigan . . . our decided and proven friend, considered the telegraph reports that England and France have ordered the withdrawal of their consuls from Mexico as the prelude to a new intervention in Mexican affairs. The European governments are deceived, he very much fears, by the noise the Democrats, and especially the New York press, are making over Maximilian's execution. Convinced that this noise expresses the sentiments of the American people and government, the European governments might be animated to prepare a new expedition in the belief that, at the very least, this time the United States will not oppose them. Therefore, he thought it absolutely necessary to make Congress express its opinion on this subject so that the European nations would understand that the United States will not permit another intervention in Mexico. To obtain this goal, Chandler wanted to present a resolution in the Senate at once, which, conceived in unobjectionable terms, would facilitate an occasion to speak about Maximilian's execution and would force other senators to speak out, thus creating the situation he desired.

I remarked that this all seemed very good to me. I would be very happy, I said, if he succeeded in his desire. Moreover, I mentioned that he had proceeded with laudable judgment and foresight in attempting immediately to ward off a grave, imminent danger.

Then Chandler asked to see Maximilian's decree of October 3, 1865, and the names of some of the principal victims so he could mention them in his resolution. I showed him all this at once. He asked the legation for a copy of the decree because he believed it better to have the whole decree inserted. This was also done. Meanwhile, Chandler drafted his resolution requesting the correspondence between the State Department, Campbell, and his successor. . . . Sumner attempted to prevent approval of this resolution. One which he had presented on the same day, Sumner claimed, was broader and encompassed Chandler's objectives among others. Nevertheless, the Senate approved Chandler's resolution.

Seeing Chandler again yesterday evening, I inquired what had prompted him to present that resolution. He responded that Wade had charged him with its presentation. This incident and the presentation of an identical resolution in the House of Representatives on the 3rd confirm my belief that, still here and desirous of absolving himself from his responsibility for having remained in New Orleans, Campbell has asked Wade to request the correspondence. I know through other means that the State Department is preparing to send the correspondence to Congress shortly. . . .

Yesterday afternoon after all the above had occurred, Senator Fowler of Tennessee came to see me. He is another of our good friends in the Senate who has cordially approved Maximilian's execution. Upon returning to the debate on this subject in today's session, he said, he intended to speak in favor of the execution. He hoped to repeat his remarks from near the end of the secret Senate session in mid-April of this year, when Senator Johnson's resolution concerning mediation between the Mexican belligerents was discussed.

To speak with greater accuracy, he requested various information about the number of persons executed under the October 3 decree, about atrocities committed by the French, such as the burning of populated areas, and about other points. I gave him all the information he desired, directing him also to the diplomatic correspondence concerning Mexican affairs which he wanted to see. This material will supply him with all the necessary factual information and documents to speak in our favor in the Senate today.

In the evening I visited Sumner, who expressed his desire for Congress to avoid occupying itself with Maximilian's execution for the present. Supposedly Congress could better limit itself to what he had already done, namely, to request all the information the government has regarding Maximilian's trial, sentencing, and execution. When these were known, then, Sumner believed, one could speak about the matter with full knowledge of the case. If his considered judgment favors the execution, he added, he would not hesitate to accept the responsibility of voicing it. Sumner's antecedents and inclinations would hardly allow him to form this opinion. We entered into a detailed conversation regarding Maximilian's execution. Sumner was surprised to learn that the trial had lasted 35 days and that all necessary facilities had been conceded to the prisoners so that their lawyers could travel from Mexico City to Querétaro, prepare their defense, and make their preparations. He had probably accepted the rumors of our enemies, which claimed that the proceedings had been modeled on the Inquisition and that the prisoners had been condemned informally and with considerable indignity.

These and other considerations convince me that the publication of the documents I have transmitted to Seward, and above all the one on the trial itself, which I truly hope will arrive while Congress is in session, would significantly contribute toward justifying our conduct by removing the illusions of people who honestly believe Maximilian was condemned informally.

I spoke with Sumner regarding Santa Anna. He was very surprised to learn that Santa Anna was arrested in the city of Sisal and not on board the *Virginia* as was reported here. This persuaded me to publicize this incident today via the Associated Press. . . .

Thaddeus Stevens . . . assured me that he approved the supreme government's conduct with respect to Maximilian. He considered the conduct in conformity with the strictest principles of international law. He was disturbed only by the possible authentication of the rumor that Santa Anna's capture had occurred in a manner violating the United States flag. After I assured him that this fear was unfounded, he seemed to be very satisfied. He also indicated that he would take the first opportunity to speak out in the House of Representatives justifying Maximilian's execution. . . .

(Note:) After concluding this note, I have learned that Stevens spoke very favorably about our affairs today.   [10:65-70]

JULY 13   In New York Grant had learned what were the plans and ramifications of the filibusters who are attempting to invade Mexico. There are two centers of action, he said, one in New York City and the other in New Orleans. Already more than 50,000 people were signed up and prepared to move, he had been assured, if the government does not impede them. He had immediately instructed Sheridan, who had sent him detailed information regarding the New Orleans circle, not to permit a single man to depart. That general will certainly and faithfully fulfill his orders, and therefore I ought to be entirely at ease in this respect. Today, Grant added, he had spoken with the secretary of war, who claimed that Seward and the whole cabinet were agreed not to permit the filibusters to depart.

Grant also informed me of Seward's decision with respect to Santa Anna and other things . . . while expressing friendship and interest for our affairs, which are only comparable with my own.   [10:130]

JULY 23   Yesterday . . . ex-minister designate of the United States to Mexico Lewis D. Campbell . . . came, spending several hours detailing everything that occurred from his departure from New York accompanied by General Sherman on board the *Susquehanna* until his resignation was accepted.

From Campbell's story, I infer he wanted to go to his destination on several occasions, but, when he could have gone, he hesitated out of timidity and because he credited the inexact and exaggerated information coming from the frontier. In my judgment, his return from Brazos to New Orleans was his most serious error. In explanation Campbell claimed that General [Mariano] Escobedo did not ask him to come along to Monterrey, while the hostile and doubtful attitude of [Servando] Canales and [Juan N.] Cortina convinced him of the danger of moving deeply into Mexico without a large escort. . . . He returned to New Orleans, Campbell continued, only to place himself in communication with his government. He intended to proceed without delay to his destination. Yet he had scarcely arrived in New Orleans when Seward instructed him not to depart again. On various occasions, Campbell claimed, he had requested authorization to go to Mexico, but Seward had insisted it was not time, until May 30 when Campbell received a peremptory order to go with no other instructions than to intercede on Maximilian's behalf. Campbell attempted to leave, but with no means of transportation provided, he could not complete the arrangements and finally had to resign.

Campbell complained of Seward. He claimed the secretary of state is attempting to present him as solely responsible for not having gone to Mexico, which is not true. As soon as the official correspondence being sent to Congress is printed, he intends to publish a defense of his conduct. He expressed sharp criticism of Plumb, secretary of the legation, whom he had excluded from legation affairs after the past January. . . .

A friend in whom I have full confidence related a frank and friendly conversation, in which Campbell had spoken very harshly about Mexicans in general, describing them as false men, without honor, dishonest, and other similar characterizations. In hindsight, I believe we should be glad Campbell did not go to Mexico.   [10:206-7]

JULY 28 On July 16 . . . Thaddeus Stevens asked me to visit him. . . . I expressed satisfaction with what I had learned of his remarks on Mexico in his recent House speech. . . .

Stevens desired to discuss the Tehuantepec business. Simon Stevens, his nephew, allegedly an agent for Marshall O. Roberts, was to arrange this matter in agreement with his uncle, Thaddeus Stevens, without affirming that he has special authority from Roberts. Nevertheless, Simon Stevens implied that Roberts would approve his actions.

Simon Stevens read what I understood to be the basis for a treaty between Mexico and the United States. This draft guaranteed Roberts the privilege to open the Tehuantepec road, adjusting the terms of the Louisiana Company's concession by the following modifications:

1st) Roberts would have the right to commence the railroad at the mouth of the Goatzacoalcos and not from Minatitlán;

2nd) he would have the right, as I understand it, to canalize the whole river to make it navigable for deep-draft steamers from its source; and

3rd) the United States would have the right to establish naval stations at the two terminal ports.

I explained to Stevens that I had no authorization to discuss or to decide these points, nor sufficient time to consider them in order to express my private opinion regarding them. If he intended to declare the Louisiana Company's concession in force, I added, my government would probably not accede to this because it had solemnly declared that concession void, although it would probably concede all necessary facilities to make the transit easier and more comfortable. Regarding the naval depots, at the time I was uncertain what rights the United States government would acquire and what obligations would be imposed on Mexico with a stipulation like the one the Louisiana Company proposed, and therefore, I could not express any opinion regarding it. With all possible clarity, I made him aware of the difficulty involved in Roberts, who had solicited and obtained concessions from Maximilian, appearing now as the personal benefactor of another concession. In my judgment, I continued, it would be most prudent for the two companies to unite in soliciting the concession. If this is not possible, and [Charles] Knapp clearly could not carry the undertaking to completion, Roberts could form a new company without using his name to solicit the concession.

[Simon] Stevens said he would alter his project in light of my remarks, and he would send me a copy when modified. I expected to receive the revised draft for transmission in this mailing, thus enabling me to refer to it. Before this draft document could be sent, however, Congress adjourned and [Thaddeus] Stevens left Washington. Later, Simon Stevens indicated that he had modified the project, but now he would not give me the proffered copy.   [10:217-18]

SEPTEMBER 9   The last time I was in New York, Banks came from Massachusetts to see me, he claimed in order to learn what would be our government's policy in respect to the United States. He expressed great interest in us and an explicit desire to concede us the necessary or material assistance to consolidate. He also spoke of the opening of the Tehuantepec route as the first necessary step toward this result. Above all, he added, the different people interested in constructing the road ought to combine. He considered Marshall O. Roberts the most appropriate person to undertake and carry this enterprise to completion.

After having seen Banks, a friend of his informed me that Banks was seriously considering accompanying me to Mexico and returning here in time for the next congressional elections. . . . I asked Banks then if he was really considering going to Mexico. He replied affirmatively. Then I declared how very pleased I would be if we could travel together, adding that I would notify him as soon as I could set the date of my departure. He also stated that he was considering informing Seward of his desire to go to Mexico.

Without a doubt, Banks's trip to the Republic would produce very good results. Hence I will arrange for him to make the trip, so we can extract the greatest possible advantage from it. Thus among this country's public men, one in a very elevated position will be interested in our affairs. Having been in Mexico and having been treated courteously by our public men, he will return as our friend, and his voice will be in our favor in places where otherwise we would not be heard.   [10:326-27]

SEPTEMBER 15   Wishing to speak with Seward privately and extraofficially on several points of interest, I went to his house today. . . .

In view of our cordial relations, I considered it necessary to inform him that several friends in New York wished to invite me to a dinner before I left this country to express their sympathy for our cause and to rejoice in our success. . . . These same friends wished me to discuss various specific matters. I asked him to look at and give me his opinion regarding a brief speech I had prepared. He would gladly do so, he replied, telling me his thoughts after reading my manuscript. This speech contains nothing hostile to this government. Therefore, consulting Seward about it risked nothing, but, in a certain sense, could give the speech character. . . .

Then I told Seward that Banks desired to travel to Mexico with me. I had already suggested we could travel together, I added, and Senator

[Oliver] Morton of Indiana had similarly been invited when I learned that he also desired to visit Mexico. We may hope that all the public men of this country who desired to go to Mexico would go to become acquainted with and study that country. Certainly Mexico as well as the United States would profit from this. I would be pleased if Seward shared my opinion on this point. Seward agreed with me in this, desiring to go to Mexico himself as soon as he could.

Finally, I spoke to Seward about the Tehuantepec business, informing him of the current state of affairs. I requested his opinion regarding how we should conduct ourselves so as not to wound susceptibilities in this country. I also inquired about how this question could affect our relations with the United States government. He agreed that the best arrangement would be for Marshall O. Roberts, Charles Knapp, and all other interested parties to unite, soliciting a new unopposed concession. Seward offered to write to his friend Thurlow Weed to work toward this arrangement. Regarding how this matter could affect our relations with this government, Seward told me that although the United States was greatly interested in the establishment of communications between both seas via Tehuantepec, he doubted any difficulty would arise if this were not effected immediately.

This is a faithful resumé of a conversation lasting more than two hours. [10:338]

OCTOBER 5 Today at midday I went to the White House to take leave informally of President Johnson. . . . Shortly after I arrived at the White House, Johnson received me. I regretted having to leave this country, where I have so many friends and unforgettable memories, I told him, but I considered it my duty to return to my country. I carried with me, I added, the most agreeable memories of his fine treatment of me in our official relations, of the sympathy he had professed for our cause, and of his very distinguished service to us from his high position. I told him I would take the greatest pleasure in testifying about this to my government and to my fellow citizens.

Johnson thanked me with some emotion for these sentiments. He was not very demonstrative, he told me, but his sincerest sympathies have always been with us. Although he did not speak as much as others, he added, he believed no one exceeded him in sympathy for Mexico. He was pleased and satisfied with the result [of the intervention], believing the developments were the most favorable for Mexico. Very sincerely desiring us to consolidate peace in the Republic now, he judged, we needed only peace to become a prosperous, happy nation. The Liberal party's preponderance, he thought, now seemed sufficiently strong to maintain the factions in check and to consolidate the peace. In conclusion, he wished me a happy voyage and a quick return.

I thanked Johnson for his kind remarks and took leave of him. His sincere manner and his cordial and frank words persuaded me that his sympathy for us had been and is more profound and sincere than generally believed.   [10:428]

Epilogue
Romero, Mexican-American
Liberal Lobbyist

Both the United States and Mexico experienced liberal revolutions in the mid-nineteenth century. Both became obsessed with free-market rhetoric extolling growth, development, and a belief that material progress would resolve any problems within their social orders. The two nations experienced a warm relationship in the last years of the 1850s before the Civil War erupted in the United States and the French, Spanish, and British intervened in Mexico in 1861. President James Buchanan's administration had reacted to the Liberal ouster of the Conservatives with considerable sympathy and had wished to negotiate commercial and transit agreements with Liberal Mexico.

Against this background, Matías Romero initially presumed that Abraham Lincoln and the Republican party shared similar ideology and goals with Mexico's Liberal faction under Benito Juárez. The Lincoln administration's policy proved disappointing. After Lincoln's assassination, Romero initially thought President Andrew Johnson was a true liberal and friend of Mexico, but again Romero's expectations were disappointed. Romero believed that Secretary of State William H. Seward dominated both Lincoln and Johnson and that his policy toward the French intervention would result in little of the assistance Romero desired. Romero's friendship with General Ulysses S. Grant during 1865 and 1866 encouraged his hopes, and, indeed, Grant delivered considerable moral and material aid to the beleaguered Mexican Liberals. In 1867, Romero's mission to secure aid against the French became moot. The French troops withdrew, and several weeks later Maximilian was a prisoner of Juárez's government.

The execution of Maximilian on June 19, 1867, opened the final act of the multifaceted Mexican–United States relationship during the mid-nineteenth century. The debate focused on two questions initially raised during years of the Civil War and French intervention. Was the French venture in Mexico purely foreign interference in the New World, a clear violation of the Monroe Doctrine? Or was it an effort to achieve stability and order in a society lacking those attributes? Were the Civil War and the French intervention ideologically and tangibly part of the same conflict? Or were they two separate struggles that simply happened at the same time? The debate in the U.S. Congress and in the American media suggests that the French were attempting to undermine U.S. penetration and influence in Mexico and Latin America and that the two wars were thus part of a broad conflict between liberalism, the ideological and world view of industrial capitalism, and the conservative remnants of mercantilistic, paternalistic, and agrarian institutions supporting monarchical and aristocratic management of society.

Many North American leaders feared the execution of Maximilian might provoke renewed French or Austrian intervention in the New World. After the Liberals regained authority in Mexico City, Seward ordered the U.S. minister in Mexico, Marcus Otterbourg, not to press for collection of claims of U.S. citizens against Mexico so the Liberals could have breathing space to straighten out their affairs. This respite was brief, however, because by late 1868 a claims treaty was signed and ratified, and the claims commission was preparing to hear petitioners.

Matías Romero considered his lobbying successful and so, apparently, did the Mexican government. He resigned in 1867 but was urged to return to Washington in 1868 to finalize the claims treaty. About fifteen years later, after serving as Mexican senator and twice as secretary of the treasury in Mexico and spending several years in private life as a planter, Romero was persuaded by General Porfirio Díaz to return to the United States as Mexican minister. He held this post for more than fifteen years until his death in 1898, except for one brief period when he again served temporarily as Mexican secretary of the treasury.

U.S. relations with Mexico blossomed under Romero's influence. Trade between the two nations which had risen sharply during the 1860s and then waned in the late 1860s and early 1870s, gained momentum beginning in the late 1870s. Commercial exchange rose in absolute amounts and as a percentage of either Mexican or U.S. foreign trade regularly after the mid-1870s. Moreover, the view Romero emphasized for forty years—that the two liberal societies shared ideological perspectives and goals with regard to growth, social and economic opportunity, and other liberal objectives—laid the basis for Mexico and Cuba to become the chief investment targets for U.S. excess capital.

Future problems resulted from an imbalance which Romero recognized but misjudged. He knew that Mexico was the weaker of the two partners. The United States was the model, the teacher, provider of the master plan for Mexican social, economic, and political growth and development. Within a liberal framework of competition, individualism, and growth, such an imbalance between two unregulated, free-market interactors produces exploitation, marginalization, and extraction of wealth. United States and other foreign firms and capitalists controlled the distribution of Mexico's major wealth and initiated the development projects that exploited Mexican wealth. Finally, in the twentieth century, a reaction of antiforeignism and nationalism emerged in Mexico.

By 1860, the United States had devoted its energy to territorial expansion in quest of its continental empire for three-quarters of a century. The liberal revolution during the 1860s launched a new empire based on industrialism, nationalism, and market expansion. After a brief healing period U.S. capitalists moved to full development of the domestic market and capital accumulation with an eye to world-scale market expansion. Both Mexican and U.S. liberals expected their cooperation and mutual sympathy would lead to a widening of the marketplace. It was not an accident that U.S. capital as well as trade began to penetrate Mexico extensively in the 1870s and 1880s. This was the future Romero had envisioned and had lobbied for incessantly for more than forty years.

Romero had not envisioned the major social revolution that would occur just over ten years after his death, justifying itself by blaming much of Mexico's misfortune on foreign exploitation and abuse of Mexico's political economy and citizens. It also blamed a *comprador* Mexican elite—lawyers, businessmen, politicians, intellectuals, and military figures whose wealth, status, and power were derived from foreign investors and firms—for many of the injustices within Mexico. Romero apparently did not expect international exchange based on liberal social transformations to cause revolution and social unrest. But that he worked so hard to promote liberalism in Mexico and to link it with the United States makes it appropriate to question to what extent the world Romero sought to build in the 1860s contributed to the Mexico of the 1910s and 1920s.

Essay on Sources

Matías Romero had a significant role in United States–Mexican relations as well as in internal Mexican history between 1858 and 1898. It is therefore surprising that little attention has been given to his life from either side of the Rio Grande, especially because vast quantities of his personal and public papers are readily available.

Romero published about forty books and a large number of essays and articles. A list of his publications follows this essay. His most imposing and significant publication, from which the documents translated in this book are taken, is *Correspondencia de la legación mexicana en Washington durante la intervención extranjera, 1860-1868*, 10 vols. (Mexico: Imprenta del Gobierno, 1870-92). These volumes contain almost all his dispatches and their annexes sent to his government. The originals are available in the Archivo de la Secretaría de Relaciones Exteriores, Mexico City, which also holds a personal file on Romero's diplomatic career. Several of Romero's other works are also collections of documents.

Romero's official correspondence with the United States government can be found in the National Archives, Notes to Foreign Legations (Microfilm 99) and Notes from Foreign Legations (Microfilm 54) for the years he was chargé d'affaires, minister, or ambassador. Much of his formal correspondence relating his meetings and exchanges with Seward is published in U.S. Department of State, *Papers Relating to the Foreign Relations of the United States* (various volumes, 1861-), and in Senate or House Documents (for example, Senate Executive Document 1, 37th Cong., 1st sess.; House Executive Document 100, 37th Cong., 2d sess.; House Executive Documents 1 and 54, 37th Cong., 1st sess.; House Executive Document 1, 39th Cong., 2d sess.; House Executive Document 29, 40th Cong., 1st sess.; House Executive Document 1, 40th Cong., 1st sess.; Senate Executive Document 20, 40th Cong., 1st sess.). These and other U.S. government publications, often published at Romero's instigation, document much of the interchange between Romero and his foreign ministry.

The record of the official side of Romero's life can be supplemented by a truly amazing body of private correspondence. In 1952, the Banco de México purchased Romero's private papers, a collection of well over one hundred thousand items about evenly divided between correspondence received and sent. To guide scholars in the use of the vast Archivo Histórico de Matías Romero, the Banco de México decided to publish a multivolume catalog. So far, Guadelupe Monroy Huitrón has edited two volumes, covering the years 1837-84, which have been published under the title *Archivo histórico de Matías Romero: Catálogo descriptivo, correspondencia recibida*, 2 vols. (México: Banco de México, 1965, 1970). A third volume should appear shortly, concluding the series of correspondence received. Then a projected four-volume catalog of correspondence sent will be initiated. The Banco de México also permitted the publication of the *Diario personal de Matías Romero, 1855-1865*, edited by Emma Cosío Villegas (México: El Colegio de México, 1960). In addition to this main collection, dozens of private collections in Mexico and the United States contain Matías Romero materials. For example, two collections of Edward Lee Plumb Papers, located in the Library of Congress and at Stanford University, the Hiram Barney Papers

at the Huntington Library, and the James W. Beekman Papers in the New York Historical Society contain numerous letters from Romero and drafts of letters to him.

Yet in spite of this vast body of manuscript and printed source material, no
adequate biography of Romero has yet been written. Nor have his papers been used
extensively to help describe United States–Mexican relations in the last half of the
nineteenth century. The only biography of Romero is the inadequate Harry Bern-
stein, *Matías Romero, 1837-1898* (México: Fondo de Cultura Económica, 1973). The
best introduction to Romero, both as a person and as a diplomat, can be extracted
from Daniel Cosío Villegas, *Historia moderna de México: El porfiriato, la vida política
exterior*, vols. 5 and 6 (México: Editorial Hermes, 1960, 1963). His attempts to promote United States investment are mentioned frequently in David Pletcher, *Rails,
Mines and Progress: Seven American Promoters in Mexico, 1867-1911* (Port Washington,
N.Y.: Kennikat Press, 1972). Romero's brief contact with Mexico's internal economy
during his tenures as secretary of treasury is described in Francisco R. Calderón,
Historia moderna de México: La república restaurada, la vida económica, vol. 2 (México:
Editorial Hermes, 1955).

Four doctoral dissertations and one master's thesis have used Romero's papers
to study him and his diplomatic labors. These are Robert W. Frazer, "Matías Romero
and the French Intervention in Mexico" (Ph.D. dissertation, University of California,
Los Angeles, 1941), John Patton Ogden, "The Labors of Matías Romero, 1861-
1868" (M.A. thesis, Duke University, 1941), Robert Ryal Miller, "Mexican Secret
Agent in the United States, 1861-1867" (Ph.D. dissertation, University of California,
1960), which should be compared closely with Robert B. Brown, "Guns over the
Border: American Aid to the Juárez Government during the French Intervention"
(Ph.D. dissertation, University of Michigan, 1951), and Thomas Schoonover, "Mexican–United States Relations, 1861-1867" (Ph.D. dissertation, University of Minne-
sota, 1970), now expanded, revised, and published in book form *Dollars over Dominion: The Triumph of Liberalism in Mexican–United States Relations, 1861-1867* (Baton
Rouge: Louisiana State Univ. Press, 1978).

Robert W. Frazer and Robert R. Miller have published articles taken from their
dissertations, which draw heavily upon Romero's official or private correspondence.
These articles are Robert W. Frazer, "The Ochoa Bond Negotiations of 1865-1867,"
Pacific Historical Review 11 (December 1942): 397-414; R. W. Frazer, "Trade between
California and the Belligerent Powers during the French Intervention in Mexico,"
Pacific Historical Review 15 (December 1946): 390-99; R. W. Frazer, "The United
States European and West Virginian Land and Mining Company," *Pacific Historical
Review* 13 (March 1944): 28-40; Robert R. Miller, "Gaspar Sanchez Ochoa: A Mex-
ican Secret Agent in the United States," *Historian* 23 (May 1962): 316-29; R. R.
Miller, "Herman Sturm: Hoosier Secret Agent for Mexico," *Indiana Magazine of History* 58 (March 1962): 1-15; R. R. Miller, "Plácido Vega: A Mexican Secret Agent in
the United States," *Americas* 19 (October 1962): 137-48; and R. R. Miller, "Lew Wallace and the French Intervention in Mexico," *Indiana Magazine of History* 59 (March
1963): 31-50.

Aspects of Romero's activity in the United States and his efforts to influence
United States policy are described in Dexter Perkins, *The Monroe Doctrine, 1826-1867*
(Baltimore: Johns Hopkins Univ. Press, 1933); Robert R. Miller, "Matías Romero:
Mexican Minister to the United States during the Juarez–Maximilian Era," *Hispanic
American Historical Review* 45 (May 1965): 222-45; Marvin Goldwert, "Matías Ro-
mero and Congressional Opposition to Seward's Policy toward the French Interven-
tion in Mexico," *Americas* 22 (July 1965): 22-40; Thomas Schoonover, "The Mexi-

can Minister Describes the 'Swing around the Circle,'" *Civil War History* 19 (June 1973): 149-61; Thomas Schoonover, "Mexican Affairs and the Impeachment of President Andrew Johnson," *East Tennessee Historical Society Publications* 46 (1974): 76-93; and Thomas Schoonover, "Dollars over Dominion: Developing United States Economic Interests in Mexico, 1861-1867," *Pacific Historical Review* 45 (February 1976): 23-45. The last two articles appear in revised form as part of the monograph, Thomas Schoonover, *Dollars over Dominion.* Robert Ryal Miller's *Arms across the Border: United States Aid to Juárez during the French Intervention in Mexico, Transactions of the American Philosophical Society,* vol. 63, pt. 6 (1973), discusses Romero's role in Juárez's efforts to obtain arms from the United States. All of Miller's writing on Mexican–U.S. relations in the 1860s should be compared with Robert B. Brown's dissertation cited above. Two other articles that touch briefly Romero's relationship to the United States in the Civil War era are Thomas Schoonover, "Anteproyecto de Thomas Corwin para un tratado comercial en 1861," *Historia Mexicana* 28 (April-June 1979): 596-609; and Thomas Schoonover, "Misconstrued Mission: Expansionism and Black Colonization in Mexico and Central America during the Civil War," *Pacific Historical Review* 49 (November 1980): 607-20.

For the reader who wishes to go beyond the story Romero presents, there are several starting points. James G. Randall and David Donald, *The Civil War and Reconstruction* (Boston: Little, Brown, 1969), remains the best single volume on this period, and its bibliography is extensive. A good, if European-oriented, narrative of Civil War diplomacy is Donald P. Crook, *Diplomacy during the American Civil War* (New York: John Wiley, 1975). Several good general histories supply background for understanding the context of U.S.–Mexican relations in the 1860s, alternative interpretations, and bibliographic guidance. The best one-volume study is Josefina Zoraida Vázquez and Lorenzo Meyer, *México frente a Estados Unidos: Un ensayo histórico, 1776-1980* (México: El Colegio de México, 1982); English translation *The United States and Mexico* (Chicago: Univ. of Chicago Press, 1985). One can also turn to Karl M. Schmitt, *Mexico and the United States, 1821-1973: Conflict and Coexistence* (New York: John Wiley, 1974), and Howard Cline, *The United States and Mexico, 1821-1963,* 3d ed. (Cambridge, Mass.: Harvard University Press, 1963). Also useful, although in Spanish, is Luis G. Zorrilla, *Historia de las relaciones entre México y los Estados Unidos de América, 1800-1958,* 2 vols. (México: Porrua, 1965-66). Two fine recent bibliographies, however, can best guide the reader to sources and secondary literature: Richard Dean Burns, ed., *Guide to American Foreign Relations since 1700* (Santa Barbara: ABC–Clio, 1983), and David Trask, Michael Meyer, and Roger Trask, comps. *A Bibliography of United States–Latin American Relations since 1810,* 1 vol. and supplement (Lincoln: University of Nebraska Press, 1968, 1979).

Bibliography of Works by Matías Romero

Books or pamphlets written, compiled, or edited

Apuntes para formar un bosquejo histórico del regreso a la República por los Estados Unidos de algunos de los prisioneros mexicanos deportados a Francia; acompañados de documentos oficiales para rectificar los Apuntes del Sr. de. Epitacio Herta. México: Imprenta del Gobierno, 1868. 335pp.

Artículos sobre México, publicados en los Estados Unidos de América por Matías Romero en 1891-1892. México: Oficina impresora de estampillas, 1892. 332 pp.

Banquete dado en obsequio del señor don Matías Romero, enviado extraordinario y ministro plenipotenciario de México en los Estados–Unidos, por ciudadanos de Nueva York, el 2 de octubre de 1867. México: Imprenta del Gobierno, 1868. 80 pp.

Biografía del ciudadano Benito Juárez. Puebla: N.p., 1867.

Bosquejo histórico de la agregación a México de Chiapas y Soconusco y de las negociaciones sobre límites entablados por México con Centro–América y Guatemala. Colección de documentos oficiales que sirve de respuesta al opúsculo de d. Andres Dardon, intitulado "La cuestión de límites entre México y Guatemala." Vol. 1, 1821-31. México: Imprenta del Gobierno, en palacio, a cargo de F. Mata, 1877. 795 pp.

Circulares y otras publicaciones hechas por la legación mexicana en Washington, durante la guerra de intervención, 1862-1867. 2 vols. in l. México: Imprenta del Gobierno, 1869.

Coffee and India–Rubber Culture in Mexico; Preceded by Geographical and Statistical Notes on Mexico. New York: G. P. Putnam's Sons, 1898. 417 pp.

Comisionados de la República Mexicana en los Estados Unidos, dos notas del Señor Romero a Mr. Seward. Baltimore: John Murphy, 1867. 79 pp.

La conferencia internacional americana. México: Imprenta del Gobierno Federal, 1890. 128 pp.

Contratos hechos en los Estados Unidos por los Comisionados del Gobierno de México durante los años de 1865 y 1866. México: Imprenta del Gobierno, 1868. 590 pp.

Correspondencia de la legación mexicana en Washington con el Ministerio de Relaciones Exteriores de la República y el Departamento de Estado de los Estados Unidos, sobre la captura, juicio y ejecución de Don Fernando Maximiliano de Hapsburgo. 2 vols. México: Imprenta del Gobierno, 1868.

Correspondencia de la legación mexicana en Washington durante la intervención extranjera. 10 vols. México: Imprenta del Gobierno, 1870-92.

Correspondencia Oficial de la Legación Mexicana en Washington, con el Ministerio de Relaciones Exteriores de la República y el Departamento de Estado en Washington, sobre la conducta de don Jesús González Ortega, 1865-1866. México: Imprenta del Gobierno, 1869.

Cultivo del café en la costa meridional de Chiapas. 4th ed. México: Oficina tipografía de la Secretaría de fomento, 1893. 163 pp.

El cultivo del café en la república mexicana. 2d ed. México: Oficina tipografía de la Secretaría de fomento, 1893. 127 pp.

Dinner to Señor Matías Romero, Envoy Extraordinary and Minister Plenipotentiary from Mexico, on the 29th of March, 1864. New York: N.p., 1866. 49 pp.

El estado de Oaxaca. Barcelona: Tipolitografía de Espasa y Compañía, 1886. 212 pp.

Estudio sobre la anexión de México a Estados Unidos. México: Imprenta del Gobierno Federal, 1890. 112 pp.

Expediente de la secretaría de hacienda respeto de las medidas propuestas y acordadas para impulsar el desarrollo de los elementos de riqueza agrícola del Departamento de Soconusco en el Estado de Chiapas, 1870-1871. México: Imprenta del Gobierno, 1871. 186 pp.

Expediente informativo formado por la sección del gran jurado del congreso de la Unión con motivo de la acusación presentada por D. Juan Andrés Zambrano contra el c. ministro de hacienda, Matías Romero. México: Imprenta del Gobierno, 1868. 382 pp.

Exposición de la secretaría de hacienda de los Estados Unidos Mexicanos de 15 de enero de 1879 sobre la condición actual de México, y el aumento del comercio con los Estados Unidos. México: [Imprenta del Gobierno,] 1879. 349 pp.

Exposición que el ejecutivo federal dirige al Congreso de la Unión, dando cuenta del uso que ha hecho de las facultades que le concedió el artículo 3º de la ley de 1º de diciembre de 1871, y del estado que guarde la hacienda federal, el 1º de abril de 1872. México: Imprenta del Gobierno, 1872. 465 pp.

Exposición que el ejecutivo federal dirige al Congreso de la Unión el 1º de abril de 1871 sometiéndole un proyecto de arreglo de la deuda pública y dándole cuenta del estado de la hacienda federal en el primer semestre del año económico cuadragesimosexto. (México: Imprenta del Gobierno, 1871. 39 pp.

El ferrocarril de Tehuantepec. México: Oficina tipografía de la Secretaría de fomento, 1894. 30 pp.

Geographical and Statistical Notes on Mexico. New York: G. P. Putnam's Sons, 1898. 286 pp.

Gran banquete dado al ministro de la República mejicana, por varias de las personas más distinguidas de la ciudad de Nueva York, para expresar su simpatía por la causa de Méjico y su oposición a la intervención francesa. New York: N.p., 1864. 32 pp.

Historia de las intrigas europeas que ocasionaron la intervención francesa en México. Nota del Sr. Romero a Mr. Seward, el 2 de octubre de 1862. México: Imprenta del Gobierno, J. M. Sandoval, 1868. 259 pp.

Importancia del cultivo del hule en el porvenir de la República. 3d ed. México: Secretaría de Fomento, 1898. 51 pp.

Informe del Matías Romero al gobernador del estado de Oaxaca respeto de la compañía que organizó para construir el ferrocarril de Oaxaca, y del traspaso que le hizo de la concesión de 25 de agosto de 1880. México: F. Mata, impresor, 1881. 60 pp.

Informe que el ciudadano Matías Romero rindó al ministerio de guerra y marina, de la comisión que se le confió para la compra, en los Estados Unidos, de armas con los adelantos modernos, para el ejército de la república. México: Imprenta del Gobierno, 1868. 87 pp.

Mexico and the United States. A Study of Subjects Affecting Their Political, Commerical and Social Relations, Made with a View to Their Promotion. Vol. 1. New York: G. P. Putnam's Sons, 1898. 759 pp.

Minutes of the International American Monetary Commission. Actas de la Comisión Monetaria Internacional Americana. Washington, D.C.: [U.S. Government Printing Office?], 1891. 123 pp.

Proceedings of a Meeting of Citizens of New York, to Express Sympathy and Respect for the Mexican Republican Exiles, Held at Cooper Institute, July 19, 1865. With an Appendix

Containing the Speeches of the Hon. Matías Romero. New York: J. A. Gray and Green, 1865. 60 pp.

Railways in Mexico: An Article by Senator Don Matías Romero, Mexican Minister to Washington, in Answer to an Article of the Hon. John Bigelow Entitled "The Railway Invasion of Mexico," Pub. in Harper's New Monthly Magazine for October, 1882. Washington, D.C.: W. H. Moore, 1882. 31 pp.

Reciprocidad Comercial entre México y los Estados Unidos. México: Oficina tipografía de la Secretaría de fomento, 1890. 350 pp.

Refutación de las inculpaciones hechas al C. Matías Romero por el gobierno de Guatemala. México: Imprenta poliglota de C. Ramiro y Ponce de León, 1876. 374 pp.

Responsabilidades contraídas por el Gobierno Nacional de México en los Estados Unidos en virtud de los Contratos celebrados por sus agentes, 1864-1867. México: Imprenta del Gobierno en Palacio, 1867. 32. pp.

The Silver Standard in Mexico. Reprinted from "The North American Review" for June, 1897, with Introductory Remarks. . . . New York: [Knickerbocker Press], 1898. 64 pp.

The Situation of Mexico: Speech, Delivered by Señor Romero . . . at a Dinner in the City of New York, on the 16th of December, 1863. New York: W. C. Bryant & Co., 1864. 12 pp.

Speech of Señor Don Matías Romero . . . Read on the 65th Anniversary of the Birth of General Ulysses S. Grant, Celebrated at the Metropolitan Methodist Episcopal Church, of the City of Washington, on the 25th of April, 1887. New York: W. Lowey, 1887. 16 pp.

Tabla sinóptica de los tratados y convenciones celebrados por la República Mexicana con naciones extranjeras. Tabasco: Imprenta del Gobierno, 1859. 78 pp.

The Tehuantepec Isthmus Railway. Washington, D.C.: N.p., 1894. 30 pp.

Articles

"Cartas de Don Matías Romero a Don José Alfonso, 1890-1896." *Revista chilena de historia y geografía* 123 (1954-55): 143-67.

"Criminal Jurisprudence, Roman and Anglo-Saxon." *North American Review* 162 (January 1896): 33-47.

"Fall of the Second Empire." *Century Magazine* 54 (May 1897): 138.

"The Free Zone in Mexico." *North American Review* 154 (April 1892): 459-71.

"The Garza Raid and Its Lessons." *North American Review* 155 (September 1892): 324-37.

"Mexico." *Bulletin of the American Geographical Society* 27 (1896): 327-86.

"Mexico: A Country of Central America." *Journal of the American Geographical Society* 26 (1894): 32-37.

"Mr. Blaine and the Boundary Question between Mexico and Guatemala." *Bulletin of the American Geographical Society* 29 (1897): 281-330.

"Pan-American Conference." *North American Review* 156 (September 1890): 354-66.

"Pan-American Conference." *North American Review* 156 (October 1890): 407-21.

"The Philosophy of the Mexican Revolutions." *North American Review* 162 (January 1896): 33-47.

"Settlement of the Mexico-Guatemala Boundary Question." *Bulletin of the American Geographical Society* 29 (1897): 123-59.

"The Silver Standard in Mexico." *North American Review* 160 (June 1895): 704-11.

"The United States and the Liberation of the Spanish-American Colonies." *North American Review* 165 (July 1897): 70-86.

"The United States and the Spanish-American Colonies." *North American Review* 165 (November 1897): 553-71.

"Wages in Mexico." *North American Review* 154 (January 1892): 33-49.

"Wages in Mexico." *North American Review* 154 (March 1892): 382-83.

Index

www.ingramcontent.com/pod-product-compliance
Lightning Source LLC
Chambersburg PA
CBHW031509270326
41930CB00006B/325